The New American
Poetry of Engagement

The New American Poetry of Engagement

A 21st Century Anthology

Edited by ANN KENISTON
and JEFFREY GRAY

McFarland & Company, Inc., Publishers
Jefferson, North Carolina, and London

LIBRARY OF CONGRESS CATALOGUING-IN-PUBLICATION DATA

The new American poetry of engagement : a 21st century
anthology / edited by Ann Keniston and Jeffrey Gray.
        p.   cm.
Includes index.

ISBN 978-0-7864-6467-8
softcover : acid free paper ∞

1. American poetry — 21st century.   I. Keniston, Ann, 1961–
II. Gray, Jeffrey, 1944–
PS617.N49 2012
811'.608 — dc23   2012021540

BRITISH LIBRARY CATALOGUING DATA ARE AVAILABLE

On the cover: The exterior support columns from the lower level of
the south tower of the World Trade Center after the September 11
attack (FEMA photographer Bri Rodriguez)

Manufactured in the United States of America

*McFarland & Company, Inc., Publishers
    Box 611, Jefferson, North Carolina 28640
    www.mcfarlandpub.com*

For our children —
Paul and Jeremy Novak
and
Pablo and Maira Duarte Quiroga

Table of Contents

Acknowledgments   xi
Introduction: Saying What Happened in the 21st Century   1

Rae Armantrout   New 17 • Previews 18 • Bubble Wrap 18
  • Action Poem 19

Frank Bidart   Curse 20 • The Soldier Who Guards the Frontier 21
  • To the Republic 22 • Inauguration Day 23

Robert Bly   Call and Answer 23 • Let Sympathy Pass 24 • The Stew
  of Discontents 25 • Those Being Eaten 26 • Here the Sleepers
  Sleep 27

Bruce Bond   The Altars of September 28 • Flag 29 • Ringtone 32

Joel Brouwer   Lines from the Reports of the Investigative Committees 32

Timothy Donnelly   Partial Inventory of Airborne Debris 34
  • Dream of Arabian Hillbillies 38

Carolyn Forché   The Ghost of Heaven 41

Katie Ford   Flee 43 • Earth 44 • Fish Market 44 • The Vessel
  Bends the Water 45

Forrest Gander   Background Check 46

Peter Gizzi   Protest Song 47

Louise Glück   October 47

Albert Goldbarth   Some Common Terms in Latin That Are Larger Than
  Our Lives 53

Kenneth Goldsmith "A1" from *The Day* 54

Jorie Graham Little Exercise 61 • Praying (*Attempt of June 14 '03*) 62 • Guantánamo 64 • Employment 66

Linda Gregerson Sweet 68 • Father Mercy, Mother Tongue 70 • Still Life 72 • The Selvage 76

Eamon Grennan Y2K 78

Marilyn Hacker Letter to Hayden Carruth 78 • *From* Names 80 • Ghazal: *min al-hobbi m'a qatal* 82

Forrest Hamer Aftermath 83 • What Happened 84 • Conference 84

Robert Hass I am Your Waiter Tonight and My Name is Dmitri 85 • Ezra Pound's Proposition 88 • On Visiting the DMZ at Panmunjom: A Haibun 89 • Some of David's Story 89

Bob Hicok Happy Anniversary 93 • Full Flight 94 • Troubled Times 96 • In the Loop 97 • Stop-loss 98

Brenda Hillman *From* Nine Untitled Epyllions 99 • Reportorial Poetry, Trance & Activism 102 • In a Senate Armed Services Hearing 102 • Request to the Berkeley City Council Concerning Strawberry Creek 105 • In High Desert Under the Drones 107

Galway Kinnell When the Towers Fell 107

Yusef Komunyakaa From "Love in the Time of War" 112 • Grenade 113 • The Towers 113 • Heavy Metal Soliloquy 115 • The Warlord's Garden 115 • Surge 116 • Clouds 117

Maxine Kumin Extraordinary Rendition 118 • On Reading *The Age of Innocence* in a Troubled Time 119 • Entering Houses at Night 120 • Still We Take Joy 120 • Just Deserts 121

Ann Lauterbach Victory 122 • Hum 123 • Echo Revision 125

Ben Lerner Didactic Elegy 129

Timothy Liu Ready-Mades 134 • Vita Breva 135 • Beauty 135 • Elegy for Oum Kolsoum Written Across the Sky 135

John Matthias Column I, Tablet XIII 136

J. D. McClatchy Jihad 137

Raymond McDaniel   Assault to Abjury 139 • Sen Jak's Advice to the
Tropically Depressed 139

Sandra McPherson   On Being Transparent: Cedar Rapids Airport 140

W. S. Merwin   To the Light of September 142 • To the Words 143
• To the Grass of Autumn 143 • To Ashes 144 • To the Coming
Winter 145

Philip Metres   From "Hung Lyres" 146 • Asymmetries 146
• Testimony 147 • Compline 148 • From "Homefront/
Removes" 149

Naomi Shihab Nye   Dictionary in the Dark 149 • Interview, Saudi
Arabia 150 • I Never Realized They Had Aspirations Like Ours 150

Geoffrey O'Brien   A History 151

Sharon Olds   September, 2001 153

Robert Pinsky   Poem of Disconnected Parts 154 • The Forgetting 156
The Anniversary 157

Kevin Prufer   National Anthem 159 • Dead Soldier 160 • Those
Who Could Not Flee 161 • Recent History 163 • God Bless Our
Troops 164

Claudia Rankine   From *Don't Let Me Be Lonely: An American Lyric*:
"Cornel West makes the point" 165 • "Timothy McVeigh died at
7:14 A.M." 166

Donald Revell   Given Days 167 • Vietnam Epic Treatment 172
• Election Year 174

Frederick Seidel   God Exploding 174 • The Black-Eyed Virgins 175
• Eurostar 176 • Song: "The Swollen River Overthrows Its
Banks" 176 • The Bush Administration 177

Hugh Seidman   Found Poem: Microloans 179 • Thinking of
Baghdad 180

Lisa Sewell   The Anatomy of Melancholy 181

Susan Stewart   When I'm crying, I'm not speaking 183 • When I'm
speaking, I'm not crying 184 • Elegy Against the Massacre at the
Amish School in West Nickel Mines, Pennsylvania, Autumn 2006 184

David Wagoner　In Rubble 187

C. K. Williams　War 188　•　Fear 189　•　The Future 191
　•　Cassandra, Iraq 192　•　Lies 193

Eleanor Wilner　Found in the Free Library 193　•　In a Time of War
　194　•　Back Then, We Called It "The War" 195　•　The Show Must
　Go On 197　•　Rendition, with Flag 198　•　Colony Collapse
　Disorder (CCD) 199

C. D. Wright　From *Rising, Falling, Hovering*: "He slept with the dead
　then" 200　•　"One bright night" 200　•　"I was just thinking" 201

Robert Wrigley　Exxon 202

The Poets: Profiles and Statements　　　　　　　　　　　　　　205
Index　　　　　　　　　　　　　　　　　　　　　　　　259

Acknowledgments

We wish to acknowledge the generous support of the Scholarly and Creative Activities Grants Program of the College of Liberal Arts at the University of Nevada, Reno, and the English Department at Seton Hall University.

We are grateful to the research assistants who helped us locate poems, obtain permissions, track down poets, and assemble and proofread the manuscript. At the University of Nevada, Reno, Sarah Stewart helped locate poems; Brian Baaki extended this research and obtained relevant anthologies; special thanks are due to S. Laurel Griffiths, who painstakingly checked and assembled the typescript and to editorial assistant Eric Stottlemyer, who researched and obtained many of the permissions. At Seton Hall University, we wish to thank Dejon Turner and especially Valerie Falk, who, in addition to numerous organizational labors, helped assemble the manuscript, proofread it, and created the index.

We also wish to thank the publishers who granted us permission to reprint these poems, virtually all at drastically reduced fees or gratis. This book would not be possible without their generosity and support.

Our greatest debt is to the poets whose work we include. We are grateful for their poems and for their generosity in allowing us to reprint them, and also for their prose statements, which together offer what may be the first comprehensive account of the state of U.S. poetics of the early 21st century.

We here acknowledge the following publishers, which have allowed us to reprint previously published poems.

Rae Armantrout, "New," "Previews," "Bubble Wrap" from *Versed* (Wesleyan University Press, 2009). © 2009 by Rae Armantrout and reprinted by permission of Wesleyan University Press. "Action Poem" appeared in *Shampoo*. Used by permission of the author.

Frank Bidart, "To the Republic" from *Watching the Spring Festival* by Frank Bidart. Copyright © 2008 by Frank Bidart. "Curse" and "The Soldier Who Guards the Frontier" from *Star Dust* by Frank Bidart. Copyright © 2005 by Frank Bidart. Reprinted with the permission of Farrar, Straus, and Giroux. "Inauguration Day" appeared in *Slate*. Used by permission of the author.

Robert Bly, "Call and Answer" from *My Sentence Was a Thousand Years of Joy* by Robert Bly. Copyright © 2005 by Robert Bly. Reprinted by permission of HarperCollins Publishers. "Let Sympathy Pass," "The Stew of Discontents," "Those Being Eaten," and "Here the Sleepers Sleep" from *The Insanity of Empire: A Book of Poems Against the Iraq War* by Robert Bly. Copyright 2004. Used by permission of Robert Bly and Ally Press.

Bruce Bond, "The Altars of September" from *Cinder*. Copyright © 2003 by Bruce Bond. Reprinted with the permission of The Permissions Company, Inc. on behalf of Etruscan Press, www.etruscanpress.org. Bruce Bond, "Ringtone" from PEAL. Copyright © 2009 by Bruce Bond. Reprinted with the permission of The Permissions Company, Inc. on behalf of Etruscan Press, www.etruscanpress.org. "Flag" from *Blind Rain*. Copyright 2008 by Bruce Bond. Reprinted with the permission of Louisiana State University Press and the author.

Joel Brouwer, "Lines from the Reports of the Investigative Committees" appeared in *Poetry*. Used by permission of the author.

Timothy Donnelly, "Partial Inventory of Airborne Debris" and "Dream of Arabian Hillbillies" from *The Cloud Corporation*. Copyright 2010. Reprinted with the permission of Wave Books and the author.

Katie Ford, "Flee," "Earth," "The Vessel Bends the Water" and "Fish Market" from *Colosseum*. Copyright © 2008 by Katie Ford. Reprinted with permission of The Permissions Company, Inc. on behalf of Graywolf Press, Minneapolis, Minnesota, www.graywolfpress.org.

Forrest Gander, "Background Check" appeared in *La Siega Revista* online journal. Used by permission of the author.

Peter Gizzi, "Protest Song" from *The Outernationale* (Wesleyan University Press, 2007). © 2007 by Peter Gizzi and reprinted by permission of Wesleyan University Press.

Louise Glück, "October" from *Averno* by Louise Glück. Copyright © 2006 by Louise Glück. Reprinted with the permission of Farrar, Straus and Giroux. Copyright © 2004, 2006 by Louise Glück, reprinted in the UK by permission of The Wylie Agency LLC.

Albert Goldbarth, "Some Common Terms in Latin That Are Larger Than Our Lives" appeared in *Poetry*. Used by permission of the author.

Kenneth Goldsmith, excerpt from "The Day," which appeared as *The Day* from Figures Books. Copyright © 2003 by Kenneth Goldsmith. Used by permission of the author and Figures Books.

Jorie Graham, "Praying (Attempt of June 14 '03)," "Little Exercise" from *Overlord* by Jorie Graham. Copyright © 2005 by Jorie Graham. Reprinted by permission of HarperCollins Publishers. "Guantánamo" from *Sea Change* by Jorie Graham. Copyright © 2008 by Jorie Graham. Reprinted by permission of HarperCollins Publishers. "Employment" first appeared in the *London Review of Books*. Reprinted by permission of the author.

Linda Gregerson, "Sweet" and "Father Mercy, Mother Tongue" from *Magnetic North: Poems* by Linda Gregerson. Copyright © 2007 by Linda Gregerson. Reprinted by permission of Houghton Mifflin Harcourt Publishing Company. All rights reserved. "The Selvage" first appeared in *Poetry* and "Still Life" first appeared in *The New Yorker*. Both used by permission of the author.

Eamon Grennan, "Y2K" from *Out of Sight: New and Collected Poems*. Copyright © 2010 by Eamon Grennan. Reprinted with the permission of Graywolf Press, Minneapolis, Minnesota, www.graywolfpress.org.

Marilyn Hacker, "Ghazal: min al-hobbi m'a qatal," "Names," "Letter to Hayden Carruth," from *Names: Poems* by Marilyn Hacker. Copyright © 2010 by Marilyn Hacker. Used by permission of W.W. Norton & Company, Inc.

Forrest Hamer, "Aftermath," "What Happened," "Conference" from *Rift* © 2007 by Forrest Hamer. Reprinted with permission of Four Way Books. All rights reserved.

Robert Hass, three poems ("I am Your Waiter Tonight and My Name is Dmitri," "Ezra Pound's Proposition," "On Visiting the DMZ at Panmunjom: A Haibun") from *Time and Materials: Poems 1997–2005* by Robert Hass. Copyright © 2007 by Robert Hass. Reprinted by permission of HarperCollins Publishers. "Some of David's Story" from *The Apple Trees at Olema* by Robert Hass. Copyright © 2010 by Robert Hass. Reprinted by permission of HarperCollins Publishers.

Bob Hicok, "Stop-loss, "Troubled times," and "In the loop" from *Words for Empty and Words for Full*, by Bob Hicok, © 2010. Reprinted by permission of the University of Pittsburgh Press. "Happy anniversary" and "Full flight" from *This Clumsy Living*, by Bob Hicok, © 2007. Reprinted by permission of the University of Pittsburgh Press.

Brenda Hillman, "Nine Untitled Epyllions" from *Pieces of Air in the Epic* (Wesleyan University Press, 2007). Copyright © 2007 by Brenda Hillman and reprinted by permission of Wesleyan University Press. "Reportorial Poetry," "In a Senate Armed Services Hearing," "Request to the Berkeley City Council" by Brenda Hillman from *Practical Water* (Wesleyan University Press, 2009). © 2009 by Brenda Hillman and reprinted by permission of Wesleyan University Press. "In High Desert Under the Drones," published in the *Chronicle of Higher Education*, is used by permission of the author.

Galway Kinnell, "When the Towers Fell" from *Strong Is Your Hold: Poems* by Galway Kinnell. Copyright © 2006 by Galway Kinnell. Reprinted by permission of Houghton Mifflin Harcourt Publishing Company. All rights reserved.

Yusef Komunyakaa, "Here the old masters of Shock & Awe" (From "Love in the Time of War"), "Grenade," "The Towers," "Heavy Metal Soliloquy," "The Warlords' Garden," "Surge," and "Clouds" from *Warhorses* by Yusef Komunyakaa. Copyright © 2008 by Yusef Komunyakaa. Reprinted with the permission of Farrar, Straus, and Giroux.

Maxine Kumin, "Extraordinary Rendition," "On Reading the Age of Innocence in a Troubled Time," "Still We Take Joy," "Entering Houses at Night," from *Still to Mow* by Maxine Kumin, Copyright © 2007 by Maxine Kumin. Used by permission of W.W. Norton & Company, Inc.

Ann Lauterbach, "Hum," "Victory," from HUM by Ann Lauterbach, copyright © 2005 by Ann Lauterbach. Used by permission of Penguin, a division of Penguin Group (USA) Inc. "Echo Revision," from *Or To Begin Again* by Ann Lauterbach, copyright © 2009 by Ann Lauterbach. Used by permission of Penguin, a division of Penguin Group (USA) Inc.

Ben Lerner, "Didactic Elegy" from *Angle of Yaw*. Copyright © 2006 by Ben Lerner. Reprinted with the permission of The Permissions Company, Inc. on behalf of Copper Canyon Press, www.coppercanyonpress.org.

Timothy Liu, "Ready Mades," "Vita Breva," "Beauty," and "Elegy for Oum Kolsoum Written Across the Sky" from *For Dust Thou Art* by Timothy Liu. Copyright © Timothy Liu, reprinted with permission of Southern Illinois University Press.

Robert Lowell, "Epilogue," from *Day by Day* by Robert Lowell. Copyright © 1977 by Robert Lowell. Reprinted with the permission of Farrar, Straus and Giroux.

John Matthias, "Column I, Tablet XIII" from *Kedging* by John Matthias. Copyright © 2007 by John Matthias. Used by permission of Salt Publishing Ltd.

J. D. McLatchy, "Jihad" from *Hazmat: Poems* by J. D. McClatchy, copyright © 2002 by J. D. McClatchy. Used by permission of Alfred A. Knopf, a division of Random House, Inc.

Raymond McDaniel, "Assault to Abjury" and "Sen Jak's Advice to the Tropically Depressed" from *Saltwater Empire*. Copyright © 2008 by Raymond McDaniel. Reprinted with the permission of The Permissions Company, Inc. on behalf of Coffee House Press, www.coffeehousepress.com.

Sandra McPherson, "On Being Transparent: Cedar Rapids Airport" from *Expectation Days*. Copyright 2007 by Sandra McPherson. Used with permission of the poet and the University of Illinois Press.

W. S. Merwin, "To the Light of September," "To the Words," "To the Grass in Autumn," "To Ashes," and "To the Coming Winter" from *Present Company*. Copyright © 2008 by W. S. Merwin. Reprinted with permission of The Permissions Company, Inc. on behalf of Copper Canyon Press, www.coppercanyonpress.org. Electronic rights and UK rights for "To the Light of September," "To the Grass of Autumn," "To Ashes" and "To the Coming Winter" from *The Shadow of Sirius* by W. S. Merwin. Copyright © 2008 by W. S. Merwin, used by permission of The Wylie Agency LLC. Electronic rights for "To the Words" from *The Shadow of Sirius* by W. S. Merwin. Copyright © 2008 by W. S. Merwin, used by permission of The Wylie Agency LLC. UK rights for "To the Words" from *The Shadow of Sirius* by W. S. Merwin. Copyright © 2008 by W. S. Merwin, used by permission of Bloodaxe Books.

Philip Metres, "Asymmetries" appeared in *World Literature Today*, "Compline" in *Poetry*, and "Testimony" in *Field*. Used by permission of the author.

Introduction

Saying What Happened in the 21st Century

by Ann Keniston and Jeffrey Gray

> Those blessèd structures, plot and rhyme —
> why are they no help to me now
> I want to make
> something imagined, not recalled?
> I hear the noise of my own voice:
> *The painter's vision is not a lens,*
> *it trembles to caress the light.*
> But sometimes everything I write
> with the threadbare art of my eye
> seems a snapshot,
> lurid, rapid, garish, grouped,
> heightened from life,
> yet paralyzed by fact.
> All's misalliance.
> Yet why not say what happened?
> Pray for the grace of accuracy
> Vermeer gave to the sun's illumination
> stealing like the tide across a map
> to his girl solid with yearning.
> We are poor passing facts,
> warned by that to give
> each figure in the photograph
> his living name.
>   —"Epilogue," Robert Lowell

Midway through "Epilogue," the last poem of his last book, Robert Lowell memorably asks, "Yet why not say what happened?" It is a question

1

prompted by what Lowell saw as the direction of his own poetry: at the end of his career, he worried that his poems had become not the work of imagination and technique but rather mere "snapshot[s], / lurid, rapid, garish, grouped, / heightened from life, / yet paralyzed by fact." Lowell longed instead for a poetics that could resist or transform these facts, so in "Epilogue" he proposes an alternate model, one that, in going beyond reportage to "the grace of accuracy" embodied by the paintings of Vermeer, privileges what is "imagined" over what is "recalled." But this alternative also proves inadequate; Lowell turns back, toward the poem's end, to the language he used earlier, claiming that "we are poor passing facts," unable to transcend our need to chronicle what has occurred. By the end of the poem, the whole opposition has collapsed: we cannot get beyond "facts," "paralyz[ing]" though they are. Nor, in "say[ing] what happened," can we get beyond the imagination.

Lowell's anxiety can be explained partly as a symptom of a time when the imagined, the aesthetic, even the artificial were privileged over facticity and content. "Epilogue" can also be seen as a retrospective meditation, from late in the poet's career, on the role of autobiography in his own poems, as well as on the wave of poetic self-revelation those poems set off in the 1960s and 70s. But ultimately the predicament expressed by "Epilogue" is universal, one that confronts any poet who attempts to convey "what happened," whether in the private or the public sense: in being true to facts, one risks being "paralyzed" by them, yet to turn away from them is to turn away from the obligation to "give," as Lowell's last lines say, "each figure in the photograph / his living name." This problem has been central to American poetry since Lowell: poets are caught in the contradictory obligations of truth-telling, the need both to keep faith with what has occurred and to transform or transcend it.

As the nearly fifty American poets included here grapple with these issues — in their poems and in statements about their poetics (included at the end of this volume) — they offer a paradoxical response, which Lowell had begun to intuit: it is possible for poems to say what happened if in the process they question the very project of representation, acknowledging the gap between the need to tell and the limitations of the language they use. The difficulty of this predicament is made clear by the tendency of several poets — echoing Theodor Adorno's famous assertion that it is "barbaric" to write poems "after Auschwitz" — to express an aversion to poetic speech. "This is no time for poetry," writes C. D. Wright. Similarly, Sharon Olds writes with regard to the September 11 attacks, "I don't / think I could ever write about it." (The anxiety is not confined to Americans: in "The Diary of Beirut Under Siege, 1982," the Syrian poet Adonis, describing atrocities in the streets, stops and says: "Have you gone mad? Please, / Don't write about these things.")

Nevertheless, with misgivings about the problems of doing so, these poets *do* write about these events, folding those misgivings into the poems.

As editors, we have not tried to include the best poems of the first decade of the century, nor to limit ourselves to poems of a particular aesthetic or style, nor to favor emerging poets over established ones or the reverse. Rather, we have attempted to collect the strongest poems written during this period that incorporate, chronicle, or allude to public events. For clarity's sake, but also because of the epoch-making nature of September 11, 2001, we begin at the turn of the millennium. Among the events taken up in the poems are the Al Qaeda–sponsored attacks on the United States of September 11, 2001, Hurricane Katrina, the wars in Afghanistan and Iraq, the presidencies of George W. Bush and Barack Obama, the 2008 economic meltdown, the 2010 BP oil disaster, school shootings, species loss, and climate change. As often oblique as direct, these poems frequently complicate or even undermine the familiar oppositions of public and private, political and personal.

CONTEXTS. The engagement evident in the poems of *The New American Poetry of Engagement* is remarkable partly because it was not always so: most 20th-century poetry in America went in quite the other direction. Modernism, eager to break with an exhausted Victorian sentimentalism, was concerned primarily with depicting subjectivity in new ways, incorporating (especially after World War I) an awareness of fractured and traumatized consciousness, whether through fragmentation, ellipsis, free-associative dream states, or surreal imagery. We may not think of T. S. Eliot, Wallace Stevens, or André Breton as "personal" poets — indeed, Eliot made a famous claim for "impersonalism" — but their experiments and revolutions enabled an unprecedented exploration of the mind and its motions, including those just being discovered by the emerging science of psychology. The modernists' formal innovations suggested not only a new stance toward reality but also a new aesthetic, one that has influenced poets up to the present moment. American poems after the midcentury, while reacting against the erudition and difficulty of the modernists, did so in a way that turned even more emphatically away from the political: the "confessional" poetry of Robert Lowell, Sylvia Plath, Anne Sexton, and others was explicitly and candidly "personal."

These aesthetics — including the embrace both of the personal and the impersonal — shared an avoidance of the political that reflected the ethos of the New Criticism, the critical approach that arose in the 1920s and remained influential throughout much of the century. New Criticism itself reflected a social *milieu* — especially as the mid-century approached — in which political challenges to the status quo were highly unwelcome. With their emphasis on the "poem itself" ("A poem should not mean / But be," wrote Archibald MacLeish in 1926) — its dynamics, nuances, ambiguity, and tensions (to use some of their own favored terms) — the New Critics were remarkable in part for what they *left out* of discussions: history, biography, race, class, and gender.

Throughout the decades characterized above, there were nevertheless poets in the United States — not so much a coterie as important individual figures — writing socially-committed work. Voices like those of Muriel Rukeyser, Edwin Rolfe, Kenneth Rexroth, Adrienne Rich, and Allen Ginsberg, to mention some of the most famous, often did not reach a large public until the 1960s allowed or encouraged their more political vein. Indeed, during the late 1960s, much of the content excluded by the New Critics (along with poets they had ignored) burst onto the scene. The civil rights and feminist movements, the Vietnam War and the antiwar movement, the new sense of identity embraced by a range of ethnic groups — these changes demanded a powerful counterbalance to the hermeticism of much twentieth-century poetry up to that point, so much so that even the work of poets earlier celebrated for their apolitical or even anti-political poems (Plath, for example, or Elizabeth Bishop) began to seem more socially conscious, even activist, than they had earlier.

Outside the U.S., political poetry was far more visible. Through most of the 20th century, poets such as Pablo Neruda in Chile, Ernesto Cardenal in Nicaragua, Nazim Hikmet in Turkey, Anna Akhmatova and later Yevgeny Yevtushenko in Russia, and many others regularly addressed public and political issues despite consequences that included censorship, imprisonment, and exile. The poems of Hikmet, who spent much of his adult life in prison and whose poems were outlawed in his native country, have been translated into fifty languages. Neruda, at one time a political exile who sought refuge in Bolivia, Mexico, and Europe, was by the 1960s the most-read poet in the world. He frequently gave readings to audiences of thousands in South America, including one to 100,000 in São Paolo's Pacaembu stadium, the largest stadium in the world. In terms of the commitment of his poetry together with its wide popular reception, Neruda has had no parallel in English-speaking countries.

Many of the Latin American, Polish, Turkish, Russian, and other poets had been writing "political" poetry since the 1930s, but their poetry made it to American shores only decades later. Newly translated by American poets in the 1960s, it provided a new model for U.S. poets. At first, the translations seemed to affect a minority of American poets, albeit important ones, including W. S. Merwin and Robert Bly, both included in the present anthology. But this poetry in translation became increasingly central to American poetry and poetics, shaping and extending what was possible in the American idiom.

Another indication that U.S. tastes in poetry were changing toward the end of the twentieth century was the publication in 1993 of *Against Forgetting,* edited by Carolyn Forché. This best-selling anthology compiled what Forché, herself the author of influential poems about El Salvador and U.S. involvement there, called in the book's subtitle "Twentieth-Century Poetry of Witness." Forché first introduced the phrase "poetry of witness" in 1981. It appeared in another form in Czeslaw Milosz's 1984 book-length essay *The Witness of Poetry*; it also recalls discussion of Latin American *testimonio*, the genre that emerged out of the situation of victims of military regimes during the Cold War, particularly in the 1980s in Central America. It is by now an indispensable term of our poetic and critical vocabulary.

Forché required that the poets included in her anthology "must have personally endured conditions of extremity," a criterion that emphasizes biography (and may explain why the bulk of the 150 poets in her collection are from Eastern Europe and Latin America). At the same time, however, she notes that "not all poems address extreme conditions," a remark that would seem to place primary value not on the life but on the poem. In her more recent writing on the subject, Forché, looking back on her work in El Salvador in the 1980s, has emphasized that poetry of witness "is a mode of reading rather than of writing, of readerly encounter with the literature of that-which-happened," and warns that we should be wary of seeing poems "in purely evidentiary terms." While this shift to defining witness through the eye of the beholder is significant, the notion that poetry could — and perhaps should — bear witness to extreme and even hitherto unspeakable events marks a larger cultural shift toward a view of poetry as responsive to and responsible for the world outside the self.

In spite of influences from international poetry and in spite of voices from within the United States, a certain suspicion of politically engaged poetry has lingered, no longer out of a New Critical credo that would keep politics out of poetry but rather out of an epistemological sense that witness itself, and its associations with truth and authenticity, is not possible in the 21st century. A quite different and more recent trend extends this idea, one that reveals a shift not only in the subject matter of poetry but in its form. This shift is evident in the 2009 anthology *American Hybrid,* whose title suggests its agenda: to chronicle the recent tendency of American poetry to bridge the gap of the last thirty-odd years between an experiential aesthetic, often associated with the confessional movement, and an experimental poetics indebted to the Language movement of the 1970s and its modernist precursors. Such divisions have become uninteresting, if not obsolete, to poets and readers alike. Instead, as *American Hybrid* and characterizations of recent poetry as "elliptical" (in Stephen Burt's term) or "skittery" (in Tony Hoagland's) have shown, U.S. poetry has increasingly combined aspects of the experimental with elements drawn from more traditional poetic traditions.

There are therefore several possible answers to the question of how and why, after a century of relative apoliticism, American poetry has changed in the first years of the new millennium. Certainly events themselves — 9/11 most conspicuously — disrupted and threw into question the "personal" concern of much poetry. At the same time, responding to hitherto neglected strands of radicalism in earlier American poetry and to the literatures reaching us through translation, U.S. poetry began to "catch up" in this regard with that of other nations, a trend accelerated by the interest here as abroad with the possibility that poetry could bear witness to actual events. Moreover, as suggested above, American poets have grown restless with the attempt to split poetry into the two warring camps of the experiential (i.e., subjective) and the experimental (i.e., linguistic); the turn toward a more engaged poetry seems to suggest an alternative.

ENGAGED POETRY. The new poetry is political with a difference. It can be most usefully described not in terms of a genre or subgroup but as a tendency or trope to be found in a range of formally and tonally diverse poems. It bears traces of post-confessional, political, experimental, and modernist. We prefer the general term "engaged poetry" to describe this mode of poetry. While this term recalls the French *littérature engagée* and the Spanish *literatura de compromiso* (that last word meaning "commitment," not "compromise"), engaged poems are seldom as overt in their claims or charges as the South American and European poetry described earlier. Contemporary engaged poems tend not to espouse a stance of witness. In fact, they often insist that their speakers have *not* directly witnessed or participated in the events they describe. They reveal, in short, a distance between event and subjectivity. In her statement, Maxine Kumin writes, "To state the obvious: images and reports of events do not bring us closer to events; they serve only to make us conscious of them." Several of the poets here reveal neither a compulsion nor an inability to speak, but rather an awareness of the particular dangers of doing so, which include self-aggrandizing and (the old bugaboo of modernism) didacticism. One has to be careful, writes Linda Gregerson,

> simply because there are so many ghastly ways of going wrong. I'm always worried — I think it's essential to be worried — about the possibilities of trespass. We've all seen work that hitches an easy ride on the sufferings of others, that borrows intensity from large-scale trauma only to reduce it to the scale of self.

Katie Ford notes in her statement the "horrible risk ... of sensationalizing violence, the risk of sentimentalizing human loss." Nevertheless, given the stakes, these risks must be run: she cites Milton's plea to God in "On the Late Massacre in Piedmont" to "record their groans." Ford writes, "The poet, too, ought to take up this task: Preserve the groans of the dead, despite the warnings against it."

While the poems of *The New American Poetry of Engagement* often reveal postmodern or "hybrid" tendencies, they do not do so for principally aesthetic or formal reasons. Rather, such strategies offer an antidote to postmodernism's decontextualization. Timothy Donnelly chronicles just such a movement away from an embrace of the postmodern in his own career: his early poems were, he says, "formally complex, loud with music, full of pyrotechnics and wordplay and foreign words and phrases. Maybe they were hermetic. Quite possibly they were frivolous." But his work shifted, Donnelly claims, partly because the incursions of reality proved unignorable: "I found that admitting reality into my work as a springboard or foil allowed for the kind of tonal complexity and amped-up artfulness I couldn't forsake."

The opening lines of Susan Stewart's "When I'm Speaking, I'm Not Crying" directly undermine the old distinction between the political and the personal: "The personal is artificially political just as / the political is artificially personal." Similarly, Kevin Prufer asserts in his statement that one needs to "think of poetry as a public sort of speech, an act of communication about our responsibilities as citizens, our simultaneous culpability and helplessness"; for Peter Gizzi, "the political is always implicit to real writing."

A question persists in this hybrid poetry of engagement: how can a poem be informed by postmodern destabilizations of identity and reality while remaining committed if not to witness then at least to Lowell's attempt to "give / each figure in the photograph / his living name"? One way to clarify the problem is to consider the ways this poetry deploys the trope of irony. The poetry of witness and trauma has been, until recently, largely an irony-free zone. In postmodernism, on the other hand, irony abounds, tending toward the witty and parodic, if not the flippant and trivial. In fact, irony can deflect and displace real-life references so drastically that, as Frank Bidart has said of some postmodern poetry, it works like "armor," encouraging a playing on surfaces without the drive to probe deeper. Bruce Bond, in his statement, goes further, referring to

> the poetry of an adolescent culture, where it is just too embarrassing to aspire to be sincere or wise, to be authentic and yet still write a poem of great wonder, surprise, intellectual/emotional precision, and lovely difficulty.

Yet the poetry in this anthology reveals something different: irony can also function something like a Freudian screen memory, concealing painful or unassimilable content behind other images. Irony thus may function as a survival technique. Engaged poetry certainly entails an indirect stance — or many different stances — toward reality. Eamon Grennan writes, "I've found it necessary for the most part to 'tell it slant.'": "I shy away from — as I think many poets do — explicit and direct handlings of the political, of public events, probably wary of the kind of hollow rhetorical gestures that such direct confrontations can generate." Emily Dickinson's awareness that the "Truth" must be told "slant," that it is always filtered through subjectivity and language, is here extended, and many poems in *The New American Poetry of Engagement* imply that figuration, paradox, and equivocation are the only ways to approach extremity.

SUBJECTIVITY. The poets included here, in the face of these dangers, often interrogate the notion of a fixed or reliable speaker. A number of them — Brenda Hillman, Robert Hass, Bidart, Galway Kinnell, Yusef Komunyakaa, Donnelly, and others — include a first person but undermine its unity or stability. In a few instances, "we" begins in collective witness, as in the opening of Kinnell's "When the Towers Fell": "From our high windows, we saw the towers." Kinnell then undermines this position, reverting first to unreliable reportage ("someone said"), and then to more radical doubt ("I wish I could say"). The unidentified "we" in Raymond McDaniel's "Assault to Abjury," in Kevin Prufer's "God Bless Our Troops" and in several other poems invites readers to evaluate the authenticity of the voice. Hillman's "In a Senate Armed Services Hearing" begins with a human witness — "From my position as a woman / i could see" — then shifts to what "the fly / could ... foresee" and to what the first-person speaker sees "[f]rom my position as the fly," "from my position / as a thought," and "from my / position as a molecule." Midway through Komunyakaa's "Surge," a parenthetical, italicized interjection — *"(A pause)"* — reveals that the poem is not spoken by the poet. The final phrase of Eleanor Wilner's "Found in the Free Library" uses a parenthetical, italicized comment — *"(but here the document is torn)"* — to a similar end.

Still other poems juxtapose two different vantage points — a present position of safety and domesticity inhabited by the speaker with a distant, calamitous place that the speaker learns of through the news. In this way, the first-person voice implies the incommensurability and inexpressibility of geographically distant events, while also suggesting a painful sense of complicity. In Hugh Seidman's "Thinking of Baghdad," the opposition is explicitly identified as one between "here" (where "I resented the price of a loaf of bread" and "I sat on a park bench in the sun") and "there" ("city, just past imploded brick / ... just past the trope for black holes"). Wilner's "Rendition, with Flag," juxtaposes a domestic scene of setting out nets "to catch ... beavers / who have been teething on the trees" with one, occurring at the same time, where "a US soldier smokes, while Fallujah burns."

Such scenes implicate the domestic "I" while indicating that what is occurring "there"—in most of these cases Iraq—cannot be represented fully or directly. In C. D. Wright's fragment beginning "One bright night," the poem's unidentified protagonists learn of horrors occurring elsewhere on television while "passing through the lobby." Poems such as this imply, without overtly articulating, a critique of American insularity and smugness, while also suggesting, as Gregerson's "Still Life" does, that the safe and remote speaker cannot or should not convey what is occurring elsewhere since "through my lucky and // ignorant life I have never so much as / encountered the scent // of explosives." Moreover, the subject's "here" is most often incommensurate with the event's "there": as Ann Lauterbach notes in her statement, "My near is not your near."

Yet another group of poems excises the speaker altogether in ways that recall the elisions of imagism. In Eamon Grennan's "Y2K," a series of sentence fragments establishes contrasts rather than coherent scenes. The poem begins by juxtaposing a picturesque scene of fog-shrouded chapels with an apparent oil spill: "Mutation of bells. Chapels vanishing in fog. / A cormorant, oil encased. Smoke, more smoke." Timothy Liu's poems juxtapose immediate observations of the aftermath of the 9/11 attacks with political language and cliché while refusing to impose an "I" that might analyze or connect the pieces, revealing the limitations of first-person witness in the face of overwhelming events.

In the process, many of these poems directly challenge the authority of the poet as witness. Donnelly's "Partial Inventory of Airborne Debris" begins with the speaker looking at his reflection: "Small wonder I recoil / even from my own / worn image looking back," then proceeds to critique the familiar lyric stance of introspective self-regard: "I / myself must somehow be // the wolf, and all the rest / must just be television."

As Donnelly's example of the self as wolf indicates, the speaking subject can be alienated and disturbed. The eccentric and deranged narrators of Frederick Seidel's poems provide extreme examples. In "The Bush Administration," a predatory America is out to kill terrorists, to "whiten darkness" ("America will pay any price to whiten darkness") and conquer the "bush" in the other sense of the word—that is, the untamed non–American world. But the speaker, far from being an observer, much less a critic, of political horrors, is an actor at their center:

> I crawl into a crocodile
> And I go native.
> The white cannibals in cowboy boots
> Return to the bush
> And the darkness of the brutes.

> I am on all fours eating grass.
> So I can throw up because I like the feeling.
> I crouch over a carcass and practice my eating.

Here, as in other Seidel poems included in this anthology, the speaker is a bundle of pathologies held up for the reader's horror and fascination. The effect, arguably, is not to inspire outrage or pity so much as to show, as Thomas Hardy said literature should, the sorriness of the world (by which he meant not sorrow but shabbiness).

APPROPRIATED LANGUAGE. Even more often than unfamiliar subjects, contemporary engaged poetry contains unfamiliar language. This language is often not "poetic" but rather found, processed, even official. Poets use this appropriated language in different ways — to critique it, alternate or juxtapose it with other language, or simply present it whole, as found object. J. D. McClatchy's "Jihad" cites italicized Koranic citations. Forrest Hamer's "Conference" includes citations from various participants at a 2001 conference in South Africa on racism. Lisa Sewell's "The Anatomy of Melancholy" juxtaposes citations from Richard Burton's 1621 text with discussions of a bombing in Tikrit and military denials of atrocities against civilians. When other poems subject appropriated language to examination and critique, they sometimes revert to just the kind of political commentary or synthesis that postmodernism has often abjured. Hillman notes that she drew on "the public record" as the "source material" for some of her poems, along with the comments of officials. Her "hope," she claims, was both to call "attention to the misuse of language" and to "transform ... their language." Several poems consider the neologisms, many of them euphemistic, that have proliferated in the 21st century. Naomi Shihab Nye's "Dictionary in the Dark" places quotation marks around words and phrases coopted for political means, including "awe" and "weapons of mass destruction," to draw attention to the kinds of misuse identified by Hillman. A similar aim seems central to Kumin's "Extraordinary Rendition," which presents the etymologies of "rend" and "render," and attempts to restore to the term "extraordinary" its older association with wonder.

Poems such as these, in exposing the implications of official or otherwise commodified language, directly critique American insularity and attempts at omniscience. Other poems, however, engage in what critic Linda Hutcheon has called "complicit critique," a mode in which suspect language is used by a speaker who does not pretend to be aloof from it; that is, a given discourse or subject position is interrogated even as the speaker is revealed to be inexorably bound up with it. This appropriation is a familiar feature of postmodernism. In fact, postmodernism is often defined in terms of the replacement of reality with what Jean Baudrillard and others have called simulacra, copies of reality and copies of those copies. Thus, some of the poems here, rather than emphasizing the trivial or parodic aspect of appropriation, depict experience as accessible *only* through already interpreted or politically manipulated forms — especially the media. They incorporate denatured or dishonest language in part to demonstrate that engagement is not about experience or subjectivity as much as it is about language itself.

The epigraph of Joel Brouwer's "Lines from the Reports of the Investigative Committees," for example, comes from a 2010 BP statement, and the poem does not distinguish between reportorial and lyric language. As a result, "actual" events — Lowell's "fact" — seem indistinguishable from their representations. Brouwer makes a related point in his statement when he links the difficulty of "learning what had happened" after a recent tornado in his town to the simultaneous work of two "crews." The job of "crew one" is to clean up debris and put the material world in order, while "crew two," consisting of various scientific, charitable, meteorological, academic, and journalistic institutions and authorities, constructs coherent narratives about that world. But "the historiographical ministrations of crew two" in fact alter the sense of what really happened and thus impel us to "forfeit at least a portion of the confusion which is our natural state."

Brouwer in this way implies questions similar to those more explicitly posed by Rae Armantrout's statement: how can "we process this [institutional, governmental] deception and how is it processed for us by our popular culture?" Armantrout's own poems often consist entirely of various appropriated phrases or modes of speech — what her statement goes on to call "ideology, of one sort or another, and ... what Marxist theorists call 'false consciousness.'" "Bubble Wrap," for example, mixes a first-person speaker's questions ("'Want to turn on CNN, / see if there've been any /disasters?'") with a series of phrases ("Ponzi scheme," "'astro-turf' calls") drawn from contemporary popular discourse: we cannot locate in this barrage of language a fixed speaker or voice.

By far the most extreme example of the incorporation of existing discourse into a poem is Kenneth Goldsmith's "The Day," which contains nothing but found text: the poem transcribes verbatim the *New York Times* of September 11, 2001. Goldsmith writes in his statement that

> in their self-reflexive use of appropriated language, conceptual writers [like himself] embrace the inherent and inherited politics of the borrowed words: far be it for conceptual writers to morally or politically dictate words that aren't theirs. The choice or machine that makes the poem sets the political agenda in motion, which is often times morally or politically reprehensible to the author.

The power of "The Day" derives from the entirely implicit juxtaposition of the ordinary news of that day with what has not yet occurred, which the reader anticipates and recalls. With all meta-language elided from the poem, the reader is forced to provide it. This mode of appropriation is, arguably, millennial. It recalls but revises the modernist interest in collage: while found objects — for example, Apollinaire's menu from a Chinese restaurant or Duchamp's urinal — were recontextualized at the beginning of the 20th century, early 21st century poems present found objects without intervention or comment, and, in Goldsmith's case, without humor or parody. Goldsmith's, unlike some early 20th century examples, is not a collage of different sources but a single nonpoetic source rendered into poetry.

In short, these poems juxtapose source materials sometimes to mount a critique of them but just as often to achieve a sense of lived reality *through* them.

DIACHRONICITY. The importance of Goldsmith's poem derives in large part from the date of the *New York Times* he transcribes, the day of the attacks on the Trade Towers. Other poems create similar tensions through the use of dates. Donald Revell's "Given Days," C. K. Williams's "Fear," and W. S. Merwin's series of odes involve a tension between the generally mundane, domestic, or natural topics on which the poems focus and the dates they include — in these cases, all around September 2001.

Other poems open up a larger diachronic view: they temporally juxtapose the present and the past in ways that imply not only analogies between these two moments but continuities through history. Prufer uses ancient Roman history, as well as science fiction, to illuminate the present, which his statement says is "swimming away from the immediacy of the events around me ... into now timeless, neutral imagined territory." In an even more pronounced example of this technique, Williams's "War" includes Mayan scribes in A.D. 900, Greek and Trojan gods of the ancient world, and fighter pilots of the present day, all of whom participate in an ongoing and parallel rhythm. The "season's ceaseless wheel," as Williams writes in this poem, suggests the nonlinearity not only of the seasons but of the catastrophe at the heart of the poem: the victims' faces, the smoke, and the "columns of nothingness." In Kinnell's "When the Towers Fell," noted above, a similarly diachronic vision structures the poem: the events of 9/11 alternate with catalogues and allusions spread across centuries, with particular focus on the 20th. Here the allusions — to, among others, Walt Whitman, François Villon, and Paul Celan — do not, as Kinnell explicitly comments in the poem, imply analogies but instead create what he calls "a corollary" and a "lineage": these antecedent scenes, he writes, "come before us now not as a likeness, / but as a corollary, a small instance in the immense / lineage of the twentieth century's history of violent death —"

In evoking history, these poems paradoxically reveal the difficulty of speaking about recent events out of context, a practice that risks either elevating or obscuring the importance of these same events. They also imply that describing a traumatic event in isolation may obscure larger forces at work over long stretches of time. The power of diachronicity in these poems thus does not inhere in their historical specificity as much as in their webbing of poetry, prophecy, and history and in their collapsing of multiple times and locales. The poems do not deny eventness; we live, C. K. Williams writes, in a "particle of time." But they offer an understanding of that particle that is unavailable when it is seen in isolation. The diachronicity of the poems also reveals the deadliness of repetition, which as Wilner notes, is "the context in which today's wars and atrocities are set, a pattern [my] poems record and whose blindness and waste they mourn."

FORM. Our emphasis on content rather than form in the foregoing paragraphs reveals something significant about engaged poetry: this poetry challenges the still-pervasive legacy of the New Criticism, manifest in the tendency to read postmodern and "experimental" poems primarily in formal terms, focusing, that is, on their innovative materiality, on how they sound and look, on their diction, syntax, and style. (This emphasis may be surprising given that many experimental authors profess an oppositional and overtly political stance in their prose. Their reconfiguring of language is meant not for its own sake but to alter ideological assumptions.) We do not mean to imply, however, that form is secondary. Rather, these poems reveal a strikingly wide array of formal choices, whose diversity is bound to the difficulties of representing "what happened."

The use of familiar forms may have a special function where the poetry of trauma is concerned: by containing, confining, or distancing content that would otherwise be inadmissible, form may allow that content to be expressed. Certainly a number of poems here employ traditional forms, including the sonnet, ghazal, villanelle, haibun, and — a form that has found a new life in postmodernity — the pantoum, in which alternating pairs of lines are repeated verbatim. One appeal of such forms may have to do with their repetitiveness: they insist, as does the diachronicity of other poems, on the not-newness of what is occurring. Kumin offers another reason: "The rigors of writing within a pattern somehow seem to free me to speak out. I'm sure there are other poets who feel the same." But formal "rigors" do not only manage the unmanageable; they transform, displace, contextualize, and hybridize contraband content.

Other formal features here — including the mixture of documentary prose and photos in Claudia Rankine's poems and the collages and ellipses of Rae Armantrout — evoke a fragmentation and intertextuality familiar from modernism and often renovated in postmodernism. Like Pound's and Eliot's disjunctive poetics, which are sometimes read as responses to post–World War I trauma, contemporary discontinuities of form enact discontinuities of consciousness. The old techniques, after the millennium, once again help convey the unrepresentability of events and of our responses to them.

The long poem or sequence also recalls modernist modes. But length in the poems of *The New American Poetry of Engagement* seems to serve different purposes than it did for Whitman or William Carlos Williams. Kinnell, for example, incorporates catalogues not of abundance but of trauma and deprivation. In Louise Glück's "October," the speaker herself seems traumatized, unable to name or elaborate on the unnamed event that has recently occurred. Ben Lerner's "Didactic Elegy" depicts the 9/11 attacks in the voice of an unidentified, highly analytic speaker who seems to exemplify the quality of didacticism, while Goldsmith's "The Day," as we have indicated, comprises already-written text, uninterrupted by a speaker or voice.

SAYING WHAT HAPPENED IN THE 21ST CENTURY. What does it mean, then, to write poems that consider the problem of saying what happened? For some of the poems here, the engagement entails addressing the world of poetry itself, its readings, and its audience. Pinsky's "The Forgetting" describes the public reading of an inflammatory and anti–Semitic poem (almost certainly Amiri Baraka's "Somebody Blew Up America"), at which the members of the audience "were applauding and screaming, they were happy" but "they just weren't listening." Pinsky then modifies this claim, considering the possibility that they were listening but in a way that facilitates "an ecstasy of forgetting." By contrast, Jorie Graham's "Praying (Attempt of June 14 '03)" describes an audience listening to a poet, perhaps in ancient Mycenae, who "sing[s] of what has happened," "waiting. Listening for the terrible outcome." In a direct evocation of Lowell, Graham suggests that poetry can say "what has happened" but that the act is meaningful only when it is heard. Here the affirmation of listening mitigates what we have noted as a topic in many poems: the difficulty of writing, the refusal to "ever write about it" and the need to "tell it slant."

In fact, affirmations of the need to write, especially for a particular audience, recur. Pinsky describes the act of writing in "Poem of Disconnected Parts" via a Guantánamo inmate who "incised his Pashto poems into styrofoam cups," a scene that impels the poet to affirm his own commitment to his audience, which in this case includes the dead. Philip Metres's "Testimony (After Daniel Heyman)" blacks out some of its lines, suggesting censorship or the unspeakable. But this tactic of self-censoring, rather than shutting down the poem, affirms the poet's need to "write very quickly / So I do not lose the thread of the story."

It is consistent with the range of strategies these poems use to destabilize witness, subjectivity, tone, and form that such affirmations tend to be curtailed and hesitant. But they also affirm the necessity of attempting to convey "what happened." Forrest Hamer's poem of that title introduces things that "could not be spoken" but goes on to affirm "a word, but not many," then "more words but not what happened." "What happened," the poem concludes, is "a kind of speech, but not yet." While what happens may elude the poet, it enables the poem. In the succinct opening line of W. S. Merwin's "To the Words," which addresses, like all the poems of his we have included, its subject, "when it happens you are not there." (It is significant that Merwin does not specify what "it" is.) But if words are not there when whatever it is happens, they also exist "to say what could not be said," and the poet's job is to impel them to "say it."

Read together, the poems of *The New American Poetry of Engagement* say what happened while enacting the obstacles to doing so. These poems are conscious of the problems involved in representation, but they employ this consciousness not to avoid facts but to get closer to them. In the process, events themselves seem different: rather than being discrete in time and space, they perform the drift and errancy that has long characterized poetry itself. Some of the poems, as they grapple with such issues, get stalled, as Lowell did in his attempt to delineate a poetics of both accuracy and imagination, and that getting stalled becomes part of the subject of the poem. If sometimes the poems approach the luminous clarity ascribed by Lowell to Vermeer, just as often they find in the contradictory demands of their task a poetics committed neither entirely to what happened nor to its imaginative transformation but to the process of shifting between them. It is this friction that has engendered the group of poems collected here, poems that reveal the diversity and commitment, as well as the anxieties, of 21st century American poetry.

Rae Armantrout

New

If yellow
is the new black,

the new you
is a cartoon

spokesman
who blows his lines

around bumptious 3-D
Hondas,

apologizes often,
and remains cheerful.

*

The new pop song
is about getting real:

"You had a bad day.
The camera don't lie."

But they're lying
to you
about the camera.

*

Since Fallujah
is the new Antigua,

sunlight nibbles
on pre-
charred

terrain
in the electric fireplace.

Previews

AMERICA

The playboy scion of a weapons company repents. His
company, he sees now, is corrupt, his weapons being
sold (behind his back) to strong men. Alone, he builds a
super weapon in the shape of a man. Now, more powerful and more innocent than ever before, he attacks.

HAPPENING

The train halts. An engineer tells us we're stopped because we've lost touch with the outside world. Things
are happening ahead, but we don't know what they are.
This could represent an act of war. We stand in a field,
no longer passengers.

Bubble Wrap

"Want to turn on CNN,
see if there've been any
disasters?"

*

In the dream,
you slip inside me.

Ponzi scheme; rhyme scheme.

The child wants his mother
to put her head
where his is, see
what he sees.

*

In the dream
inside the dream,

our new roommates
are arguing:

"These are not
'astro-turf' calls,

and we're all populists
now."

*

Now an engine's
single indrawn breath.

(The black hole
at the heart
of it
is taking it

all back.)

*

An immigrant
sells scorpions
of twisted electrical wire
in front of the Rite-Aid.

Action Poem

1
On screen
men discover
that their mothers
are imposters,
that their world's
unreal.

Substitution
is eerie.

(We discover *this* again.)

2

America
has a lucid dream.

She's falling
from level
to collapsing level
in someone else's (whose?)
terrain, through
floorboards, off bridges,
firing desperately.

Someone says, "Dream
bigger," handing us
an RPG.

Frank Bidart

Curse

May breath for a dead moment cease as jerking your

head upward you hear as if in slow motion floor

collapse evenly upon floor as one hundred and ten

floors descend upon you.

May what you have made descend upon you.
May the listening ears of your victims   their eyes   their

breath

enter you, and eat like acid
the bubble of rectitude that allowed you breath.

May their breath now, in eternity, be your breath.

*

Now, as you wished, you cannot for us
not be. May this be your single profit.

Of your rectitude at last disenthralled, you
seek the dead. Each time you enter them

they spit you out. The dead find you are not food.

Out of the great secret of morals, *the imagination to enter*
the skin of another, what I have made is a curse.

The Soldier Who Guards the Frontier

On the surface of the earth
despite all effort I continued
the life I had led in its depths.

So when you said cuckoo
hello and my heart
leapt up imagine my surprise.

From its depths some mouth
drawn by your refusals of love
fastened on them and fattened.

It's 2004; now the creature
born from our union in 1983
attains maturity.

He guards the frontier.
As he guards the frontier he listens
all day to the records of Edith Piaf.

Heroic risk, Piaf sings. Love
is heroic risk, for what you are impelled
to risk but do not

kills you; as does, of course this voice
knows, risk. He is addicted
to the records of Edith Piaf.

He lives on the aroma, the intoxications
of what he has been spared.
He is grateful, he says, not to exist.

To the Republic

I dreamt I saw a caravan of the dead
start out again from Gettysburg.

Close-packed upright in rows on railcar flat-
beds in the sun, they soon will stink.

Victor and vanquished shoved together, dirt
had bleached the blue and gray one color.

Risen again from Gettysburg, as if
the state were shelter crawled to through

blood, risen disconsolate that we
now ruin the great work of time,

they roll in outrage across America.

You betray us is blazoned across each chest.
To each eye as they pass: *You betray us.*

Assaulted by the impotent dead, I say it's
their misfortune and none of my own.

I dreamt I saw a caravan of the dead
move on wheels touching rails without sound.

To each eye as they pass: *You betray us.*

Inauguration Day

(January 20, 2009)

Today, despite what is dead

staring out across America I see since
Lincoln gunmen
nursing fantasies of purity betrayed,
dreaming to restore
the glories of their blood and state

despite what is dead but lodged within us, hope

under the lustrous flooding moon
the White House is still
Whitman's White House, its
gorgeous front
full of reality, full of illusion

hope made wise by dread begins again

Robert Bly

Call and Answer

August 2002

Tell me why it is we don't lift our voices these days
And cry over what is happening. Have you noticed
The plans are made for Iraq and the ice cap is melting?

I say to myself: "Go on, cry. What's the sense
Of being an adult and having no voice? Cry out!
See who will answer! This is *Call and Answer!*"

We will have to call especially loud to reach
Our angels, who are hard of hearing; they are hiding
In the jugs of silence filled during our wars.

Have we agreed to so many wars that we can't
Escape from silence? If we don't lift our voices, we allow
Others (who are ourselves) to rob the house.

How come we've listened to the great criers — Neruda,
Akhmatova, Thoreau, Frederick Douglass — and now
We're silent as sparrows in the little bushes?

Some masters say our life lasts only seven days.
Where are we in the week? Is it Thursday yet?
Hurry, cry now! Soon Sunday night will come.

Let Sympathy Pass

1.

People vote for what will harm them; everywhere
Borks and thieves, bushes hung with union men.
Things are not well with us. Some deep-
Reaching covetousness rules the countryside.
The greedy one begins to eat Alaska,
The Caribbean Islands, the rainforests, the Tigris.
What did Whitman say a hundred years ago?
"Let sympathy pass, a stranger, to other shores!"

2.

When was it we wanted the holy mountains,
The Black Hills, what did we want them for?
Tamburlaine inhabits the autumnal woods;

Lame in one leg, half-mad, the old man
Inhabits the chambers of inaccessible oaks.
Didn't our race make a deal with the old man
So that the boy in the upper room would live?
Now boars rush in and out of the dusky surf.

3.

The two Bushes come. They say clearly they will
Make the rich richer, starve the homeless,
Tear down the schools, short-change the children,
And they are elected. Millions go to vote,
Vote to lose their houses, their pensions,
Lower their wages, bring themselves to dust.
All for the sake of whom? Oh you know —
That Secret Being, the old rapacious soul.

The Stew of Discontents

1.

Northern lights illumine the storm-troll's house.
There men murdered by God promenade.
The buffalo woman plays her bony flute calling
The lonely father trampled by the buffalo god.
The foreskins of angels shelter the naked cradle.
The stew of discontents feeds the loose souls.
And the owl husbands the moors, harries the mouse,
Beforehand, behindhand, with his handsome eyes.

2.

The White House Administrator sits up late at night
Cutting his nails, and the backs of black whales, the tip
Of the mink's tail, the tongue that appears between lips,
All of these testify to a soul that eats and is eaten.

Pushed on by the inner pressure of teeth,
Some force, animal-born, is slippery, edgy,
Impatient, greedy to pray for new heavens,
Unforgiving, resentful, like a fire in dry wood.

3.

What will you say of our recent adventure?
Some element, Dresdenized, coated with Somme
Mud and flesh, entered, and all prayer was vain.
The Anglo-Saxon poets hear the whistle of the wild
Gander as it glides to the madman's hand.
Spent uranium floats into children's lungs.
All of the sake of whom? For him or her
Or it, the greedy one, the rapacious soul.

Those Being Eaten

The cry of those being eaten by America,
Others pale and soft being stored for later eating.

What of Jefferson
Who saw hope in new oats?

The wild houses go on
With long hair growing from between their toes.
The feet at night get up
And run down the long white roads by themselves.

Dams reverse themselves and want to go stand alone in the
    desert.

Ministers dive headfirst into the earth:
And the pale flesh
Spreads guiltily into new literatures.

That is why these poems are so sad:
The long dead running over the fields,

The mass sinking down,
The light in children's faces fading at six or seven.

The world will soon break up into small colonies of the saved.

Here the Sleepers Sleep

1.

Here the sleepers sleep, here the Rams and the Bears play.
The old woman weeps at night in her room at the Nursing Facility.
There are no bridges over the ocean.
She sees a short dock, and ahead of that darkness, hostile waters,
    lifting swells,
Fitfully lit, or not lit at all.
Tadpoles drowse in the stagnant holes.
The gecko goes back to this home in the cold rain.

2.

The wife of the Chrysler dealer is in danger of being committed
    again.
She left the hospital hopeful, she struggles hard,
She reads Laing and Rollo May;
But nothing works, she dreams she is interred in Burma.
Cars go past her house at night, Japanese soldiers at the wheel.
Nothing can be done, the kernel opens, all is swept away;
She is carried out of sight.
The doctor arrives; once more she leaves dry-eyed for the hospital

3.

We wake, no dream is remembered, the scenes gone into smoke.
We are in some enormous place, abandoned,
Where Adam Kadmon has been forgotten, the luminous man is
    dissolved.
The sarcophagus contains the rotted bones of the monks; so many
    lived in the desert.
None are alive, only the bones lie in the dust.
My friend goes to Philadelphia to claim his father's body.

It lies in an uncarpeted room in the ghetto, there was no one else
  to claim the body.
The time of manifest destiny is over, the time of grief has come

---

Bruce Bond

The Altars of September

That night she closed her eyes and saw
the trapped birds of voices shatter
against the crumbling walls, like a scene
in a movie replaying the disaster,
lighting up the back of the brain.
With each collapse the glass rose up,
restored, bright with sky, the fist
of God a shadow-plane approaching.

And it felt so distant, the numb
comfort that would bear this image
into the first cold regions of sleep,
the blackboard of the body wet
and remless, as if those towers
fell still deeper through the floor
of the mind, gone the way of the pill
she took in faith, swallowing the world.

However many nights she clicked
her TV off, its spark of light
dwindling into the clear stone,
it would take time for any shape
slipping through her hands to lie
down in clay or paper, any lip
of paint to redden her brush.
White was its own confession.

She always imagined the distance
between a painting of a day

and the day behind it as a path
that carries us into our lives,
giving us more room, more reason
to move, luring us on and in
like sleep so deep in the body
all we see is of the body.

In time, looking out this way
through the window of her canvas,
every cloud dragging its anchor
becomes a burden of the flesh,
not hers alone, but the skin
of what no solitary gaze
can tear there from heaven's fire,
what no frame can ever shelter.

Just that morning before she heard
the news, she took the shore drive south,
set up her easel, all the while
an unaccountable strangeness
drawn down over the folding cliffs,
a stillness unlike any day,
the uneasy silence of the skies
that hour tender as an eye.

Flag

These nights in all their smoke
and armor, the great concussions

of bad faith thumping the horizon,
the epileptic flash inside the cloud

giving it depth, reach, weight to pull
as we move about our drowsy city,

I keep seeing my mother's room
at dusk, small, fading, lit by the ice

of television glass; how brief a life,
how long the hours, how fretful

the mother who picks the spice
grain by grain from a plate of meat,

who presses her palms against her eyes
as if to bury the world in the world.

Any wonder I too turn the pages
of my linens, bathed in ink,

that I sink my face in my pillow
and read. And whose world is it

that leans so close to blow out
the stray candles of my words,

to pare the evening horror down
to human size, to the crumpling

sound of spring rain; whose hand is this
that cracks the window of a book,

its Buddha hemmed in flags of fire,
a hub in the mind's wide *wheel* of fire.

Be in the world but not of it,
says the book — or is it the other way —

*be lodged in the ring of flames
so deep there's no retreating.*

I could be somewhere between this
wakefulness and another country,

in the no-fly zone of near-sleep
where ceilings buckle, sigh, click

into place, where the clock bleeds
a little nightlight, humming,

where over and over the wind gives
its briefing to the alders,

and who am I to talk, I say,
as if God burned the letters that we sent.

My flag is not my flag
draped on the face of a tyrant statue.

Its colors are no brighter
than a song I sang badly as a boy.

No song, says the world, *not now.*
No mooning over a troubled covenant.

No song for the beast of the literal
heart thrashing in its irons.

And then it comes to me:
my father's weariness at the end

of day, eyes glazed, his body
bearing what I could not fathom.

It is 1954; somewhere still
ash settles on a village in Korea.

Bombs shake the Nevada sand.
Birds drop out of the sky in cinders.

Be in the world but not of it,
says the body, the eye, the ring of flames.

My father blankets the grass,
tunes the somber radio and falls

asleep, drowned in violins —
hello in there, we whisper —

that gentle snore like a cleft chain
dragging across the ocean floor.

Ringtone

As they loaded the dead onto the gurneys
to wheel them from the university halls,
who could have predicted the startled chirping
in those pockets, the invisible bells
and tiny metal music of the phones,
in each the cheer of a voiceless song.
Pop mostly, Timberlake, Shakira, tunes
never more various now, more young,
shibboleths of what a student hears,
what chimes the dark doorway to the parent
on the line. Who could have answered there
in proxy for the dead, received the panic
with grace, however artless, a live bird
gone still at the meeting of the strangers.

Joel Brouwer

Lines from the Reports of the Investigative Committees

The Department of the Interior and Department of Homeland Security announced a joint enquiry into the explosion and sinking of the Transocean Deepwater Horizon on April 22. The U.S. House of Representatives Committee on Energy and Commerce Subcommittee on Oversight and Investigations and Senate Committee on Energy and Natural Resources have also announced investigations.

Last week BP launched its own investigation into the incident and has an investigation team at work in Houston, Texas.
— bp.com, April 28, 2010

Beneath three thousand feet, the sea is wholly dark.
The shuttle feeds hydraulics to the blind shear ram
and represents a single failure point for disconnect.
Recommendation: Declare selected points on earth
invisible. Affected communities have been provided
with limited quantities of powdered milk
and other staples. Many questions remain. Some

close their eyes under water instinctively.
Imagination can create a sense of peril where
no real peril exists. Safety equipment tests
were necessarily imaginary; mechanisms in question
were wholly inaccessible. A journalist sinking
into the mud was told to toss his camera
to a colleague and hold extremely still. In this
sense, we are our own prisoners. Investigators
have salt in their hair and sand in their teeth.
The hotel pool is empty. Yet questions remain.
Barbeque billboards depict grinning pigs in aprons
and toques. Cleanup crews recover thousands
of plastic milk jugs from the shallows. Do these
images appeal to the death drive? Care should be
taken to ensure the highest possible reliability
from that valve. Thousands in affected communities
have been evicted and live in tents. Demonstrators
have prevented investigators from accessing
hotel stairwells. 1900: Rudolf Diesel
demonstrates an engine fueled by peanut oil
at the Paris World's Fair. The Vietnamese owner
of Bad Bob's bbq Buffet tells a journalist
she last drank powdered milk in a refugee camp
"a thousand years ago." Items available only
in limited quantities are found in Appendix C.
Cleanup crews have stacked thousands of drums
of dispersant in hotel parking lots. Dominant
failure combinations for well control suggest
additional safety mechanism diversity
and redundancy provide additional reliability.
Bank of America will offer limited foreclosure
deferments in affected communities. Thousands
of years ago, a pronghorn ram slipped beneath
the surface of a tar pit, jerking its snout
for air. Recommendation: Live at inaccessible
elevations. Recommendation: Close your eyes.
Recommendation: Prevent access to the invisible.
Engineering reports noted required safety
mechanisms were unlikely to function yet were
required for safety's sake. If the committee
may offer an analogy, a blind surgeon is dangerous,

an imaginary surgeon harmless. Still, questions
remain. BP's 2010 Q1 replacement cost profit
was $5,598 million, compared with $2,387 million
a year ago, an increase of 135%. Unlimited
quantities of peanuts are available. However,
care must be taken to ensure continued high
reliability of the shuttle valve, since it is
extremely critical to the overall disconnect
operation. Phenomena not meant to be accessed
or imagined are found in Appendix E. Cleanup crews
are sometimes idled for lack of fuel. 1913: Diesel
found dead, drowned under suspicious circumstances.
The investigators' hotel toilets won't flush.
Midas turned everything he touched to gold.
In this sense, seabirds cloaked in oil are rich.
Cleanup crews live in tents and are provided
with limited quantities of barbeque and wear
white canvas jumpsuits like prisoners on furlough.
If the committee may offer an analogy, the death
drive resides at wholly dark depths of imagination
and fuel issues from a wound we've opened there.

Timothy Donnelly

Partial Inventory of Airborne Debris

Small wonder I recoil
    even from my own
worn image looking back

where I always find it
    looking like it's trying
to warn me something

unspeakable is coming:
    Item. I stand before me
in a haze where people

can be made to want to
　　make people stand
precariously on boxes,

arms wide open, strange
　　hoods pulled down
over human faces, little live

wires hooked to various
　　parts of the bodies
ridden on like donkeys,

smeared in feces, stacked
　　one on top the other
for a photo to prolong

the swell an accomplishment
　　like that engenders.
Item. What kept us from

discovering our selves'
　　worst wasn't the lack
of evidence so much as

a failure of delivery, a kink
　　overcome through
the push in technology

we've all had a hand in
　　one way or the other.
Item. Looks like anyone

can be led as soon astray
　　as to slaughter, disappearing
down the long ill-lit

institutional corridor
　　misadventure unfolds
one synapse at a time —

and to presume immunity
　　may be a symptom.
Item. In time I begin to

lose sensation, thoughts,
    I'm not complaining,
dropped a sedative in

tapwater and watched
    its demonstration on
what we have in common

with a sunset, gradual
    change and all the rest,
difficult to paraphrase

to be honest but I'm not
    complaining, it's like being
detained indefinitely

but with three meals a day
    on a tropical island!
Item. Looks like what's

done in my defense, or in
    its name, or in my
interest or in the image

of the same, no matter how
    distorted, fattened up
for laughs or plain dead-on,

connects to me by virtue
    of an invisible filament
over which I can claim

no know-how, no management,
    no muscle to speak of
(anatomical or spiritual),

what can I do, I can feel it
    tugging again, what have I
done: rotisserie chicken,

homestyle gravy, mac
    and cheese, a hot biscuit,
sweet potato casserole —

admit it, I'm on the fat side.
   Item. As when a putz
collapses to the dance hall's

floor and the pianist stops
   his performing mid-
waltz, always an angel

in a large brown gown
   bends over the slowly
reviving body and says

Don't stop Paul we need you
   now more than ever,
whereupon Paul, without

much thought, without
   the burden of thinking,
sits back down, picks up

where he left off and plays.
   Item. Or say a dream wolf
found my room by scent,

entered it, climbed upon
   my sleeping throat
and camped there just to prove

its point, and when I woke
   up I feared I'd never
save myself or even under-

stand what from without a little
   alteration, meaning I
myself must somehow be

the wolf, and all the rest
   must just be television.
Item. Only in the ion-

rich atmosphere around
   a waterfall too immense
to be nostalgic did I feel

what I now know to be
    "the feel of not to feel it."
Item. Actually I'm doing

much better now, maybe
    a little, what's the word,
soporose, I guess, I think

maybe I just needed to
    work it through and now
in its wake I feel a little

what was it again, a little
    soporose, that's right,
that captures it in a way

no other word could ever
    even hope to, I suppose,
I just feel soporose, so

soporose tonight, uniquely
    soporose. You think
I should be concerned?

Dream of Arabian Hillbillies

Salutations from the all-encompassing
    arms of a hammered millionaire!
I send a blessing of watches over your body
    and a messenger to your folks

sanctifying them in a long crude eruption.
    May you journey in the security
of a huge American truck. May your enemies come
    to wither in front of this truck

allowing you and your kinfolk to occupy
    the avenue of personal interests
privately and in full style for 60,000 years.
    Talk about divine measures!

All enemy forces threatening your basic
    philosophy of life demand a helpin'
of grievous medicine: it is no longer possible
    to press letters of forgiveness

loaded with soft words and in diplomatic
    style into their hands when clearly
in their hearts they would strip you of such
    incredible resources: money out

back in important places, a wicked grip
    on the situation, pools of lost time
and no little grace ... but who can push the enemy
    underground with hospitality?

No one. Gain control of circumstances by
    taking some. Repel with mischief
raised to the utmost power, one forbidden
    behavior after another, from pure

dissociation from the feelings and prides
    of your forefathers to aggression
against the infrastructures of the sea and sky.
    Spell serious danger to their being,

y'all — only half your hoard is remaining.
    I address you now with a big torch
of guidance handed over to me by the stars
    above Texas. It is unacceptable

to assist the enemy in your dispossession.
    Be not bitten by the same snake
twice. The first explosion inspired
    the devil, and the second a gathering

of military leaders who talk to you through such
    fast moving light, one day today
is tomorrow's fear commercial, thank you
    very much. The money you pay

out for loving this world will all come back
    for the money you have left, saying

"To express hate and anger is a moral gesture
    to the future." I did *not* just say that.

Time to be enshrined in the sanctities
    of pleasure, not dragged through the streets
of the bubblin' in your head that is
    the persistence of news agencies.

Time to liberate that head from the whole
    world's behind and listen for a pen
to spell the words of your foes' humiliation.
    Why not paradise before as well as

after death, kept at a beautiful 72 degrees
    and with nothing between you
and all the privileges heapin' so high
    a neck is pinched just signing up for them?

Terrorizing the snake for twisting filthy
    text to your house is a human duty.
Let your good black shoes witness you push
    hard into the red dust of the battle

burning your intestines like a pagan tea.
    Cleanse the road to your destiny
of all idolaters and claim what they be droppin'
    for your booty. Take no captives —

or maybe one or two, should they surrender
    wealth, drink, hearts and selves
to your supremacy without hesitation.
    Paradise's nearness isn't getting any

better. May you not cave in and weep deep. May wolves
    not eat your wings. May your life
not be a lifelong movie of your life
    but a steadfast becoming other than that

which you are: a slave to the power
    fiddling among hills of fed clouds and shaken
into wonderment like a shot horse barely
    gathering will to lay down with it, y'hear?

Carolyn Forché

The Ghost of Heaven

Sleep to sleep through thirty years of night,
a child herself with child,
for whom we searched

through here, or there, amidst
bones still sleeved and trousered,
a spine picked clean, a paint can,
a skull with hair

Sewn into the hem of memory:
Fire.
God of Abraham, God of Isaac, God of Jacob,
God not
of philosophers or scholars. God not of poets.

Night to night:
child walking toward me through burning maize
over the clean bones of those whose flesh
was lifted by *zopilotes* into heaven.

So that is how we ascend!
In the clawed feet of fallen angels.
To be assembled again
in the work rooms of clouds.

She rose from where they found her lying
not far from a water urn, leaving
herself behind on the ground
where they found her, holding her arms
before her as if she were asleep.

That is how she appears to me: a ghost in heaven.
Carrying her arms in her arms.

Blue smoke from corn cribs, flap of wings.
On the walls of the city streets a *plague of initials.*

Walking through a fire-lit river
to a burning house: dead Singer
sewing machine and piece of dress.

Outside a cashew tree wept
blackened cashews over lamina.

Outside paper fireflies rose to the stars.

Bring penicillin if you can, surgical tape, a whetstone,
mosquito repellent but not the aerosol kind.
Especially bring a syringe for sucking phlegm,
a knife, wooden sticks, a surgical clamp, and plastic bags.

You will need a bottle of cloud
for anesthesia.

Like the flight of a crane
through colorless dreams.

When a leech opens your flesh it leaves a small volcano.
Always pour turpentine over your hair before going to sleep.

Such experiences as these are forgotten
before memory intrudes.

The girl was found (don't say this)
with a man's severed head stuffed
into her where a child would have been.
No one knew who the man was.
Another of the dead.
So they had not, after all,
killed a pregnant girl.
This was a relief to them.

That sound in the brush?
A settling of wind in sorghum.

If they capture you, talk.

Talk. Please yes. You heard me
right the first time.

You will be asked who you are.
Eventually, we are all asked who we are.

All who come
All who come into the world
All who come into the world are sent.
Open your curtain of spirit.

Katie Ford

Flee

When the transistor said *killing wind*
I felt myself a small noise

a call sign rubbed out
but still live where light
cut through the floorboards

and don't you think I dreamed the light a sign

didn't I want to cross
the water of green beads breaking
where one saw the other last

where the roof was torn
and the dome cried out
that the tearing was wide and far

and this is not just a lesson
of how to paint an X upon a house
how to mark one dead in the attic
two on the floor

didn't I wish
but didn't I flee

when the cries fell through
the surface of light
and the light stayed light
as if to say nothing or

what do you expect me to do

I am not human

I gave you each other
so save each other.

Earth

If you respect the dead
and recall where they died
by this time tomorrow
there will be nowhere to walk.

Fish Market

Now the suicidal drift
toward the market along the river.

Blue tarps drape the oysters
harvested from contaminated beds,
silverlings caught from trestles of the resealed lake,

their eyes against the also-open eyes
of hundreds in the sudden underneath.

What is there now to eat? Here:
fish unfold from their skins.
It is meat, you don't have
to look anymore. Disaster

eats what there is. It is
biblical: sit at the table of another

country, you must eat
what is set before you.

They didn't know they were in another country
until they were left living.

Confused by hunger,
they fill their bags.

The Vessel Bends the Water

The body begs for a system that will not break —
even to fold the warm clothes, wanting
the edges to do as they are meant to do —
                                        this is why I touched him,
I could hardly touch him, I touched him for only
a short time and not for the reason he thought.
I had been thinking of the river before, its rocks bared
and dried and deeply summered.
But then reports came back of barges breaking
the levees, skiffs bent against boulders,
aluminum glistening from above
like the wet lid of some downturned eye
that is not ashamed but about to plead
for some just realized need,
an answer to all this death. But the earth sends
only Indian paintbrush —
the feathery plant that grows where an animal has died —
not as elegy but as substitute. Last night, things made
sudden by illness, I held
onto the kitchen counter, and this seems like nothing,
how I kept my hands there. Nothing, my hands on his stomach,
where small chinks had been taken out of his skin as if by a carver's tool.
And I know there is no retrieving it back: no retrieving any of it back:
the time the body, its tree-shadowed markings,
has been racked against the walls
with no one else, just highway,
just windows.
                        Yet in those few times I touched him,
knowing one thing unfolded us both, it was my history beneath me,
my hands at least touching its skin.

Forrest Gander

Background Check

The neck and head of a horse, but with the seam of the jaw
ripped away and filled with light and the tongue, a piece of tongue,
    knifing out between remnant teeth

Above the horse, a lid closes over a fire: this is the sun extinguished

From a mass of hair a hand stretches out gripping a lantern

The figure of a woman, her neck craned
        from her crouching body, her left leg angled
wrongly and dragging behind her, her mouth
    in the light her eyes in shadow her eyes
            on the same side of her cheek

            Behind the gesturing figures, what remains of a tile roof,
        a wall, a window through which we can see —
    what can we see?

    With exclamatory silent force, two arms and a long throat
bearing a woman's upturned head are
            flung skyward
        through a break in the roof
    over a room consumed in fire

The UN diplomat draws it is not it is not war
behind the ambassador to speak draws
a curtain it is not Guernica to speak united
the curtain across the diplomat a reproduction
United States with curtain across the not war
appropriate scene right behind him it is not the
ambassador of Guernica to speak with right states
of reproduction the diplomat draws a curtain
across the scene it is not appropriate for the
ambassador of the United States to speak of war

with a reproduction of Guernica
right behind behind right behind him

Peter Gizzi

Protest Song

This is not a declaration of love or song of war
not a tractate, autonym, or apologia

This won't help when the children are dying
no answer on the way to dust

Neither anthem to rally nor flag flutter
will bring back the dead, their ashes flying

This is not a bandage or hospital tent
not relief or the rest after

Not a wreath, lilac, or laurel sprig
not a garden of earthly delights

Louise Glück

October

1.

Is it winter again, is it cold again,
didn't Frank just slip on the ice,
didn't he heal, weren't the spring seeds planted

didn't the night end,
didn't the melting ice
flood the narrow gutters

wasn't my body
rescued, wasn't it safe

didn't the scar form, invisible
above the injury

terror and cold,
didn't they just end, wasn't the back garden
harrowed and planted —

I remember how the earth felt, red and dense,
in stiff rows, weren't the seeds planted,
didn't vines climb the south wall

I can't hear your voice
for the wind's cries, whistling over the bare ground

I no longer care
what sound it makes

when I was silenced, when did it first seem
pointless to describe that sound

what it sounds like can't change what it is —

didn't the night end, wasn't the earth
safe when it was planted

didn't we plant the seeds,
weren't we necessary to the earth,
the vines, were they harvested?

2.

Summer after summer has ended,
balm after violence:
it does me no good
to be good to me now;
violence has changed me.

Daybreak. The low hills shine
ochre and fire, even the fields shine.

I know what I see; sun that could be
the August sun, returning
everything that was taken away —

You hear this voice? This is my mind's voice;
you can't touch my body now.
It has changed once, it has hardened,
don't ask it to respond again.

A day like a day in summer.
Exceptionally still. The long shadows of the maples
nearly mauve on the gravel paths.
And in the evening, warmth. Night like a night in summer.

It does me no good; violence has changed me.
My body has grown cold like the stripped fields;
now there is only my mind, cautious and wary,
with the sense it is being tested.

Once more, the sun rises as it rose in summer;
bounty, balm after violence.
Balm after the leaves have changed, after the fields
have been harvested and turned.

Tell me this is the future,
I won't believe you.
Tell me I'm living,
I won't believe you.

3.

Snow had fallen. I remember
music from an open window.

Come to me, said the world.
This is not to say
it spoke in exact sentences
but that I perceived beauty in this manner.

Sunrise. A film of moisture
on each living thing. Pools of cold light
formed in the gutters.

I stood
at the doorway,
ridiculous as it now seems.

What others found in art,
I found in nature. What others found
in human love, I found in nature.
Very simple. But there was no voice there.

Winter was over. In the thawed dirt,
bits of green were showing.

Come to me, said the world. I was standing
in my wool coat at a kind of bright portal —
I can finally say
long ago; it gives me considerable pleasure. Beauty
the healer, the teacher —

death cannot harm me
more than you have harmed me,
my beloved life.

4.

The light has changed;
middle C is tuned darker now.
And the songs of morning sound over-rehearsed.

This is the light of autumn, not the light of spring.
The light of autumn: *you will not be spared.*

The songs have changed; the unspeakable
has entered them.

This is the light of autumn, not the light that says
I am reborn.

Not the spring dawn: *I strained, I suffered, I was delivered.*
This is the present, an allegory of waste.

So much has changed. And still, you are fortunate:
the ideal burns in you like a fever.
Or not like a fever, like a second heart.

The songs have changed, but really they are still quite beautiful.
They have been concentrated in a smaller space, the space of the mind.
They are dark, now, with desolation and anguish.

And yet the notes recur. They hover oddly
in anticipation of silence.
The ear gets used to them.
The eye gets used to disappearances.

You will not be spared, nor will what you love be spared.

A wind has come and gone, taking apart the mind;
it has left in its wake a strange lucidity.

How privileged you are, to be still passionately
clinging to what you love;
the forfeit of hope has not destroyed you.

Maestro, doloroso:

This is the light of autumn; it has turned on us.
Surely it is a privilege to approach the end
still believing in something.

5.

It is true that there is not enough beauty in the world.
It is also true that I am not competent to restore it.
Neither is there candor, and here I may be of some use.

I am
at work, though I am silent.

The bland

misery of the world
bounds us on either side, an alley

lined with trees; we are

companions here, not speaking,
each with his own thoughts;

behind the trees, iron

gates of the private houses,
the shuttered rooms

somehow deserted, abandoned,

as though it were the artist's
duty to create
hope, but out of what? what?

the word itself
false, a device to refute
perception — At the intersection,

ornamental lights of the season.

I was young here. Riding
the subway with my small book
as though to defend myself against

the same world:

you are not alone,
the poem said,
in the dark tunnel.

6.

The brightness of the day becomes
the brightness of the night;
the fire becomes the mirror.

My friend the earth is bitter; I think
sunlight has failed her.
Bitter or weary, it is hard to say.

Between herself and the sun,
something has ended.
She wants, now, to be left alone;
I think we must give up
turning to her for affirmation.

Above the fields,
above the roofs of the village houses,

the brilliance that made all life possible
becomes the cold stars.

Lie still and watch:
they give nothing but ask nothing.

From within the earth's
bitter disgrace, coldness and barrenness

my friend the moon rises:
she is beautiful tonight, but when is she not beautiful?

Albert Goldbarth

Some Common Terms in Latin
That Are Larger Than Our Lives

From a description in a catalogue of rare science-fantasy titles: "Involves a
utopian society in Atlantis, war with giant apes, prehistoric creatures, dragon-
like beings, etc."

Mutant-engineered bloodsucker djinns, invisibility rays,
lost civilizations, past-life telepathic romance
— anything, finally, can fit in *et cetera*, even in
its abbreviation; much as in some story

out of Borges, where the world is the same as a library
holding all of the books in the world, and one book
holds the sentence "This is all of the books
in the world," so is, by itself, sufficient. Or

this woman on the streets of Manhattan, September 11,
2001: the look in her face is a gene
of the entire holocaustal event; fast-forward to it
any time you need to construct that whole

unbearable day. And other people are huddled
under girders, shrieking out as if to angels somewhere
at the edges of this, to presences outside of the human
— gods, and demons, and beings of the supernatural realms,

et al. And others are too dazed even for that;
they're empty now of everything except a stare
at the incomprehensible shape of things, the sky,
and what's beyond the sky, and beyond that, *ad infinitum.*

Kenneth Goldsmith

"A1" from *The Day*

"All the News
That's Fit to Print"
The New York Times
Late Edition
New York: Today, mainly sunny and noticeably less humid, high 79.
Tonight, clear, low 62. Tomorrow, sunny and cool, high 76. Yesterday,
high 86, low 73. Weather map is on Page D8.
  VOL. CL... No. 51,873
  Copyright <copy> 2001 The New York Times
  NEW YORK, TUESDAY, SEPTEMBER 11, 2001
  $1 beyond the greater New York metropolitan area.
  75 CENTS
  Photographs, clockwise from top left, by Librado Romero, Ruby
Washington, Ruth Fremson and James Estrin / The New York Times
  THE HOME STRETCH On the last day of campaigning, the mayoral
candidates scoured the city for votes. Clockwise from top Peter F. Vallone,
Alan G. Hevesi and Mark Green talked with voters in Brooklyn and
Manhattan. The polls are open from 6 A.M. to 9 P.M. Page B1
  Nuclear Booty:
  More Smugglers
  Use Asia Route
  By DOUGLAS FRANTZ
  ISTANBUL, Sept. 10— The police in Batumi, a Black Sea port in
Georgia, heard a rumor in July that someone wanted to sell several pounds
of high-grade uranium for $100,000. The most tantalizing aspect of the
tip was that one of the sellers was reportedly a Georgia Army officer.
  All sorts of scoundrels have tried nuclear smuggling in recent years.
Many are amateurs; most of what they try to peddle proves useless for
making bombs.

But the possible involvement of an army officer gave the Batumi case a measure of deadly seriousness, beyond its status as another example of how the smuggling of nuclear material has shifted to Central Asia.

On the morning of July 20, the local antiterrorist squad burst into a small hotel room near the port, just outside the Turkish border. They arrested four men, including an army captain named Shota Geladze.

On the floor of the room, in a glass jar wrapped in plastic, sat nearly four pounds of enriched uranium 235, according to Revaz Chantladze, one of the police officers. The quantity was less than is usually required for a small atomic bomb.

Subsequent analysis yielded differing opinions. A Western diplomat
Continued on Page A10
City Voters Have Heard It All
As Campaign Din Nears End
By JIM DWYER

The first time the phone rang, Victoria Ehigiator was elbow deep in a sink of soapy dishes. She dried her hands and picked up the phone. It was Al Sharpton on the line, calling about the primary election. He said his piece, and she went back to the dishes. A few minutes later, the phone rang again, and she lifted herself from the bubbles once more.

That time it was Fernando Ferrer. And then it was Gloria Davis. Followed by Adolfo Carrión.

As one digitized caller after another dropped into her home, thanks to new technology that can swamp the telephones in a ZIP code or an entire city with the actual voice of, say, Ed Koch, urging a vote for Peter Vallone, Ms. Ehigiator started to suspect that very few people in New York were not running for something — whether it was mayor, comptroller, public advocate, borough president or City Council.

And as for those few who weren't candidates, they all seemed to be calling her about those who were.

Had Bill Bradley actually phoned her about Herb Berman? And who was Herb Berman, anyway? (Psst: he's a council member running for comptroller.)

"There was another guy — his name starts with S," said Ms. Ehiglator, of Morrisania in the Bronx, offering no other clues. "I'm trying to do the Sunday dishes but I never got off the phone with all these animated voice messages. It was a real fiesta of phone calls."

Today is the end of the busiest primary campaign around here that anyone can remember, and the candidates are ganging up on the small fraction of the electorate that customarily decides such races. From the high cliffs of northern Manhattan to the ocean foam at Rockaway Beach,

New Yorkers report they are coping by slamming down the phone faster, throwing out the mail sooner,

Continued on Page B5

A Nation of Early Risers,

Morning TV Is a Hot Market

By BILL CARTER

How much morning television can one nation watch?

Ever since the owlish Dave Garroway ambled through the "Today" program on NBC starting in 1952, sometimes accompanied by a chimpanzee, television screens have greeted awakening Americans with the combination of hard news, feature reports and soft celebrity interviews that has come to be known as the morning news program.

But the competition for bleary eyes has grown more intense as media conglomerates have awakened to

the idea that changing lives, heightened interest from advertisers and other factors have made the morning one of the few areas of growth in the television business.

That trend was underscored last week when CNN raided its rival all-news cable network, Fox News, and took the anchor Paula Zahn for a new morning program it will begin next spring from inside the Time & Life Building at 50th Street on the Avenue of the Americas in Midtown Manhattan.

According to Fox executives, reading from the offer sheet they said CNN gave to Ms. Zahn, CNN agreed to triple her salary, bringing it over the $2 million mark.

The figure would be by far the most money CNN has ever paid for an anchor, far more than double what CNN agreed to pay to Aaron Brown, the anchor it has brought in from ABC to lead a prime-time newscast.

The raid and Fox's response — a lawsuit — represent the latest nasty interchange between Fox News and CNN, and serve as a proxy for a larger corporate battle between

Continued on Page C16

NEWS SUMMARY A2

Arts E1–10

Business Day C1–16

Editorial, Op-Ed A22–23

International A3–15

Metro B17

National A16–21

Science Times F1–12

Sports Tuesday D1–8

World Business W1–8
Fashion B7–8
Fashion B7–8
Health/Fitness F5–12
Obituaries C17
Weather D8
Classified Ads F9–11
Auto Exchange D4
Updated news: www.nytlmes.com
School Dress Codes vs. a Sea of Bare Flesh
By KATE ZERNIKE
MILLBURN, N.J., Sept. 7 — In the tumult of bare skin that is the hallway of Millburn High School, Michele Pitts is the Enforcer.

"Hon, put the sweater on," she barks at a pair of bare shoulders.

"Lose those flip-flops," to a pair of bare legs.

One student waves her off as Mrs. Pitts crosses her arms in a "Cover that cleavage" sign. "You talked to me already," the girl insists, then promises, "Tomorrow!" as she disappears around a corner.

Baseball caps, a taboo of yesteryear, pass by unchallenged, having slipped in severity on a list of offenses that now include exposed bellies, backs and thighs. For Mrs. Pitts, the assistant principal, there is simply too much skin to cover.

With Britney Spears and CosmoGirl setting the fashion trends, shirts and skirts are inching up, pants are slipping down, and schools across the country are finding themselves forced to tighten their dress codes and police their hallways.

This fall, New York State is requiring all public school districts to Adopt dress codes as part of a larger code of conduct. In North Carolina, the bill that allowed schools to post the Ten Commandments also required them to institute dress codes.

The days when torn jeans tested the limits are now a fond memory. Today, schools feel the need to remind students that see-through clothing is not appropriate. (The Liverpool Central School District, near Syracuse, learned this when two high school girls showed up on Halloween dressed in Saran Wrap. Only one appeared to be wearing underwear.)

In the new dress codes, spaghetti straps are forbidden (straps must be no less than an inch and a half

Don Standing
for The Now York Times
The dress code
at Millburn High

School aims to
raise standards and self-respect.
It frowns on low
necklines, bared
shoulders, flip-
flops and spa-
ghetti straps.

wide), as is clothing that "bares the private parts"; fishnet stockings and shirts; T-shirts with lewd messages; flip-flops or other clothing more suited to the beach; and skirts or shorts above mid-thigh. Boys cannot wear tank tops or

Continued on Page B7

INSIDE

Mrs. Dole to Run for Senate

Elizabeth Dole plans to announce that she will run in 2002 for the Senate seat being vacated by Jesse Helms of North Carolina. PAGE A16

Afghan Rebel's Fate Unclear

A day after a bombing aimed at the leader of the opposition to the Taliban, there were conflicting reports as to whether he survived. PAGE A15

Morgan Stanley Bias Suit

The Equal Employment Opportunity Commission filed a sex-discrimination suit against Morgan Stanley Dean Witter. BUSINESS DAY, PAGE C1

FOR HOME DELIVERY CALL 1-800-NYTIMES

0 354613937201

Giants Fail in Opener

The Giants allowed touchdowns in every quarter as the host Denver Broncos rolled to a 31–20 victory.

SPORTSTUESDAY, PAGE D1

Debate Over Shark Attacks

Commercial fishermen are at odds with scientists over the reason for a spate of highly publicized shark attacks. SCIENCE TIMES, PAGE F1

Scientists Urge
Bigger Supply
Of Stem Cells
Report Backs Cloning
to Create New Lines

By SHERYL GAY STOLBERG

WASHINGTON, Sept. 10 — A panel of scientific experts has concluded that new colonies, or lines, of human embryonic stem cells will be necessary if the science is to fulfill its potential, a finding that is likely to inflame the political debate over President Bush's decision to restrict federally financed research to the 64 stem cell lines that are already known to exist.

In a 59-page report that examines the state of human stem cell science, the panel also endorsed cloning technology to create new stem cells that could be used to treat patients. Mr. Bush strongly opposes human cloning for any reason, and the House of Representatives voted in July to outlaw any type of cloning, whether for reproduction or research.

The report by the National Academy of Sciences, perhaps the nation's most eminent organization of scientists, is scheduled to be made public on Tuesday morning at a news conference in Washington. It does not address Mr. Bush's policy directly, though it strongly supports federal financing for stem cell research.

"High quality, publicly funded research is the wellspring of medical breakthroughs," said the report, a copy of which was provided to The New York Times by Congressional supporters of stem cell research. It added that federal financing, and the government oversight that comes with it, "offers the most efficient and responsible means of fulfilling the promise of stem cells to meet the need for regenerative medical therapies."

Though the academy often issues its reports in response to requests from the government, it embarked on this study on its own earlier this year. The study was not an exhaustive review of the scientific literature in stem cells, but was rather intended to examine the prospects for the on this study on its own earlier this year. The study was not an exhaustive review of the scientific literature in stem cells, but was rather intended to examine the prospects for the research and to make policy recommendations. The report was written

Continued on Page A18

Strict Arsenic Limit Sought

Strict standards for arsenic in drinking water, suspended by the Bush administration, were justified, experts have concluded. Page A20.

KEY LEADERS TALK
OF POSSIBLE DEALS
TO REVIVE ECONOMY
BUSH IS UNDER PRESSURE
Lott Open to More Tax Cuts—
Democrat Sees Temporary
Dip Into Social Security
By ALISON MITCHELL
and RICHARD W. STEVENSON

WASHINGTON, Sept. 10— Key figures in both parties responded to the darkening economic outlook today by exploring possible compromises on additional tax cuts, and the Democratic chairman of the Senate Budget Committee suggested that such a deal could involve the politically perilous step of tapping temporarily into the Social Security surplus.

Pressure mounted on President Bush to drop his cautious approach to dealing with the weakening economy, much of it from within his own party. Republicans are voicing growing concern that the White House has underestimated public unease about the economy and the threat it poses to members of Congress up for re-election next year.

Confronted with polls showing that support for Republicans was eroding even before the government reported on Friday that the unemployment rate had surged, nervous Republicans moved on a variety of fronts.

In the House, Republican leaders agreed tonight to take up legislation in committee on Tuesday that would require automatic spending cuts if any Social Security money was spent on other government programs in the current fiscal year.

After accounting for the slowing economy and the tax cut signed into law by Mr. Bush in June, the Congressional Budget Office projected last month that the government would spend $9 billion of Social Security receipts in the fiscal year that ends Sept. 30. Both parties now expect that figure to be higher.

The White House sent a memorandum to all cabinet agencies today asking them to look for possible budget cuts as the administration develops tax and spending proposals for its next budget.

In the Senate, Trent Lott of Mississippi, the minority leader, said he was open to an idea floated by Democrats for a tax cut for workers who had not qualified for the current rebate. Workers who do not make enough money to pay federal income taxes but who still pay the payroll taxes that finance Social Security and Medicare will not receive rebate checks this year.

Mr. Lott said he would like to see

Continued on Page A20

Traced on Internet,
Teacher Is Charged
In '71 Jet Hijacking
By C.J. CHIVERS

Thirty years after a black-power revolutionary hijacked a jetliner from Ontario to Cuba and disappeared, Canadian and federal authorities matched the fingerprints he left on a can of ginger ale in the airplane with those of a teacher in Westchester County and charged the teacher with the crime yesterday.

The teacher, Patrick Dolan Critton, 54, of Mount Vernon, N.Y., was charged with kidnapping, armed robbery and extortion in United States District Court in Manhattan. He is facing extradition to Canada, where a detective had tracked him down through a simple Internet search.

The authorities said that Mr. Critton, a fugitive for 30 years, had been hiding in plain sight for the last seven years, working as a schoolteacher, using his real name, raising two sons and mentoring other children. Even one of the police officers who arrested him said he had the appearance and demeanor of a gentleman.

But as a young man, the authorities said, Patrick Dolan Critton was a revolutionary with a taste for the most daring of crimes.

By 1971, when he was 24, he was wanted by the New York City police on charges that he participated in a bank robbery that led to a frantic gun battle with the police, and that he had worked in a covert explosives factory on the Lower East Side, where the police said he made pipe bombs with other members of a black liberation group, the Republic

Continued on Page B6

Jorie Graham

Little Exercise

The screen is full of voices, all of them holding their tongues.
Certain things have to be "undergone," yes.
To come to a greater state of consciousness, yes.

Let the face show itself through the screen.
Let the organizing eyes show themselves.
Let them float to the surface of this shine and glow there.

The world now being killed by its children. Also its guests.

An oracle?—a sniper, a child beater, a dying parent in the house,

a soil so overfed it cannot hold a root system in place?
Look — the slightest wind undoes the young crop.

Are we "beyond salvation"? Will you not speak?
Such a large absence — shall it not compel the largest presence?
Can we not break the wall?
And can it please *not be a mirror* lord?

Praying *(Attempt of June 14 '03)*

This morning before dawn no stars I try again.
I want to be saved but from what. Researchers in California have
discovered a broken heart causes as much distress
in the pain center of the brain as physical injury.
The news was outside the door on the landing. I
squatted to it then came back in. Resume my
position. Knees tight, face pressed. There seems to be
a canyon. No light in it, yet it's there, but then
nothing. *Waste* comes
in, I know they are
burying our waste, that it will last hundreds of millions
of years in the mountain, that they are trying to cover it with signs they
do not know how to develop in
a language that will still communicate in that far
future saying don't open this, this is lethal beyond
measure, back away, go away, close the lid, close
the door. The canyons where my face lies full weight on the platter
of my hands have ridges and go forward only to
the buried waste. If there is beauty growing on those
flanks, beauty in detail — furred underside
of small desert leaves comes to mind but only as idea —
the sage twiggy stuff with its blue flowers — the succulent
floor plants that rise — the hundreds of crossing mucus-tracks on the walls
    where the
    snails have been
guiding the first light
down their slick avenues to some core — all of it *just in*
mind not only my closed face trying
so hard to let the thing that can save us in — if
there is beauty it is missing in its manyness is only there

in form I am trying to be honest I am not relying on
chance any more I am trying to take matters
into my own hands. Hand heart head.
Brain pain center sleep. I try to
remember. Something that *was* once is not graspable
from here. Here is all here. Is the problem. Have
tucked the body away. Am all alone on this
floor. In a city in America. To make a
sacrifice. Of what. Save my beloveds. Save my
child. Save her right now. Destroy this carpeting these
windows the walls take the whole of what is wrong
in payment from us. Let me fall through the air.
Save the will to live, save the constituent part of
the human. No. What is constituent. Oh
save my child, my only child.
The more I press down onto the rung the more we move up the
canyon. In Mycenae we moved up this canyon too,
up, up through the city to the throne room at the top.
The columns still standing. The view of two oceans and over two
ranges. Where the King and his retinue are receiving the news. Here. The
poet ushered in. To sing of what has happened. Right here.
On this floor. The voice telling its story. Long, slow, in detail. All of them
waiting. Listening for the terrible outcome. In detail. The opening
of the singer at the throat. The still bodies of the
listeners, high on this outpost, 3,000 years ago, the house of
Agamemnon, the opening of the future. There. Right through the open
mouth of the singer. What happened, what
is to come. And the stillness surrounding them when it is done,
the song. And the singer still. And the chalices empty.
Dawn about to open it all up again. Dawn about to
move it from inside the mind back out. Light almost visible
on the far hills. Oh who will hear this. When it comes it will be time only for
action. Keep us in the telling I say face to the floor.
Keep us in the story. Do not force us back into the hell
of action, we only know how to kill. Once we stop singing we
only know how to get up and stride out of the room and begin
to choose, this from that, this from that, this from that, — and the pain,
the pain sliding into the folds of the brain and lodging.

Look, the steps move us up through the dark, I can hear them
even though I can't see them, we are moving further up,

this is this that and the pain sliding all along,
sliding into the fine crevices on the side walls of this brain we are
traveling up, and the pain lodging, and the pain finding the spot of
                                                  unforgetting,
as in here I am, here I am.

Guantánamo

Waning moon. Rising now. Creak, it goes. Deep
                    over the exhausted continents. I wonder says my
                    fullness. Nobody nobody says the room in which I
                    lie very still in the
darkness watching. Your heart says the moon, waning & rising further. Where
                    is it. Your
                    keep, your eyes your trigger
                    finger your spine your reasoning — also better to
                    refuse touch,
keep distance, let the blood run out of you and the white stars gnaw you, &
                    the thorn
                    which is so white outside in the field,
& the sand which is sheetening on the long beach, the soldiers readying, the
                    up-glance
                    swift when the key words, of prayer, before
                    capture, are
uttered, a shiver which has no hate but is not love, is neutral, yes, un-
                    blooded, as where for instance a bud near where
                    a hand is unlocking a
                    security-catch calls
out, & it is an instance of the nobody-there, & the sound of water darkens,
                    & the wind
                    moves the grasses, & without
                    a cry the cold flows like a watchdog's
eyes, the watchdog keeping his eye out for difference — only difference — &
                    acts being
                    committed in your name, & your captives arriving
                    at *your* detention center, there, in your
eyes, the lockup, deep in your pupil, the softening-up, you paying all your
                    attention
                    out, your eyes, your cell, your keep, your hold,
after all it is yours, yes, what you have taken in, grasp it, grasp

this, there is no law, you are not open to
prosecution, look all you'd like, it will squirm for you, there, in this rising
light, protected
from consequence, making you a
ghost, without a cry, without a cry the
evening turning to night, words it seemed were everything and then
the legal team will declare them exempt,
exemptions for the lakewater drying, for the murder of the seas, for the slaves
in their
waters, not of our species, exemption named
go forth, mix blood, fill your register, take of flesh, set fire, posit equator,
conceal
origin, say you are all forgiven, say these are only
counter-resistant coercive interrogation techniques, as in give me your
name, give it, I will take it, I will re-
classify it, I will withhold you from you, just like that, for a little while, it
won't hurt
much, think of a garden, take your mind off
things, think sea, wind, thunder, root, think tree that will hold you
up, imagine it holding you
up, choose to be who you are, quick choose it, that will help. The moon is
colder
than you think. It is full of nothing like
this stillness of ours. We are trying not to be noticed. We are in stillness as
if it were an
other life we could slip into. In our skins
we dazzle with nonexistence. It is a trick of course but sometimes it works.
If it
doesn't we will be found, we will be made to
scream and crawl. We will long to be forgiven. It doesn't matter for what,
there are no
facts. Moon, who will write
the final poem. Your veil is flying, its uselessness makes us feel there is
still time, it is about two now,
you are asking me to lose myself.
In this overflowing of my eye,
I do.

Employment

Listen the voice is American it would reach you it has wiring in its swan's neck

where it is
always turning
round to see behind itself as it has no past to speak of except some nocturnal

journals written in woods where the fight has just taken place or is about to

take place

for place

the pupils have firelight in them where the man a surveyor or a tracker still has

no idea what

is coming

the wall-to-wall cars on the 405 for the ride home from the cubicle or the
corner

office — how big

the difference — or the waiting all day again in line till your number is

called it will be

called which means

exactly nothing as no one will say to you as was promised by all eternity "ah
son, do you

know where you came from, tell me, tell me your story as you have come to this

Station" — no, they

did away with

the stations

and the jobs

the way of

life

and your number, how you hold it, its promise on its paper,

if numbers could breathe each one of these would be an

exhalation, the last breath of something
and then there you have it: stilled: the exactness: the number: your

number. That is why they
can use it. Because it was living
and now is
stilled. The transition from one state to the
other — they
give, you
receive — provides its shape.
A number is always hovering over something beneath it. It is

invisible, but you can feel it. To make a sum
you summon a crowd. A large number is a form

of mob. The larger the number the more
terrifying.
They are getting very large now.

The thing to do right
away
is to start counting, to say it is my

turn, mine to step into
the stream of blood
for the interview,
to say I
can do it, to say I
am not
one, and then say two, three, four and feel

the blood take you in from above, a legion

single file heading out in formation

across a desert that will not count.

Linda Gregerson

Sweet

Linda,
said my mother when the buildings fell,

before, you understand, we knew a thing
        about the reasons or the ways

        and means,
while we were still dumbfounded, still

bereft of likely narratives, *We cannot*
        continue to live in a world where we

        have so much
and other people have so little.

Sweet, he said.
        Your mother's wrong but sweet, the world

        has never self-corrected,
you Americans break my heart.

Our possum — she must be hungry or
        she wouldn't venture out in so

        much daylight — has found
a way to maneuver on top of the snow.

Thin crust. Sometimes her foot breaks through.
        The edge

        of the woods for safety or
for safety's hopeful lookalike. *Di-*

delphis, "double-wombed," which is
        to say, our one marsupial:

        the shelter then
the early birth, then shelter perforce again.

Virginiana for the place. The place
    for a queen

    supposed to have her maidenhead.
He was clever.

He had moved among the powerful.
    Our possum — possessed

    of thirteen teats, or so
my book informs me, quite a ready-made

republic — guides
    her blind and all-but-embryonic

    young to their pouch
by licking a path from the birth canal.

Resourceful, no? Requiring
    commendable limberness, as does

    the part I've seen, the part
where she ferries the juveniles on her back.

Another pair of eyes above
    her shoulder. Sweet. The place

    construed as yet-to-be-written-upon-
by-us.

And many lost. As when
    their numbers exceed the sources of milk

    or when the weaker ones fall
by the wayside. There are

principles at work, no doubt:
    beholding a world of harm, the mind

    will apprehend some bringer-of-harm,
some cause, or course,

that might have been otherwise, had we possessed
    the wit to see.

Or ruthlessness. Or what? Or heart.
My mother's mistake, if that's

the best the world-as-we've-made-it
can make of her, hasn't

much altered with better advice. It's
wholly premise, rather like the crusted snow.

Father Mercy, Mother Tongue

*If the English language was good enough for Jesus
Christ,* opined
the governor of our then-most-populous

state, *it is good enough for the schoolchildren
of Texas.*
Which is why, said the man at the piano, I

will always love America: the pure
products
of the Reformation go a little crazy here.

*Red bowl
of dust, correct us, we
are here on sufferance every one.*

In 1935 the very earth rose up
against us, neither
tub-soaked sheets nor purer thoughts could keep it.

out. Doorsills, floorboards, nostrils,
tongue. The sugarbowl
was red with it, the very words we spoke

were dirt.
There must have been something
to do, said my youngest one once (this
was worlds
away and after the fact).

We hoped for rain.

        We harvested thistle to feed the cows.
             We dug up soapweed. Then
           we watched the cows and pigs and chickens die. *Red*
                           bowl
of words.

        And found ourselves as nameless as
             those poor souls up from Mexico
and just about as welcome as the dust.
            Pity the traveler
        camping by a drainage ditch in someone else's

        beanfield, picking someone else's bean crop *who is here*
               and gone.

                      And look

        where all that parsing of the Latin led: plain Eunice
            in her later years refused

      to set foot in a purpose-
             built church (a cross
        may be an idol so

                  a white-
      washed wall may be one too), preferring to trust

         a makeshift circle of chairs in the parlor
                  (harbor for
the heart in its simplicity),
   her book.

               This morning

     I watched a man in Nacogdoches calling
          all of the people to quit
             their old lives, there were screens
      within screens: the one

above his pulpit (so huge
               was the crowd), the one I worked
    with my remote. *Then turn...*

              And something like the vastness of the parking lot
                 through which
they must have come (so
       huge) appeared
                      to be on offer, something

     shimmered like the tarmac on an August day

              Is this
        the promised solvent? (some were
             weeping, they were black and white).

                        A word

so broad and shallow (*Flee*), so rinsed
             of all particulars (*Flee Babel,*

    said the preacher) that translation's
              moot. The tarmac
          keeps the dust down, you must give it

that. The earth this time will have to scrape us off.

Still Life

1

His ears his mouth his
    nostrils having filled

    with ash, his cheekbones
chin (all ash) and on the ash a tide

of seawrack that cannot
    be right a trail of scum or

    vomit then and either
his shoulder's been crushed by the

blast or angled on the stretcher so
    oddly that raising

    his arm to ward us off
he seems to be more damaged than he

is, and eyes
    that should have cracked the

    camera. This was not
the current nightmare this was two

or three nightmares ago, the men
    were loading plums and

    peaches onto trucks at
Qaa. And though in my lucky and

ignorant life I have never so much as
    encountered the scent

    of explosives (I
had taken a different bus that day,

the city I live in is thicker with
    doctors than all of Bekaa

    is thick with bombs), I've
seen those eyes before exactly.

Failures of decency closer to home.

2

(The clearing of the ghetto)

Red wool, and falsely brightened, since
    we need the help.

    A child because
the chambers of the heart will hold so

little. If the filmmaker, having
    apprenticed in fables,

proposes a scale for which,
he hopes, we're apt and if

this bigger-than-a-breadbox slightly-
            smaller-than-the-microwave is

just about the vista we can
manage, let's agree to call it history, let's

imagine we had somehow seen its face
            in time. But where

in all of Kraków is
the mother who buttoned her coat?

A city steeped in harm-to-come,
            the film stock drained

to gray. The sturdy
threading-forward of a child who

might be panicked by the crowd but
            has her mind now on

a hiding place. Our
childlike conviction that she shall be

spared. Mistake that brings
            the lesson home: we lack

retention.
Chalk mark on a clouded screen.

3

But what was it like, his dying?
            It was like

a distillation.
You had morphine? We had

morphine, but he couldn't use
            the bed. *The bed?*

His lungs were so
thickened with tumors and phlegm

he had no way of breathing there.
            You'd rented the bed?

        He climbed down beside it
and asked for his tools. When something

was broken he fixed it, that had
            always been the way with him.

            So then ... We left him in his
chair. But as the day went on we thought

he needed bedding so we tried to
            lift him. That's the once

            he blamed us. *That's
the look you meant.* The why-

can't-you-people-just-leave-me-alone,
            the where-is-your-sense-

            of-shame. I will
remember it until I die myself.

You meant well. Meaning well
            was not enough.

        We meant that he
should know this wasn't lost on us.

The urn that holds his ashes does
            a better job.

                    4

Sister partridge, brother hare.
            The linen on the table

            with its hemstitch. I
have read the books on pridefulness:

the bounty of game park and sideboard
and loom, the ships

that brought the lemon trees,
the leisure that masters the view. But

I have come to think
the argument-by-likeness makes

a simpler point. The lemon,
for example, where the knife has been:

the pores, the pith, the luminescent
heart of it, each differential

boundary bound to open.
Meaning death, of course, the un-

protected flesh about to turn, but just
before the turn, while looking

can still be an act of praise.
I see you in the mirror every morning

where you wait for me. The linen,
Father, lemon, knife,

the pewter with its lovely
reluctance to shine. As though

the given world had given us
a second chance.

The Selvage

1

So door to door among the shotgun
shacks in Cullowhee and Waynesville in
our cleanest shirts and *ma'am*
and *excuse me* were all but second

nature now and this one woman comes

to the door she must have weighed
three hundred pounds Would you be
willing to tell us who you plan to vote

for we say and she turns around with
Everett who're we voting for? The
black guy says Everett. The black guy
she says except that wasn't the language
they used they used the word
we've all agreed to banish from even our
innermost thoughts, which is when
I knew he was going to win.

                    2

At which point the speaker discovers,
as if the lesson were new,
she has told the story at her own expense.
Amazing, said my sister's chairman's

second wife, to think what you've
amounted to considering where you're from,
which she imagined was a compliment.
One country, friends. Where when

we have to go there, as, depend
upon it, fat or thin, regenerate
or blinkered-to-the-end, we shall,
they have to take us in. I saw

                    3

a riverful of geese as I drove home across
our one-lane bridge. Four hundred of them
easily, close-massed against the current and
the bitter wind (some settled on the ice) and just

the few at a time who'd loosen rank to
gather again downstream. As if
to paraphrase. The fabric
every minute bound

by just that pulling-out that holds
the raveling together. You were driving
all this time? said Steven. Counting
geese? (The snow falling into the river.)

No. (The river about
to give itself over to ice.) I'd stopped.
Their wingspans, had they not
been taking shelter here, as wide as we are tall.

Eamon Grennan

Y2K

Mutation of bells. Chapels vanishing in fog.
A cormorant, oil encased. Smoke, more smoke.

Zero after zero where the families were: odd
gloves and shoes, a mattress, a child's trike.

A father carrying his daughter on one shoulder
over rocky embankments. Barbed wire on the border.

Day after day, who's chipping this Pietà?
Long time night, the usual. So forth and so on.

Marilyn Hacker

Letter to Hayden Carruth

Dear Hayden, I have owed you a letter for
one month, or two — your last one's misplaced. But I'm
    back in New York. The world is howling,
    bleeding and dying in banner headlines.

No hope from youthful pacifists, elderly
anarchists; no solutions from diplomats.

Men maddened with revealed religion
murder their neighbors with righteous fervor,

while, claiming they're "defending democracy,"
our homespun junta exports the war machine.
        They, too, have daily prayer-meetings,
        photo-op-perfect for tame reporters.

("God Bless America" would be blasphemy
if there were a god concerned with humanity.)
        Marie is blunt about it: things were
        less awful (Stateside) in 1940.

I wasn't born... I've read shelves of books about
France under Vichy after the armistice:
        war at imagination's distance.
        Distance is telescoped now, shrinks daily.

Jews who learned their comportment from storm troopers
act out the nightmares that woke their grandmothers;
        Jews sit, black-clad, claim peace: their vigil's
        not on the whistle-stop pol's agenda.

"Our" loss is grave: American, sacralized.
We are dismayed that dead Palestinians,
        Kashmiris, Chechens, Guatemalans,
        also are mourned with demands for vengeance.

"Our" loss is grave, that is, till a president
in spanking-new non-combatant uniform
        mandates a war: then, men and women
        dying for oil will be needed heroes.

I'd rather live in France (or live anywhere
there's literate debate in the newspapers).
        The English language is my mother
        tongue, but it travels. Asylum, exile?

I know where I feel more like a foreigner
now that it seems my birth country silences
        dissent with fear. Of death? Of difference?
        I know which city lightens my mornings.

You had New England; I had diaspora,
an old folk song: "Wish I was where I would be,
    Then I'd be where I am not." Would that
    joy claimed its citizens, issued passports.

"First, do no harm," physicians, not presidents,
swear when inducted. I'm tired of rhetoric,
    theirs or journalists' or my own ranting.
    I'd like to hole up with Blake and Crashaw —

but there's a stack of student endeavors that
I've got to read, and write some encouraging
    words on. Five hours of class tomorrow;
    Tuesday, a dawn flight to California.

From Names

1.

A giant poplar shades the summer square.
Breakfast shift done, Reem smooths her kinky mass
of auburn curls, walks outside, her leaf-print dress
green shadow on post-millennial bright air.
It's almost noon. I smell of sweat. I smell
despite bain-moussant and deodorant,
crumpled and aging, while recognizant
of luck, to be, today, perennial
appreciating trees. The sky is clear
as this in Gaza and Guantánamo
about which I know just enough to mourn
yesterday's dead. The elegies get worn
away, attrition crumbles them into
chasm or quicklime of a turning year.

4.

Four firelit mirrors lining the Corsican
restaurant's walls reflected divergences —
Palestinian, Syrian, Lebanese,
Russian, expat Jewish American.

A new war had begun that afternoon;
The shrinking world shrieked its emergencies
well beyond our capabilities
if not to understand, to intervene
though Mourad, who practices medicine,
has made of intervention a career.
Khaled spent decades of studying history
in the jaws, shall we say, of an emergency.
Start another bottle of rough-tongued wine,
that sanguine glitter in the midnight mirror.

     5.

Edinburgh airport seems provincial when
you're headed back to CDG/Roissy
in dusty sunlight of mid–July
midday. I had an hour. But there was Hind
(we'd been at the same conference all weekend)
who had three connections: Heathrow, Cairo,
Beirut, where the runways had been bombed
to Damascus. With airport Starbucks, we brainstormed
the thesis-in-progress she'll have to write
in English if she's going to publish it:
Lesbian writers from the Arab world.
Boarding call. I don't know if she got home.
I e-mailed her. I haven't heard from her.
The war had started five days earlier.

     6.

Noura is writing about women also: women
and war. She sends an e-mail from Mosul:
The books arrived, and they are beautiful.
I know, of course, the work of Fadwa Touqan
but since the invasion and the occupation
it is hard to find books, even in Arabic.
Attached is the synopsis of my post-doc
proposal and the draft of a translation.
I cannot visit my old teacher in Baghdad:
because I am Sunni and from Mosul
I would be immediately slain.

Through the cracked prism of Al-Andalus
we witness, mourning what we never had.
(The war goes on and on and on and on.)

7.

A waxing moon, tailwind of a return,
but to what? Life on the telephone,
letters typed on a computer screen
which no one needs to file or hide or burn
at the storm-center of emergency
where there is no coherent narrative.
With no accounting of my hours to give
black holes gape open in my memory.
If there's some story here, it isn't mine,
but one I can imperfectly discern
from what can be imperfectly expressed
by third parties in second languages.
The shots, far off, the power cut, the line
interrupted, the fact I did not learn.

Ghazal: *min al-hobbi m'a qatal*
for Deema Shehabi

You, old friend, leave, but who releases me from the love that
       kills?
Can you tell the love that sets you free from the love that
       kills?

No mail again this morning. The retired diplomat
stifles in the day's complacency from the love that kills.

What once was home is across what once was a border
which exiles gaze at longingly from the love that kills.

The all-night dancer, the mother of four, the tired young
       doctor
all contracted HIV from the love that kills.

There is pleasure, too, in writing easy, dishonest verses.
Nothing protects your poetry from the love that kills.

The coloratura keens a triumphant swan-song
as if she sipped an elixir of glee from the love that kills.

We learn the maxim: "So fine the thread,
so sharp the necessity" from the love that kills.

The calligrapher went blind from his precision
and yet he claims he learned to see from the love that kills.

Spare me, she prays, from dreams of the town I grew up in,
from involuntary memory, from the love that kills.

Homesick soldier, do you sweat in the glare of this
    checkpoint
to guard the homesick refugee from the love that kills?

Forrest Hamer

Aftermath

Somewhere there are omens.
Somewhere all the bodies have been buried, and survivors keep watch
Over skeletons they also had been.
The children are raising each other.

Bodies are buried; survivors keep watch.
Somewhere the earth is burning, eager for new skin.
Each child is raising another;
Music and meaning are patient.

The earth is just burning.
There are terrible questions —
Somewhere music is patient, and meaning.
Somewhere those who had been slaughtered feel unanswerable longing.

We have terrible questions,
And those who slaughtered have longing.
Those who have been slaughtered lie unanswered.
Languages lift from ashes like these

And those who slaughtered feel the same longing.
Hope comes home, somewhere in us;
Language lifts from ash.
Rightly, we are cautious.

Somewhere hope hovers over
What we would have done, whatever did we do.
Rightly, we are cautious;
Stories everywhere.

What Happened

To say about it one thing. No, two. It was a horror. It could not be spoken.
So first there was the problem of recovering speech.
Calling out to it, listening each other.
We looked to the assurances of nature — regular violence, regular relief.
Color splayed before us — yellows, rhythms of red.
Faces and patterns in faces. Patience.
Finally, a word, but not many.
Silence again, longing.
More words but not what happened; words we had already said.
Horror holding, a black hole. Opening a little,
Then a little more, then: we could think about the horror: what happened
A kind of speech, but not yet.

Conference
Durban, 2001

On South African TV, the nightly news is broadcast four times —
Once each in Zulu, English, Afrikaans, and Xhosa.
Watching them in sequence offers the sense young countries are forged
On very old land, peoples fighting to make of the news what might last.

Once each in Zulu, English, Afrikaans, and Xhosa,
Someone said, *The self can be a dangerous thing —*
People fight to make of themselves what might last.
There is always an other, and we don't always know what to make of it.

Someone said, *The self can be a dangerous thing,*
But if the self is also an us and one becomes lost to it,
There are always others. What do we make of them?
How do they settle our grief?

The self is an us and the self can get lost.
Our table was too small. Some of us sat at the sides of the wall
Seeking to settle old griefs.
Hearing some things but not others, people demanded to speak.

The roundtable was small. Some sat at the sides of the wall.
There were wounds they were wearing, marks of the many not there.
Everyone needed to speak and be heard, but
Horrors had happened; there wasn't room for them all.

There were wounds upon wounds, marks of the many not there.
We were expecting many, not the many who came;
Horrors had happened and no one had room for them all.
A stranger stood, cautioning, *We should not presume.*

He'd been waiting for many, the many who came;
He wanted to body them in.
And though he'd come far, he couldn't hold hopes;
Their gravity held him back.

We have to work at it, work for it, body it in.
Are you talking about peace, I ask him, and he says back to us,
Even a stone is in movement. I stopped for a moment, taking it in.
We have to keep going.

But, do we move towards peace, I ask him, and he says to me,
A self becomes formed by the other it hates;
We have to question our nature;
There's some other story to tell.

Robert Hass

I am Your Waiter Tonight and My Name is Dmitri

Is, more or less, the title of a poem by John Ashbery and has
No investment in the fact that you can get an adolescent
Of the human species to do almost anything (and when adolescence
In the human species ends is what The Fat Man in *The Maltese Falcon*
Calls a "a nice question, sir, a very nice question indeed")
Which is why they are tromping down a road in Fallujah

In combat gear and a hundred and fifteen degrees of heat
This morning and why a young woman is strapping
Twenty pounds of explosives to her mortal body in Jerusalem.
Dulce et decorum est pro patria mori. Have I mentioned
That the other law of human nature is that human beings
Will do anything they see someone else do and someone
Will do almost anything? There is probably a waiter
In this country so clueless he wears a T-shirt in the gym
That says Da Meat Tree. Not our protagonist. American amnesia
Is such that he may very well be the great-grandson
Of the elder Karamazov brother who fled to the Middle West
With his girl friend Grushenka — he never killed his father,
It isn't true that he killed his father — but his religion
Was that woman's honey-colored head, an ideal tangible
Enough to die for, and he lived for it: in Buffalo,
New York, or Sandusky, Ohio. He never learned much English,
But he slept beside her in the night until she was an old woman
Who still knew her way to the Russian pharmacist
In a Chicago suburb where she could buy sachets of the herbs
Of the Russian summer that her coarse white nightgown
Smelled of as he fell asleep, though he smoked Turkish cigarettes
And could hardly smell. Grushenka got two boys out her body,
One was born in 1894, the other in 1896,
The elder having died in the mud at the Battle of the Somme
From a piece of shrapnel manufactured by Alfred Nobel.
Metal traveling at that speed works amazing transformations
On the tissues of the human intestine; the other son worked
          construction
The year his mother died. If they could have, they would have,
If not filled, half-filled her coffin with the petals
Of buckwheat flowers from which Crimean bees made the honey
Bought in the honey market in St. Petersburg (not far
From the place where Raskolnikov, himself an adolescent male,
Couldn't kill the old moneylender without killing her saintly sister,
But killed her nevertheless in a fit of guilt and reasoning
Which went something like this: since the world
Evidently consists in the ravenous pursuit of wealth
And power and in the exploitation and prostitution
Of women, except the wholly self-sacrificing ones
Who make you crazy with guilt, and since I am going
To be the world, I might as well take an axe to the head

Of this woman who symbolizes both usury and the guilt
The virtue and suffering of women induces in men,
And be done with it). I frankly admit the syntax
Of that sentence, like the intestines slithering from the hands
Of the startled boys clutching their belly wounds
At the Somme, has escaped my grip. I step over it
Gingerly. Where were we? Not far from the honey market,
Which is not far from the hay market. It is important
To remember that the teeming cities of the nineteenth century
Were site central for horsewhipping. Humans had domesticated
The race of horses some ten centuries before, harnessed them,
Trained them, whipped them mercilessly for recalcitrance
In Vienna, Prague, Naples, London, and Chicago, according
To the novels of the period which may have been noticing this
For the first time or registering an actual statistical increase
In either human brutality or the insurrectionary impulse
In horses, which were fed hay, so there was, of course,
In every European city a hay market like the one in which
Raskolnikov kissed the earth from a longing for salvation.
Grushenka, though Dostoyevsky made her, probably did not
Have much use for novels of ideas. Her younger son,
A master carpenter, eventually took a degree in engineering
From Bucknell University. He married an Irish girl
From Vermont who was descended from the gardener
Of Emily Dickinson, but that's another story. Their son
In Iwo Jima died. Gangrene. But he left behind, curled
In the body of the daughter of a Russian Jewish cigar maker
From Minsk, the fetal curl of a being who became the lead dancer
In the Cleveland Ballet, radiant Tanya, who turned in
A bad knee sometime early 1971, just after her brother ate it
In Cao Dai Dien, for marriage and motherhood, which brings us
To our waiter, Dmitri, who, you will have noticed, is not in Bagdad.
He doesn't even want to be an actor. He has been offered
Roles in several major motion pictures and refused them
Because he is, in fact, under contract to John Ashbery
Who is a sane and humane man and has no intention
Of releasing him from the poem. You can get killed out there.
He is allowed to go home for his mother's birthday and she
Has described to him on the phone — a cell phone, he's
Walking down Christopher Street with such easy bearing
He could be St. Christopher bearing innocence across a river —

Having come across a lock, the delicate curl of a honey-
Colored lock of his great-grandmother's Crimean-
Honey-bee-pollen. Russian-spring-wildflower-sachet-
Scented hair in the attic, where it released for her
In the July heat and raftery midsummer dark the memory
Of an odor like life itself carried to her on the wind.
Here is your sea bass with a light lemon and caper sauce.
Here is your dish of raspberries and chocolate; notice
Their subtle transfiguration of the colors of excrement and blood;
And here are the flecks of crystallized lavender that stipple it.

Ezra Pound's Proposition

Beauty is sexual, and sexuality
Is the fertility of the earth and the fertility
Of the earth is economics. Though he is no recommendation
For poets on the subject of finance,
I thought of him in the thick heat
Of the Bangkok night. Not more than fourteen, she saunters up to you
Outside the Shangri-la Hotel
And says, in plausible English,
"How about a party, big guy?"

Here is more or less how it works:
The World Bank arranges the credit and the dam
Floods three hundred villages, and the villagers find their way
To the city where their daughters melt into the teeming streets,
And the dam's great turbines, beautifully tooled
In Lund or Dresden or Detroit, financed
By Lazard Frères in Paris or the Morgan Bank in New York,
Enabled by judicious gifts from Bechtel of San Francisco
Or Halliburton of Houston to the local political elite,
Spun by the force of rushing water,
Have become hives of shimmering silver
And, down river, they throw that bluish throb of light
Across her cheekbones and her lovely skin.

On Visiting the DMZ at Panmunjom: A Haibun

The human imagination does not do very well with large numbers.
More than two and a half million people died during the Korean
War. It seems that it ought to have taken more time to wreck so many
bodies. Five hundred thousand Chinese soldiers died in battle, or of
disease. A million South Koreans died, four-fifths of them civilians.
One million, one hundred thousand North Koreans. The terms are
inexact and thinking about them can make you sleepy. Not all "South
Koreans" were born in the south of Korea; some were born in the
north and went south, for reasons of family, or religion, or politics,
at the time of the division of the country. Likewise the "North
Koreans." During the war one half of all the houses in the country
were destroyed and almost all industrial and public buildings.
Pyongyang was bombarded with one thousand bombs per square
kilometer in a city that had been home to four hundred thousand
people. Twenty-six thousand American soldiers died in the war.
There is no evidence that human beings have absorbed these facts,
which ought, at least, to provoke some communal sense of shame. It
may be the sheer number of bodies that is hard to hold in mind. That
is perhaps why I felt a slight onset of nausea as we were moved from
the civilian bus to the military bus at Panmunjom. The young soldiers
had been trained to do their jobs and they carried out the transfer
of our bodies, dressed for summer in the May heat, with a precision
and dispatch that seemed slightly theatrical. They were young men.
They wanted to be admired. I found it very hard to describe to
myself what I felt about them, whom we had made our instrument.

> The flurry of white between the guard towers
>   — river mist? a wedding party?
> is cattle egrets nesting in the willows.

Some of David's Story

"That first time I met her, at the party, she said,
'I have an English father and an American mother
and I went to school in London and Providence, Rhode Island,
and at some point I had to choose,
so I moved back to London and became the sort of person
who says *puh-son* instead of *purr-son*.'
For the first *person* she had chosen an accent

halfway between the other two.
It was so elegant I fell in love on the spot. Later,
I understood that it was because I thought
that little verbal finesse meant
she had made herself up entirely.
I felt so much what I was and, you know,
that what I was was not that much,
so she just seemed breathtaking."

*

"Her neck was the thing, and that tangle of copper hair.
And, in those days, her laugh, the way
she moved through a room. Like Landor's line —
she was meandering gold, pellucid gold."

*

"Her father was a philosopher,
fairly eminent in that world, and the first time
I was there to dinner, they talked about California wines
in deference to me, I think, though it was a subject
about which I was still too broke to have a thing to say,
so I changed the subject and asked him
what kind of music he liked. He said, 'I loathe music.'
And I said, 'All music?' And he said —
he seemed very amused by himself but also
quite serious, 'Almost all music, almost all the time.'
and I said 'Beethoven?' And he said
'I loathe Beethoven, and I loathe Stravinsky, who loathed Beethoven.'"

*

"Later, in the night, we talked about it.
'It's feelings,' she said, laughing. 'He says
he doesn't want other people putting their feelings into him
any more than he wants,' and then she imitated
his silvery rich voice, 'them putting their organs
into me at great length and without my consent.'
And she rolled onto my chest and wiggled herself
into position and whispered in my ear,
'So I'll put my feelings in you, okay?'
humming it as if it were a little tune."

*

"Anyway, I was besotted. In that stage, you know,
when everything about her amazed me.
One time I looked in her underwear drawer.
She had eight pair of orange panties
and one pair that was sort of lemon yellow, none of them
very new. So that was something
to think about. What kind of woman
basically wears only orange panties."

*

"She had the most beautiful neck on earth.
A swan's neck. When we made love, in those first weeks,
in my grubby little graduate student bed-sit,
I'd weep afterward from gratitude while she smoked
and then we'd walk along the embankment to look at the lights
just coming on — it was midsummer — and then we'd eat something
at an Indian place and I'd watch her put forkfuls of curry
into that soft mouth I'd been kissing. It was still
just faintly light at midnight and I'd walk her home
and the wind would be coming up on the river."

*

"In theory she was only part-time at Amnesty
but by fall she was there every night, later and later.
She just got to be obsessed. Political torture, mostly.
Abu Ghraib, the photographs. She had every one of them.
And photographs of the hands of some Iranian feminist journalist
that the police had taken pliers to. And Africa,
of course, Darfur, starvation, genital mutilation.
The whole starter kit of anguished causes."

*

"I'd wake up in the night
and not hear her sleeper's breathing
and turn toward her and she'd be looking at me,
wide-eyed, and say, as if we were in the middle of a conversation,
'Do you know what the report said? It said
she had been raped multiple times and that she died
of one strong blow — they call it blunt trauma —
to the back of her head,
but she also had twenty-seven hairline fractures

to the skull, so they think the interrogation
went on for some time.'"

*

"— So I said, 'Yes, I can tell you exactly
what I want.' She had her head propped up on one elbow,
she was so beautiful, her hair
that Botticellian copper. 'Look,' I said,
'I know the world is an awful place, but I would like,
some night, to make love or walk along the river
without having to talk about George fucking Bush
or Tony fucking Blair.' I picked up her hand.
'You bite your fingernails raw.
You should quit smoking. You're entitled, we're entitled
to a little happiness.' She looked at me,
coolly, and gave me a perfunctory kiss
on the neck and said, 'You sound like my mother.'"

*

"We were at a party and she introduced me
to one of her colleagues, tall girl, auburn hair,
absolutely white skin. After she walked away,
I said, 'A wan English beauty.' I was really thinking
that she was inside all day breathing secondhand smoke
and saving the world. And she looked at me
for a long time, thoughtfully, and said,
'Not really. She has lymphoma.'
I think that was the beginning of the end.
I wasn't being callow, I just didn't know."

*

"Another night she said, 'Do you know
what our countrymen are thinking about right now?
Football matches.' 'Games,' I said. She shook her head.
'The drones in Afghanistan? Yesterday they bombed a wedding.
It killed sixty people, eighteen children. I don't know
how people live, I don't know how
they get up in the morning.'"

*

"So she took the job in Harare and I got ready
to come back to Berkeley, and we said we'd be in touch

by e-mail and that I might come out in the summer
and we'd see how it went. The last night
I was the one who woke up. She was sleeping soundly,
her face adorably squinched up by the pillow,
a little saliva — the English word spittle came to mind —
a tiny filament of it connecting the corner of her mouth
to the pillow. She looked so peaceful."

*

"In the last week we went to hear a friend
perform some music of Benjamin Britten.
I had been in the library finishing up, ploughing
through the back issues of *The Criterion* and noticing
again that neither Eliot nor any of the others
seemed to have had a clue to the coming horror.
She was sitting beside me and I looked at her hands
in her lap. Her beautiful hands. And I thought about
the way she was carrying the whole of the world's violence
and cruelty in her body, or trying to, because
she thought the rest of us couldn't or wouldn't.
Our friend was bowing away, a series of high, sweet,
climbing and keening notes, and that line of Eliot's
from *The Wasteland* came into my head:
'*This music crept by me upon the waters.*'"

Bob Hicok

Happy Anniversary
March 16, 2006

There is a war.

This is a brand of minimalism: there are many wars.

Whenever you are reading this, this is the case:
people running and screaming and sharp things and dull pains.

A softness of phantom limbs marching through the forest.

Arms attached to legs, legs attached to dream.

Whenever you are reading this, you may be killing, you may be dead.

I was thinking, I should mow the lawn, buy milk, stop the war.

Let's all add that to our lists: learn Spanish, meet Jesus,
stop the war.

All past lists and future lists, all notions of mind,
all wonderings above the frost-wounded daffodils —
will they make it, doctor, will they pull through? —
should include the unsophisticated breath.

There is my war in the now and your war in the then.

Other things I can predict: snow, lava, vowels, the heat-seeking
qualities of money.

Stop.

Long enough to enter the cratered, the moon fields and marionette
the dead, to wear them on your body as your body,
as if you've reeled-in your shadow, as if you're holding
how you'll be forgotten in your arms.

Until the word empty whispers, *I am full.*

Until the shadow fits.

Full Flight

I'm in a plane that will not be flown into a building.
It's a SAAB 340, seats 40, has two engines with propellers
is why I think of beanies, those hats that would spin
a young head into the clouds. The plane is red and loud
inside like it must be loud in the heart, red like fire
and fire engines and the woman two seats up and to the right
resembles one of the widows I saw on TV after the Towers
came down. It's her hair that I recognize, the fecundity of it
and the color and its obedience to an ideal, the shape
it was asked several hours ago to hold and has held, a kind
of wave that begins at the forehead and repeats with slight

variations all the way to the tips, as if she were water
and a pebble had been continuously dropped into the mouth
of her existence. We are eighteen thousand feet over America.
People are typing at their laps, blowing across the fog of coffee,
sleeping with their heads on the windows, on the pattern
of green fields and brown fields, streams and gas stations
and swimming pools, blue dots of aquamarine that suggest
we've domesticated the mirage. We had to kill someone,
I believe, when the metal bones burned and the top
fell through the bottom and a cloud made of dust and memos
and skin muscled across Manhattan. I remember feeling
I could finally touch a rifle, that some murders
are an illumination of ethics, that they act as a word,
a motion the brain requires for which there is
no syllable, no breath. The moment the planes had stopped,
when we were afraid of the sky, there was a pause
when we could have been perfectly American,
could have spent infinity dollars and thrown a million
bodies at finding the few, lasering our revenge
into a kind of love, the blood-hunger kept exact
and more convincing for its precision, an expression
of our belief that proximity is never the measure of guilt.
We've lived in the sky again for some years and today
on my lap these pictures from Iraq, naked bodies
stacked into a pyramid of ha-ha and the articles
about broomsticks up the ass and the limbs of children
turned into stubble, we are punchdrunk and getting even
with the sand, with the map, with oil, with ourselves
I think listening to the guys behind me. There's a problem
in Alpena with an inventory control system, some switches
are being counted twice, switches for what I don't know —
switches of humor, of faith — but the men are musical
in their jargon, both likely born in New Delhi
and probably Americans now, which is what the flesh
of this country has been, a grafted pulse, an inventory
of the world, and just as the idea of embrace
moves chemically into my blood, and I'm warmed
as if I've just taken a drink, a voice announces
we've begun our descent, and then I sense the falling.

Troubled Times

Each shot three times at least, thrice
we don't say much, I just now remember
I was trying to write that morning

about a goose being chased
in the field by cows, it suggests,
I remember just now I don't want to feel

what it suggests, I've been here,
at this point of failure about to picture him
in the hall, in a room, and refusing

that presence in the life, though I can't go back
to the goose, the phalanx of udders,
I think I was writing "the cows lean forward

like cannon," refusing to water
the images, let them grow, it suggests
diligence, this is not a meditation,

they were funny, tons of waddle
chasing feathers, I don't want his face
behind my eyes, it's too easy to let him be

how I see the sun, I left a blank space
behind me a moment ago, I had to go back
and write "diligence" where nothing was,

nor will I strike a line across the word
to suggest my doubt, I'll just come right out
and admit my imperfections, that I am adrift

right here, in needing to talk about
but not wanting to glorify him, the parents
have lost everything, I've lost

something, I don't know what, it suggests
_____, now I'll leave blanks, will be
pointless, as if moo could trap honk,

my thoughts want to be bucolic,
they have these "pick your own" places
around here for apples and grief

I imagine grows from the brain seeing itself
one day in a shop window as it passes,
so many problems because we know we exist,

let us not know we exist, let us be blank,
three times each, I keep starting to see him,
an arm, a shoe, don't think of the blue unicorn,

the pink elephant, I can never remember
how that goes, the chartreuse aardvark,
how to unmind what's in mind, how to mine,

use, remove, to hold, so much to hold,
I bend to pick up the memo and cockroaches
in my arms go free, disgusting, what I know now,

what do I know now, the goose got away, I am here
but here isn't here, the sky worn by the hours
like a cap that fits some other head

In the Loop

I heard from people after the shootings. People
I knew well or barely or not at all. Largely
the same message: how horrible it was, how little
there was to say about how horrible it was.
People wrote, called, mostly e-mailed
to say, there's nothing to say. Eventually
I answered these messages: there's nothing
to say back except of course there's nothing
to say, thank you for your willingness to say it.
Because this was about nothing. A boy who felt
that he was nothing, who erased and entered
that erasure, and guns that are good for nothing,
and talk of guns that is good for nothing,
and spring that is good for flowers, and Jesus
for some, and scotch for others, and "and"
for me in this poem, "and" that is good
for sewing the minutes together, which otherwise

go about going away, bereft of us and us
of them, like a scarf left on a train
and nothing like a scarf left on a train,
like the train, empty of everything but a scarf,
and still it opens its doors at every stop,
because this is what a train does,
this is what a man does with his hand on a lever,
because otherwise why the lever, why the hand,
and then it was over, and then it had just begun.

Stop-loss

Absolutely, I agree. It's what we all
want to do. Unless by we
I mean Thanatos, but I just asked,
I do not mean Thanatos. I mean you

holding your daughter's hand,
thinking darkly, despite yourself,
to when you're dead and she's old
and alone. That's a loss you want

to stop, of optimism, the present tense,
of just being with here as you wait
for the bus, watching her watch a blackbird
that doesn't have to go to school.

The man beside you in fatigues, camouflaged
from Wednesday, holding his son's hand
for the last time before he returns
to shooting at people, being shot at

in a war he thought he was done with,
I mean him: he wants to stop loss.
What a beautiful phrase for the army
to support. In it, I hear

that we're through with the grenades,
the violent enterprise of steel,
we're on to the new war, the war against
the cannibalism of war. Hurrah for us,

for you, fighting the impulse
to see the end in everything,
this spring day, the giant steps
of the bus she has to climb, literally

as you would a mountain, not thinking,
for once, she will fall, but feeling,
for an instant, she will make it,
without ropes, in a pink dress, laughing.

Brenda Hillman

From Nine Untitled Epyllions

[2]

I made a winged

creature, and when they

bring it through each

desert on a flag

of bar codes and minus signs

in poverty of fact

through their present freedom,

it is then my

sweet-beaked creature stands for

nothing; it is then

in the frail startfulness

the creature dreams its

situations through the O

blood river it cannot

cross nor the *y*

in abyss, sleeps for

the them whose helmets

lost their eyes in

the s/hell oil past

the nineveh tent — though,

actually it isn't dreaming

yet; you better start

the other flag, assassin

air, now, citizen syllable.

[4]

I am a seamstress.

I have no country.

So when I count

our dying hero's breaths

as stitches carrying Trotsky

south, it seems cloth

is a state though

every century changes what

cloth is. Now you

might enter: what kind

of cloth is your

soul, do you think.

This world's violent, comforting

machine has made it

general. The lost one

is everywhere; you won't

recover him. Hero, machine —

vowels color things but

only you provide distinction:

the curved dove back
and fourth vowel bells —
any sounds, actually — which
because they are uneven
call you from suffering —

[6]
After their freedom had
started I fled for
the flatness I felt
had no horizon then:
their global killed people
it would never see;
a dove with Nike
checkmarks on its wings
flies from 16th-century scenes
where we're making glass
& flax in the countryside::
ferrule of plows::: bronze
backgrounds for new towns —;
do you feel this
we in you sometimes?
I hope that you
do. Haunted by the
need to work, blinded
by cloth, I take
my needle through gates
of ivory and gates
of horn, I sew,

I push the little

bright thing on through —

Reportorial Poetry, Trance & Activism
An Essay

Reportorial poetics can be used to record detail with immediacy while one is doing an action & thinking about something else.

Experience crosses over with that which is outside experience; the unknown receives this information as an aquifer receives replenishing rain. Meditative states can be used to cross material boundaries, to allow you to be in several places at once, such as Congress & ancient Babylon.

i recorded notes in Washington while attending hearings & participating in actions to make the record collective & personal. Working with trance while sitting in the Congressional hearings i recorded details in a notebook.

If bees can detect ultraviolet rays, there are surely more possibilities in language & government. The possible is boundless.

Whether or not you have the strength to resist official versions that are devastating the earth & its creatures, you could in any case send back reports. If political parties will not provide solutions, the good can occur when people gather in small groups to work for justice in each community using imagination without force.

People could leave their computers at least briefly to engage with others in public spaces. It is then the potential of each word comes forward.
If you have no time or strength, act without time or strength because they may follow. In the meantime you could imagine that you have them.

In a Senate Armed Services Hearing

From my position as a woman
  i could see
    the back of the General's head, the prickly
intimate hairs behind his ears,

the visible rimless justice raining down
from the eagle on the national seal,
        the eagle's claw-held pack of arrows
              & its friends. A fly was making its for-sure-maybe-
algebra cloud in the Senate chamber; it fell to us
              to see how Senators
re-shuffled papers, the pity of
        the staples, to sense when someone coughed after
                    the about-to-be-czar General said *I don't foresee a long*
role for our troops, there was a rose vibration in the rug.
        From its position on the table the fly
could then foresee
                    the soon-to-be-smashed goddess as in
    Babylon. More perception had to be, began to be.
        Filaments rose from the carpet as the General spoke,
the Senators were stuck. What
              were they thinking sitting there
        as dutiful as lunch patrols
in junior high. From my position as the fly
i could foresee as letters issued
from their mouths like *General I'd be interested*
    to know, some of the letters regretted that.
                              Fibers in the carpet
        crouched. From
the floor arose the sense
              the goddess Ishtar had come down
    to bring her astral light with a day-wrinkled plan. From my position
        as a thought i thought she might. She might
        come in to rain her tears
on Senator Bayh & Senator Clinton, on Senator Warner
              in his papa tie & Senator Levin, on Senator Reed &
Senator Hill — rain tears into their water glasses, Ishtar
        from Babylon they had not met
        before they smashed her country now or never.
              Then someone — Clinton i think it was
but it might have been Bayh — asked whether this confirmation *will*
              give breathing space for the new
    General to unoccupy (*how do the dead breathe, Senator,* from my position
              as a fly) & i forget who asked what isn't even
    in the same syntax of this
language i'm trying to make no progress in, asked

how the army would unoccupy, by north or south?
A voice beside my insect ear
said, these Senators all have their lives:
kids with stuff to do, folks with cancer, some
secret shame in a quotidian —
the thing in front always producing
panic, — just like yours, the voice went, just like your life.
i tried to think if this was true but was too weak from
flying above this notebook to pity them. From my
position as a molecule i could foresee
twelve Senate water glasses, each bubble had an azure
rim, the ovals on
the Senators' heads were just like them, the breath they used
when saying °° *A* °° for *American interests* made the *A* stand still,
it had a sunset clause.
They tried to say °°° *Safety* °°° but the *S* withdrew,
the *S* went underground. Would not
be redeployed. Refused to spell. Till all the letters stopped
in astral light, in dark love for their human ones —

Request to the Berkeley City Council Concerning Strawberry Creek

After George Herbert

From hills, from storm drains
meeting tumbled–below molecules of Berkeley
tap water & rain, past Center & Shattuck to the cool straight
waves of the Bay, Council, daylight that Creek. Near CementHenge
of the B of A with the Shattuck Cinemas' mild butter Saturday matinee
popcorn redolence meets downtown Peets' decaf, daylight. Daylight possible lizards, raccoons, beetles which starts with be, their esplanade & vision. Corridors would return for vision citizens, also dew on finches flying
to Dwight. Council, apply your   wisdom. We swear by the seven
creeks of Berkeley, as by our   poetry — for e.g. A's, AW's, B's, B
H's, Bateau Group's, XX's C's, CS's, D's, D's, E's, F's, FH's, G's, G's, GG's
& GO's, XX's & I's, J's, JB's & JC's, JF's, JJ's, JM's, K's & KS's, L's, LH's,
LM's, LS's, M's, MP's, N's, P's, XX's & PD's, PS's, R's, RS's, RP's who
moved, S's, SK's, T's, U–Z's, XX's, XX's, all students living over windows who walk near spearmint nooses of campus creeksides,
who write little or much, in water as in poetry — that we
are one body. (Shelley noted this.) The invisible
is lined with the visible.
(We also noted this.) Aren't you mostly water
yourselves? We walked to campus on Watershed Day against
our national government. Water creatures are against war. Even
the swordfish nearby knows not to send its sword into another swordfish unless it's going to eat it. So water leaped to brown. The soul of the
poet, healing, saw the leaping. Be on the side of leaping, Council. Aren't
the first two letters of Be   rkeley legally curved? So the dryads
living near this Creek leave   oaky ghost menus, words of ancestors CM, JM, JS, TG & letters from the east, from A–Z, C & F who
should have moved here, N & J, J & B who did move — So the visible
improves in a School where they said daylight the creek, day-light.
& the Aging sheen caught the Bay. We don't know how to live
but water thinks it through, a syntax tangled to renew, H_2O =
one-third forever & two-thirds good sense. Spirals & hips,
eyelashed willows, we're yours; what else lives? In
water, we stop stopping it —

There's so much about the mind
we don't know yet between the mem-
orable & the forgotten which is why
we need water words. The clogged-for-50-
years-creek tumbled along badly when the
father & brother of the brenda who transcribes
this worked on campus; when the first husband
worked here, the creek was dirty — just a dump —
& in the era of the second husband, clearing began.
They tried bunchgrass & a Study formed. Live oaks dropped their spiky leaves on down, Council, & the creek had a
chance, its numbers & properties like mythic figures — Daphne
& her agitators — in M's word, to *toggle* back & forth between new
things they said. Wholeness lives in parts like those water striders,
triremes of golden insects, Council. (It's up to you to make brave government imagine things.) Sacramento suckers had returned, hitch-
minnow, the raccoon who fished them out; & the egret that fished
was probably even helping the salmon. Maybe you'll put porous
pavers for the Berkenstocks, my dears. This great stream
of Strawberry Creek, with its stickle-backs like the
letter E at the end of Mother Tuolumne carrying the muskrat from Cascadia's borderland,
is three point five miles long, Council. We are
not on the side of extra starts but of inner freedom. Let's note to each lover of rain-checks that
economy & strains of longing come from the same
place. Feed creatures. Dolphins near Monterey dive,
Council, when the creek's mysterious ochre balances
in health. Fine mist is curling in the brenda hairs.
The lyric grew in strength & the water grew less dead.
Some have a moment of mood when they stand on the bridge
near the U.C. Life Sciences Building. The cottonwood says twenty-
five things & a lamp. Monarchs will come back from Reno & Win-
nemuca; buckeye, father of the camphor tree, would talk. Nymphs
would make do with celebrate. Sisters & brothers of the Council,
bring light, beauty & order to the edge; we the writers & readers,
griots with lyres & harps, in you, by you & for the generations,
ask that you day light that creek day, day ○ light ○ that ○ Creek

In High Desert Under the Drones

We are western creatures; we can stand for hours in the sun. We read poetry near an Air Force base. Is poetry pointless? Maybe its points are moving, as in a fire. The enlisted men can't hear. Practice drones fly over-head to photograph our signs; they look like hornets [*Vespula*] with dangly legs dipping in rose circles with life grains. They photograph shadows of the hills where coyotes' eyes have stars. They could make clouds of white writing, cilia, knitting, soul weaving, spine without nerves, dentures of the west, volcano experiments, geometry weather breath & salt. Young airmen entering the base stare from their Hondas; they are *lucky to have a job* in *an economy like this.* The letters of this poem are also lucky to have a job for they are insects & addicts & thieves. Volcanic basalt recalls its rock star father. Creosote & sage, stubby taupe leaves greet the rain. We hold our signs up. We're all doing our jobs. Trucks bring concrete for the landing strip they've just begun.

                                      A cliff stands out in winter
         Twin ravens drop fire   from its eyes
My inner life is not so inner & maintains the vascular system of a desert plant. I'm grateful to Samuel Beckett & to my high school boyfriend whose drunk father yelled when we closed the door & read *The Unnamable* during the Tet offensive. A sense of the absurd can always help. Outside the base we see borax mines in the distance — the colors of flesh, brown, black, peach, pink, bronze. We stand there as the young airmen settle into their routine. The Gnostics noted it is difficult to travel between spheres, you've had to memorize the secret names & the unnamable haunts every aspect of your routine. The names grow heavier as you carry them between the spheres.

Galway Kinnell

When the Towers Fell

From our high window we saw them
in their bands and blocks of light
brightening against a fading sunset,
saw them in the dark hours glittering
as if the spirits inside them sat up

calculating profit and loss all night, saw
their tops steeped in the first yellow
of sunrise, grew so used to them
often we didn't see them, and now,
not seeing them, we see them.

*

The banker is talking to London.
Humberto is delivering breakfast sandwiches.
The trader is working the phone.
The mail sorter starts sorting the mail.
The secretary arrives, the chef,
the gofer, the CEO ... *povres et riches*
Sages et folz, prestres et laiz
Nobles, villains, larges et chiches
Petiz et grans et beaulx et laiz ...[1]

*

The plane screamed low, down lower Fifth Avenue,
lifted at the Arch, someone said, shaking the dog walkers
in Washington Square, drove for the North Tower,
struck with a heavy thud and a huge bright gush
of blackened orange fire, and vanished, leaving behind
a hole the size and shape a cartoon plane might make
passing through and flying away, on the far side
back into the realm of the imaginary.

*

Some with torn clothing, some bloodied,
some limping at top speed like children
in a three-legged race, some half dragged,
some intact in neat suits and dresses,
many dusted to a ghostly whiteness
with eyes rubbed red as the eyes of a zahorí,
who can see the dead under the ground,
they swarm in silence up the avenues.

*

[1]   ...poor and rich
Wise and foolish, priests and laymen
Noblemen, serfs, generous and mean
Short and tall and handsome and homely
— Francois Villon, from *The Testament*

Some died while calling home to say they were OK.
Some called the telephone operators and were told to
    stay put.
Some died after over an hour spent learning they would die.
Some died so abruptly they may have seen death from
    inside it.
Some burned, their faces caught fire.
Some were asphyxiated.
Some broke windows and leaned into the sunny day.
Some were pushed out from behind by others in flames.
Some let themselves fall, begging gravity to speed them to
    the ground.
Some leapt hand in hand that their fall down the sky might
    happen more lightly.

                    *

At the high window where I've often stood
to think, or to elude a nightmare, I meet
the single, unblinking, electric glare
lighting the all-night lifting
and sifting for bodies, pieces of bodies, a thumb, a tooth,
    anything that is not nothing.

                    *

She stands on a corner holding his picture.
He is smiling. In the heavy smoke
few pass. Sorry sorry sorry.
She startles.
Suppose, across the street, that headlong stride ...
or there, that man with hair so black it's purple ...

                    *

And yet, suppose some evening I forgot
The fare and transfer, yet got by that way
Without recall — lost, yet poised in traffic —
Then I might find your eyes ...[2]

Sorry sorry good luck thank you.
On this side it is "amnesia," or forgetting the way home;
on the other, "invisibleness," or never entirely returning.

[2]And yet, suppose some evening I forgot...
— Hart Crane, from "For the Marriage of Faustus and Helen"

Hard to see past the metallic mist
or through the canopy of supposed reality
cast over our world, bourn that no creature ever born
can pry its way back through, that no love can tear.

                        *

All day the towers burn and fall, and burn and fall.
In a shot from New Jersey they seem like smokestacks
    spewing earth's oily remnants.
Schwarze Milch der Frühe wir trinken sie abends
wir trinken sie mittags und morgens wir trinken sie nachts
wir trinken und trinken[3]

                        *

They come before us now not as a likeness,
but as a corollary, a small instance in the immense
lineage of the twentieth century's history of violent death —
black men in the South castrated and strung up from trees,
soldiers advancing through mud at ninety thousand dead
    per mile,
train upon train of boxcars heading eastward shoved full to
    the corners with Jews and Roma to be enslaved or
    gassed,
state murder of twenty, thirty, forty million of its own,
state starvation of a hundred million farmers,
atomic blasts erasing cities off the earth, firebombings
    the same,
death marches, assassinations, disappearances,
entire countries become rubble, minefields, mass graves.

Wir schaufeln ein Grab in den Lüften da liegt man nicht eng.[4]

                        *

Burst jet fuel, incinerated aluminum, steel fume, crushed
    marble, exploded granite, pulverized drywall, mashed

[3]Black milk of daybreak we drink it at nightfall
we drink it at midday at morning we drink it at night
we drink it and drink it
— Paul Celan, from *Death Fugue*

[4]We're digging a grave in the sky there'll be plenty of room to lie
    down there
— Paul Celan, from *Death Fugue*

concrete, berserked plastic, crazed chemicals, scoria,
  rotting flesh, vapor
of the vaporized — draped over
our island up to streets regimented
into numerals and letters, breathed across
the great bridges to Brooklyn and the waiting sea —
astringent, miasmic, empyreumatic, sticky,
air too foul to take in, but we take it in,
too gruesome for seekers of lost beloveds
to breathe, but they breathe it and you breathe it.

                    *

The man doesn't look up.
Her photograph hangs from his neck.
He stares at the sidewalk of flagstones
laid down in Whitman's century, curbside edges rounded
by the rasps of wheels of iron and steel:
the human brain envying the stones:
Nie staja sie sa.
Nic nod to, myslalem,
zbrzydziwszy sobie
wszystko co staje sie.[5]

                    *

I thought again of those on the high floors
who knew they would burn alive and then, burned alive.
As if there were mechanisms of death
so mutilating to existence that no one
gets over them, ever, not even the dead.

                    *

I sat down by the waters of the Hudson
and saw in steel letters welded to the railing posts
Whitman's words written when America
was plunging into war with itself: *City of the world!...*
Proud and passionate city — mettlesome, mad, extravagant city![6]

[5]They do not become, they are.
Nothing but that, I thought,
finally secretly loathing
everything that becomes.
— Aleksander Wat, from *Songs of a Wanderer*
[6]*City of the World!...*
— Walt Whitman, from "City of Ships"

But when the war was over and Lincoln dead
and the dead buried, Whitman remembered:
I saw battle-corpses, myriads of them,
And the white skeletons of young men, I saw them,
I saw the debris and debris of all the slain soldiers of the war,
But I saw they were not as was thought.
They themselves were fully at rest— they suffer'd not,
The living remain'd and suffer'd, the mother suffer'd,
And the wife and the child and the musing comrade suffer'd.[7]

*

In our minds the glassy blocks succumb over and over,
slamming down floor by floor into themselves,
blowing up as if in reverse, exploding

downward and rolling outward,
the way, in the days of the gods, a god
might rage through the streets, overtaking the fleeing.

As each tower goes down, it concentrates
into itself, transforms itself
infinitely slowly into a black hole

infinitesimally small: mass
without space, where each light,
each life, put out, lies down within us.

Yusef Komunyakaa

From "Love in the Time of War"

Here, the old masters of Shock & Awe
huddle in the war room, talking iron,
fire & sand, alloy & nomenclature.
Their hearts lag against the bowstring
as they daydream of Odysseus's bed.
But to shoot an arrow through the bull's-eye

[7] I saw battle-corpses, myriads of them...
— Walt Whitman, from "When Lilacs Last in the Door-yard Bloom'd"

of twelve axes lined up in a row
is to sleep with one's eyes open. Yes,

of course, there stands lovely Penelope
like a trophy, still holding the brass key
against her breast. How did the evening star
fall into that room? Lost between plot
& loot, the plucked string turns into a lyre
humming praises & curses to the unborn.

Grenade

There's no rehearsal to turn flesh into dust so quickly. A hair-trigger, a cocked hammer in the brain, a split second between a man & infamy. It lands on the ground — a few soldiers duck & the others are caught in a half-run — & one throws himself down on the grenade. All the watches stop. A flash. Smoke. Silence. The sound fills the whole day. Flesh & earth fall into the eyes & mouths of the men. A dream trapped in midair. They touch their legs & arms, their groins, ears & noses, saying, What happened? Some are crying. Others are laughing. Some are almost dancing. Someone tries to put the dead man back together: "He just dove on the damn thing, sir!" A flash. Smoke. Silence. The day blown apart. For those who can walk away, what is their burden? Shreds of flesh & bloody rags gathered up & stuffed into a bag. Each breath belongs to him. Each song. Each curse. Every prayer is his. Your body doesn't belong to your mind & soul. Who are you? Do you remember the man left in the jungle? The others who owe their lives to this phantom, do they feel like you? Would his loved ones remember him if that little park or statue erected in his name didn't exist, & does it enlarge their lives? You wish he'd lie down in that closed coffin, & not wander the streets or enter your bedroom at midnight. The woman you love, she'll never understand. Who would? You remember what he used to say: "If you give a kite too much string, it'll break free." That unselfish certainty. But you can't remember when you began to live his unspoken dreams.

The Towers

Yes, dear son   No,
dead, but not gone,   none,
some were good, ordinary   not a single one
people who loved a pinch of salt   possessed wings as agile

on a slice of melon. Good,
everyday souls gazing up
at birds every now & then,
a flash of wings like blood
against the skylights. Well,
others were good as gold
certificates in a strongbox
buried in the good earth. Yes,
two or three stopped to give
the homeless vet on the corner
a shiny quarter or sliver dime,
while others walked dead
into a fiery brisance, lost
in an eternity of Vermeer.
A few left questions blighting
the air. Does she love me?
How can I forgive him?
Why does the dog growl
when I turn the doorknob?
Some were writing e-mails
& embossed letters to ghosts
when the first plane struck.
The boom of one thousand
trap drums was thrown against
a metallic sky. A century of blue
vaults opened, & rescue workers
scrambled with their lifelines
down into the dark, sending up
plumes of disbelieving dust.
They tried to soothe torn earth,
to stretch skin back over the
pulse beat. When old doubts
& shame burn, do they smell
like anything we've known?
When happiness is caught off
guard, when it beats its wings
bloody against the bony cage,
does it die screaming or laughing?

& unabashedly decorous as yours,
son. Not even those lovers who
grabbed each other's hand & leapt
through the exploding windows.
Pieces of sky fell with the glass,
bricks, & charred mortar. Nothing
held together anymore. Machines
grunted & groaned into the heap
like gigantic dung beetles. After
planes had flown out of a scenario
in Hollywood, few now believed
their own feet touched the ground.
Signed deeds & promissory notes
floated over the tangled streets,
& some hobbled in broken shoes
toward the Brooklyn Bridge.
The cash registers stopped on
decimal points, in a cloud bank
of dead cell phones & dross.
Search dogs crawled into tombs
of burning silence. September
could hardly hold itself upright,
but no one donned any feathers.
Apollo was at Ground Zero
because he knows everything
about bandaging up wounds.
Men dug hands into quavering
flotsam, & they were blinded by
the moon's indifference. No,
Voice, I don't know anything
about infidels, though I can see
those men shaving their bodies
before facing a malicious god
in the mirror. The searchlights
throbbed. No, I'm not Daedalus,
but I've walked miles in a circle,
questioning your wings of beeswax
& crepe singed beyond belief.

Heavy Metal Soliloquy

After a nightlong white-hot hellfire
of blue steel, we rolled into Baghdad,
plugged into government-issued earphones,
hearing hard rock. The drum machines
& revved-up guitars roared in our heads.
All their gods were crawling on all fours.
Those bloated replicas of horned beetles
drew us to targets, as if they could breathe
& think. The turrets rotated 360 degrees.
The infrared scopes could see through stone.
There were mounds of silver in the oily dark.
Our helmets were the only shape of the world.
Lightning was inside our titanium tanks,
& the music was almost holy, even if blood
was now leaking from our eardrums.
We were moving to a predestined score
as bodies slumped under the bright heft
& weight of thunderous falling sky.
Locked in, shielded off from desert sand
& equatorial eyes, I was inside a womb,
a carmine world, caught in a limbo,
my finger on the trigger, getting ready to die,
getting ready to be born.

The Warlord's Garden

He has bribed the thorns
to guard his poppies.
They intoxicate the valley
with their forbidden scent,
reddening the horizon
till it is almost as if
they aren't there.
Maybe the guns guard
only the notorious
dreams in his head.
The weather is kind
to every bloom,
& the fat greenish bulbs

form a galaxy of fantasies
& beautiful nightmares.
After they're harvested
& molded into kilo sacks
of malleable brown powder,
they cross the country
on horseback,
on river rafts
following some falling star,
& then ride men's shoulders
down to the underworld,
down to rigged scales
where moneychangers
& gunrunners linger
in their pistol-whipped hush
of broad daylight. No,
now, it shouldn't be long
before the needle's bright tip
holds a drop of woeful bliss,
before the fifth horseman of the Apocalypse
gallops again the night streets of Europe.

Surge

Always more. No, we aren't too ashamed to prod celestial beings
into our machines. Always more body bags & body counts for oath
    takers
& sharpshooters. Always more. More meat for the gibbons grinder
& midnight mover. There's always someone standing on a hill, half
    lost
behind dark aviation glasses, saying, If you asked me, buddy, you
    know
it could always be worse. A lost arm & leg? Well, you could be stone
    dead.
Here comes another column of apparitions to dig a lifetime of
    roadside graves.
Listen to the wind beg. Always more young, strong, healthy bodies.
    Always.

Yes. What a beautiful golden sunset. (*A pause.*) There's always that
    one naked soul

who'll stand up, shuffle his feet a little, & then look the auspicious,
   would-be gods
in the eyes & say, Enough! I won't give another good guess or black
   thumbnail
to this mad dream of yours! An ordinary man or woman. Alone. A
   mechanic
or cowboy. A baker. A farmer. A hard hat. A tool-&-die man.
   Almost a smile
at the corners of a mouth. A fisherman. A tree surgeon. A
   seamstress. Someone.

Clouds

The plane bobs like a cork
in an air pocket, my heart
inside my belly, & then it levels out.
The woman seated beside me
is now almost in my arms.
She smiles & says, I'm sorry
& then I see the boy soldiers
on the cover of the magazine
she's holding. Cloud-griffins
& cloud-horses pantomime the 747.

I see my face among their boyish poses
reflected in the airplane window,
& then I hear bloody toms-toms
in a deep valley, as my mind
runs along with an ancestor's
three steps into a moonless interior
before he's captured & sold
for swatches of bright cloth
& a few glass beads. A spear dance
awakens the daydreamer's blue hour.

What tribal scrimmage centuries ago
brought me here to this moment
where Georgia O'Keeffe's clouds
are flat-white against an ocean, before
the plane touches down at La Guardia

this morning? The boy soldiers
huddle around someone shot
on the ground, the raised dust
coloring their faces, clothes,
& memory the pigment of dust.

Maxine Kumin

Extraordinary Rendition

Only the oak and the beech hang onto their leaves
at the end, the oak leaves bruised the color of those
insurgent boys Iraqi policemen captured

purpling their eyes and cheekbones before
lining them up to testify to the Americans
that, no, no, they had not been beaten...

The beech leaves dry to brown, a palette of cinnamon.
They curl undefended, they have no stake in the outcome.
Art redeems us from time, it has been written.

Meanwhile we've exported stress positions, shackles,
dog attacks, sleep deprivation, waterboarding.
To rend: *to tear (one's garments or hair)*

in anguish or rage. To render: *to give what is due
or owed.* The Pope's message
this Sunday is the spiritual value of suffering.

Extraordinary how the sun comes up
with its rendition of daybreak,
staining the sky with indifference.

On Reading *The Age of Innocence* in a Troubled Time

I read this curious Victorian novel
In the suspended bliss of a mid–July night.
Moths storm the screen, longing to plaster
their frail dust against the single bulb
that lights my page. It's 1870,
Old New York. Under the orange tree
Newland Archer kisses his fiancée,
May Welland, for only the second time
in their prescribed courtship and presses down
too hard in his ardor. As Edith Wharton tells it,
the blood rose to her face and she
drew back as if he had startled her.

Reading in bed before sleep, the luxury
of entering another world as if from above…
I set it against the realities
of the breakfast table's news. Today
the *New York Times* unravels
the story of Mukhtaran Bibi, a Pakistani
woman who was raped as retribution
for something her younger brother
was said to have done, while the tribesmen
danced for joy. Gang rape. The definition
several attackers in rapid succession,
in no way conveys the fervor,
the male gutturals, the raw juice as
the treasured porcelain of her vagina
was shattered. Splintered again and again.
And after, to be jeered at.
The shame of it.

What could Wharton's good virgin say
to this illiterate, courageous survivor
who dared to press charges?
                              — As if in her day
there were no tender girls turned prostitutes,
no desperate immigrants, no used-up carthorses
beaten to the pavement, their corpses
ravaged by dogs in Old New York. Look away,
May Welland! Turn aside as best you can.

Even defended from life on the streets,
from all that was turbulent, ragged and rough,
even unacknowledged, May, history repeats.
You must have seen enough.

Entering Houses at Night

None of us spoke their language and
none of them spoke ours.
We went in breaking down doors.

They told us to force the whole scrum
— men women kids — into one room.
We went in punching kicking yelling out orders

in our language, not theirs.
The front of one little boy bloomed
wet as we went in breaking down doors.

Now it turns out that 80 percent
of the ones in that sweep were innocent
as we punched kicked yelled out orders.

The way that we spun in that sweltering stink
with handcuffs and blindfolds was rank.
We went in breaking down doors.

Was that the Pyrrhic moment when
we herded the sobbing women with guns
as punching kicking yelling out orders
we went in breaking down doors?

Still We Take Joy

While in Baghdad sewage infiltrates
the drinking water and no one dares go out
to market, or goes, *inshallah*, praying
to return, and everyone agrees

it's civil war as it was in Virgil's time,
brother Roman against brother Roman,
warrior farmers far from their barren fields,
I am reading that *pastoral of hard work,*

as Ferry calls it, introducing his
translation of *The Georgics,* still a handbook
for gardeners two millennia later.
Last winter's sooty ashes are spread

and fields are fertilized with oxen dung
much as we do today, with cow and horse manure.
It's garlic we plant in autumn, beans, yes, in spring
in this fallen world that darkens and darkens.

On January 12th, an ice-locked day,
I dig three carrots, just as the poet instructs us
to take joy in the very life of things
so that, when Zeus comes down in spring

to the joyful bridal body of the earth
and the animals all agree it is time,
I can believe the wheel will turn
once more, taking me with it or not.

Just Deserts

It is agreed that life as we know it must come to the end of its tether
by global warming or nuclear winter or cataclysmic seizure

nor will it be humans who watch the sun's demise
as it sucks Earth, Mars, and Venus inside

before it collapses from red giant to white dwarf
and we, supreme products of Darwinian selection, will have morphed

into what? backward, perhaps, to the one-celled amoebic tyro
we arose from more than four billion years ago

up from the cave drawings of auroch and bison
from the slaughter of Labrador duck, passenger pigeon

from Hiroshima and Nagasaki to lie eyes open
in Keats's *unslumbrous night.*

For however long it takes it will serve us right.

Ann Lauterbach

Victory

Reverence for that dust.
The scale is overwhelming. I
cannot envision this ever getting done.
They took a lot away from us.
World rattles its harness.
Among, within us, too many injuries
as if in caves in mountains in snow. The train
whistled, a thing of air,
and the chorale also ceased.
Night took over even as the moon
came up blushing and round to lead us on.
The philosopher with the poker was in a rage.
Sebald perished in a crash. I looked up
to find the stars rambling across the sky and
the starlings,
the starlings, I have nothing to say about starlings.

The body does not appear; enthusiastically, the guitar strums.
Shoes wander; vertiginous ascent, pathology of disorder
in which nothing is under the overlay
of a high-velocity near. The kids are on their snowmobiles.
I could kill them. I could speak of killing the kids
and not mean it. I could kill the snowmobiles
and ask the kids to look at the copulating
dolls hung from threads
and then at solace.

If form is recurrence, who sighs at the
spoken? *Ah ah ah,* the anecdotal takes
sunset and moonrise into a regime.

To speak outside the retro-fit of
a target's eye, blinking, hands waving as the ship pulls out,
empathy like a shadow on an object's pyre,
the object's stench as the crowd presses
to climb the platform, snap the shutter,
watch it burn.
                        Duration slit open?
Whiplash speed rising over the skull
as an idea, any idea, say a mask,
and the shreds now
catapulting our pleasure
into this
fissure or slit through which the eye
perpetuates its claim
and all it sees is
limitless enunciation, limitless screen,
undone by the actual yet called up by
readiness: cloth, snow, page,
trees at dusk ready to disappear.
The monochrome tugs at its frame.
The news will not assuage, greets
the about-turn reckoned
as victory's norm
or sample contingent: in wartime,
reporters eat in or at the house of the vanquished.

Hum

The days are beautiful
The days are beautiful.

I know what days are.
The other is weather.

I know what weather is.
The days are beautiful.

Things are incidental.
Someone is weeping.

I weep for the incidental.
The days are beautiful.

Where is tomorrow?
Everyone will weep.

Tomorrow was yesterday.
The days are beautiful.

Tomorrow was yesterday.
Today is weather.

The sound of the weather
is everyone weeping.

Everyone is incidental.
Everyone weeps.

The tears of today
will put out tomorrow.

The rain is ashes.
The days are beautiful.

The rain falls down.
The sound is falling.

The sky is a cloud.
The days are beautiful.

The sky is dust.
The weather is yesterday.

The weather is yesterday.
The sound is weeping.

What is this dust?
The weather is nothing.

The days are beautiful.
The towers are yesterday.

The towers are incidental.
What are these ashes?

Here is the hat
that does not travel.

Here is the robe
that smells of the night.

Here are the words
retired to their books.

Here are the stones
loosed from their settings.

Here is the bridge
over the water.

Here is the place
where the sun came up.

Here is a season
dry in the fireplace.

Here are the ashes.
The days are beautiful.

Echo Revision

1.

Lest, forgetting, the branch-maiden lopped off.
Lest, forgetting, the branch-maiden lopped off.

Lest the rotund silk, flickering on a wall,
Lest the rotund silk, flickering on a wall,

Nagged by wind. Prose
Nagged by wind. Succulent prose.

Swift enough to roll downhill into the stream
Awake enough to roll downhill into the stream

(Violent, or gentle, naturalism). To claim
(Violent, or gentle, naturalism). To claim

Our attention, like soldiers, or:
Our attention, like soldiers, or:

Not like soldiers. Not like soldiers.
Not like soldiers.

And the apples and pears assembled on the white cloth
Apples and pears assembled on a white cloth

And the couple under the enormous tree — these
And the couple under an enormous tree — these

Picked out details on a chart. Then
Picked out, paused. Then,

Stumbling out from under the enunciated dirge
Stumbling out from under these forms

Of twilight's last screen
Sudden hatchings, partitions, reversals.

There were several hatchings, several namings,
The lesser and the leftover piled up

Several reversals of one into more than one.
Over the fecund industry

Had there ever been such magnitude, such spawning?
A counting of cast-off limbs.

Such counting of last limbs on the green?
To have unreason counted as reason

To have as fact unreason without crime
And only one intentional wound; to be

To covet the black eyes of the small dead rat.
Covetous of the small wakeful hour as

Adding and adding so the agenda grows
Of the black eyes of the small dead rodent.

And the blood stops running, the scar sets
Adding and adding so the agenda grew

The scar set and the tune rose into its thin retainer.
And the blood stopped running, and the scar set.

The scar set and the tune rose.

2.

A modest evocation, a simple claim. As his crimes were disbanded
A modest evocation, a simple claim.

At his death, the mourners came out from their foxholes
As his war crimes were

And the crows also.
Forgiven at death, the people

The year turned into another year overnight
Came out from their kitchens

The day turned into another day overnight
To mourn; crows agitated the air

The war was a separate entity, with its own turning dates.
And settled on kill.

The candles were lit.
The year turned into another year overnight

Nevertheless, candles were lit.
The day turned into another day overnight.

Some counting was included in the dossier of events
The war was a separate entity, with its own turning dates.

Counting seemed to ease the ambiguity of the ocean.
The candles were lit.

There are the pluses and the minuses to add and subtract.
Nevertheless candles were lit.

The issue of fewer or more. The issue of cost.
Some counting was included in the dossier of events.

But, turning away,
Counting seemed to ease the ambiguity of the ocean.

The innumerable and the inseparable
The issue of fewer or more. The issue of cost.

3.

And the incommensurate
But, turning away,

In their separate, unique garb of silver
The innumerable and the inseparable

Riding up and over the long radiant angle
In their plural garb

Like a flushed stream of mercury
Rode up and over in a long radiant angle

These seemed to make the weapons and their procedures useless
Like the flushed stream of memory

Blank came back, blank followed blank, until full.
These made the weapons and their procedures fertile.

The pathos of the hour, its desire to be spoken.
The pathos of the hours, their desire to be said.

Noon came and went and no one watched.
But noon came and went and no one spoke.

No one watched, heard, or was beseeched.
No one watched, heard, or beseeched.

Know me! called the empty bell from far off
Two hands reached up, surrendered.

And swiped its card, and drove away.
Know me! someone called from far off

And the couple stood and kissed under the boughs of the tree.
And swiped his card, and drove away.

And the old man smiled to the camera.
The couple embraced under the boughs of the tree.

The old man, now dead, had smiled to the camera.
The old man smiled to the camera.

The young man, a soldier, smiled to the camera.

Ben Lerner

Didactic Elegy

Sense that sees itself is spirit.
        Novalis

Intention draws a bold, black line across an otherwise white field.
Speculation establishes gradations of darkness
where there are none, allowing the critic to posit narrative time.
I posit the critic to distance myself from intention, a despicable affect.
Yet intention is necessary if the field is to be understood as an economy.

By *economy* I mean that the field is apprehension in its idle form.
The eye constitutes any disturbance in the field as an object.
This is the grammatical function of the eye. To distinguish between objects,
the eye assigns value where there is none.

When there is only one object the eye is anxious.
Anxiety here is comic; it provokes amusement in the body.
The critic experiences amusement as a financial return.

It is easy to apply a continuous black mark to the surface of a primed canvas.
It is difficult to perceive the marks without assigning them value.
The critic argues that this difficulty itself is the subject of the drawing.
Perhaps, but to speak here of a subject is to risk affirming
intention where there is none.

It is no argument that the critic knows the artist personally.
Even if the artist is a known quantity, interpretation is an open struggle.
An artwork aware of this struggle is charged with negativity.
And yet naming negativity destroys it.
Can this process be made the subject of a poem?

No,
but it can be made the object of a poem.
Just as the violation of the line amplifies the whiteness of the field,
so a poem can seek out a figure of its own impossibility.
But when the meaning of such a figure becomes fixed, it is a mere positivity.

*

Events extraneous to the work, however, can unfix the meaning of its figures,
thereby recharging it negatively. For example,
if airplanes crash into towers and those towers collapse
there is an ensuing reassignation of value.

Those works of art enduringly susceptible to radical revaluations are master-
    pieces.
The phrase *unfinished masterpiece* is redundant.

Now the critic feels a new anxiety in the presence of the drawing.
Anxiety here is tragic; it inspires a feeling of irrelevance.
The critic experiences irrelevance as a loss of capital.

To the critic, the black line has become simply a black line.
What was once a gesture of negativity, has lost its capacity to refer
to the difficulties inherent in reference.
Can this process be made the subject of a poem?

No,
but a poem may prefigure its own irrelevance,
thereby staying relevant
despite the transpiration of extraneous events.

This poem will lose its relevance if and when there is a significant resurgence
of confidence in the function of the artwork.
If artworks are no longer required to account for their own status,
this poem's figures will then be fixed and meaningless.

But meaninglessness, when accepted, can be beautiful
in the way the Greeks were beautiful
when they accepted death.
Only in this sense can a poem be heroic.
After the towers collapsed

*

many men and women were described as heroes.

The first men and women described as heroes were in the towers.
To call them heroes, however, implies that they were willing to accept their
   deaths.
But then why did some men and women
jump from the towers as the towers collapsed?
One man, captured on tape, flapped his arms as he fell.

Rescue workers who died attempting to save the men and women trapped in
   the towers
are, in fact, heroes,
but the meaning of their deaths is susceptible to radical revaluation.
The hero makes a masterpiece of dying
and even if the hero is a known quantity
there is an open struggle over the meaning of her death. According to the president,

any American who continues her life as if the towers had not collapsed
is a hero. This is to conflate the negative with the counterfactual.
The president's statement is meaningless
unless to be American means to embrace one's death,
which is possible.

                                  *

It is difficult to differentiate between the collapse of the towers
and the image of the towers collapsing.
The influence of images is often stronger than the influence of events,
as the film of Pollock painting is more influential than Pollock's paintings.

But as it is repeated, the power of an image diminishes,
producing anxiety and a symbolic reinvestment.
The image may then be assigned value where there is none.
Can an image be heroic?

No,
but an image may proclaim its distance from the event it ostensibly depicts,
that is, it may declare itself its own event,
and thereby ban all further investment.

The critic watches the image of the towers collapsing.
She remembers less and less about the towers collapsing
each time she watches the image of the towers collapsing.

The critic feels guilty viewing the image like a work of art,

but guilt here stems from an error of cognition,
as the critic fails to distinguish between an event
and the event of the event's image.

The image of the towers collapsing is a work of art
and, like all works of art, may be rejected
for soiling that which it ostensibly depicts. As a general rule,
if a representation of the towers collapsing
may be repeated, it is unrealistic.

*

Formalism is the belief that the eye does violence to the object it apprehends.
All formalisms are therefore sad.
A negative formalism acknowledges the violence intrinsic to its method.
Formalism is therefore a practice, not an essence.

For example, a syllogism subjected to a system of substitutions
allows us to apprehend the experience of logic
at logic's expense.

Negative formalisms catalyze a certain experience of structure.
The experience of structure is sad,
but, by revealing the contingency of content,
it authorizes hope.

This is the role of the artwork — to authorize hope,
but the very condition of possibility for this hope is the impossibility of its
    fulfillment.
The value of hope is that it has no use value.
Hope is the saddest of formalisms.

The critic's gaze is a polemic without object
and only seeks a surface
upon which to unfold its own internal contradictions.
Conditions permitting, a drawing might then be significant,
but only as a function of her search for significance.

It is not that the significance is mere appearance.
The significance is real but impermanent.
Indeed, the mere appearance of significance is significant.
We call it *politics*.

*

The lyric is a stellar condition.
The relation between the lyric I and the lyric poem
is like the relation between a star and starlight.
The poem and the I are never identical and their distance may be measured
    in time.
Some lyric poems become visible long after their origins have ceased to exist.

The heavens are anachronistic. Similarly, the lyric
lags behind the subjectivity it aspires to express. Expressing this disconnect
is the task of the negative lyric,
which does not exist.

If and when the negative lyric exists, it will be repetitious.
It will be designed to collapse in advance, producing an image
that transmits the impossibility of transmission. This familiar gesture,
like a bold black stroke against a white field,
will emphasize flatness, which is a failure of emphasis.

The critic repeats herself for emphasis.
But, since repetition emphasizes only the failure of sense,
this is a contradiction.
When contradictions are intended they grow lyrical
and the absence of the I is felt as a presence.

If and when the negative lyric exists, it will affect a flatness
to no effect.
The failure of flatness will be an expression of depth.

                              *

Towers collapse didactically.
When a tower collapses in practice it also collapses in theory.
Brief dynamic events then carry meanings
that demand memorials,
vertical memorials at peace with negativity.

Should we memorialize the towers or the towers' collapse?
Can any memorial improve on the elegance of absence?
Or perhaps, in memoriam, we should destroy something else.

I think that we should draw a bold, black line across an otherwise white field
and keep discussion of its meaning to a minimum.
If we can close the event to further interpretation
we can keep the collapse from becoming a masterpiece.

The key is to intend as little as possible in the act of memorialization.
By intending as little as possible we refuse to assign value where there is none.
Violence is not yet modern; it fails to acknowledge the limitations of its
    medium.
When violence becomes aware of its mediacy and loses its object
it will begin to resemble love.
Love is negative because it dissolves
all particulars into an experience of form.
Refusing to assign meaning to an event is to interpret it lovingly.

The meaninglessness of the drawing is therefore meaningful
and the failure to seek out value is heroic.
Is this all that remains of poetry?

Ignorance that sees itself is elegy.

Timothy Liu

Ready-Mades

Missing-persons photos plastered onto a van.

Pockets of air beneath the rubble.

Welcome then to the world community.

Candle-lit vigils held by volunteers.

As survivors circle the Armory for any news.

This the place Duchamp showed?

Morgan Stanley, Merrill Lynch.

South of Pittsburgh shot down by the Feds.

Let's smoke 'em out of their holes!

Imagine a president saying that.

Offshore where a Wildlife Preserve had been.

Vita Breva

To eke out spirits on a bomb-damaged site.

The task of earning one's daily bread.

"No matter on what grounds."

Full of leisure and pleasureful abandon.

Inventing rules to keep the spoils.

Removed from war the task.

Having made my body come again again.

Makeshift morgues sprouting up all over town.

To get ourselves "disappeared."

However the plea.

Dusted about with sentiments to soften the blow.

Beauty

Hundreds of bodies identified. Others
found only in parts. A demand
for Nostradamus on the rise: *In the city
of York, there will be a great collapse —
two twin brothers torn apart by a third
big war to begin when the city burns —*
tents from Fashion Week in Bryant Park sponsored
by Mercedes Benz now converted
into staging areas for the dead — too late
for the Emmys though Miss America
will go on as the seventy-two virgins
of Paradise welcome the martyrs in —

Elegy for Oum Kolsoum Written Across the Sky

The century's greatest Arabic voice
as cause for swoon as mourners by the millions
lined the Cairo streets to catch a glimpse
of her corpse. Gone is that most rare of wines
that spilled into a desert where caged cocks
perched on sills served as an early
warning system for chemical attacks —

aggressive tactics that delivered designer
opiates to those of us lining up
to trade our hash pipes in — pleasure reduced
to "Ala Balad El Mahboub" muzaked
through the roof. Didn't you know while women
only want to be adored, men only
want to get laid? — the gender wars hard-wired
on both sides of the globe — to don or not
to don a scarf the only question
on the minds of Muslim women who chain
themselves to those university gates
in Istanbul, never mind Iran, never mind
the Persian Gulf basking like a swimming pool
cast in the shape of a casting couch
any F-16 can see before it gets shot down —

John Matthias

Column I, Tablet XIII

(for Gilbert Loescher, UN High Commission for Refugees)

...

mostly broken, but assumed to be
a lone survivor...

      ... man called Gil
is what the paper said
if you were able to decipher the Akkadian,
cuneiform...
    A man called Gilgamesh,
was king and had a friend.

Climb along the outer wall, the inner wall,
study the foundation...
...expedition...dream
in a nether world. Apsu, the abyss

He lived next door to me for many years
and he would read beneath the tree that shaded
both our gardens. Tall Gilgamesh, he'd

play basketball with local kids and let them win.
His friend Sergio called to him
from Baghdad. Man of peace, scholar
of our failure to mend ...he went...

in schools they studied exorcism...
Sin-Lequi-Unninni wrote it down. Humbaba came
the outer walls collapsed ...inner walls

his wife Ann doing her *tai chi*
as Gil read on, then stringing wire between
our houses, hanging up a feeder for
the yellow-throated finch

Gil hanging upside down in rubble
by his broken legs, calling
for his friend. Terrible the flash of light
O terrible the thunder-blast

column ...tablet ...Enkidu

J. D. McClatchy

Jihad

A contrail's white scimitar unsheathes
Above the tufts of anti-aircraft fire.
Before the mullah's drill on righteousness,
Practice rocks are hurled at chicken-wire

Dummies of tanks with silhouetted infidels
Defending the nothing both sides fight over
In God's name, a last idolatry
Of boundaries. The sirens sound: take cover.

He has forced the night and day, the sun and moon,
Into your service. By His leave, the stars
Will shine to light the path that He has set

You to walk upon. His mercy will let
You slay who would blaspheme or from afar
Defile His lands. Glory is yours, oh soon.

Of the heart. Of the tongue. Of the sword. The holy war
Is waged against the self at first, to raze
The ziggurat of sin we climb upon
To view ourselves, and next against that glaze

The enemies of faith will use to disguise
Their words. Only then, and at the caliph's nod,
Are believers called to drown in blood the people
Of an earlier book. There is no god but God.

He knows the day of death and sees how men
Will hide. Who breaks His covenant is cursed.
Who slights His revelations will live in fire.

He has cast aside the schemer and the liar
Who mistake their emptiness of heart for a thirst
That, to slake, the streams of justice descend.

Ski-masked on videotape, the skinny martyr
Reads his manifesto. He's stilted, nervous.
An hour later, he's dropped at the market town,
Pays his fare, and climbs aboard the bus.

Strapped to his chest is the death of thirty-four —
Plus his own — "civilians" on their way
To buy or sell what goods they claim are theirs,
Unlike our fates, which are not ours to say.

Under the shade of swords lies paradise.
Whom you love are saved with you, their souls
In His hand. And who would want to return to life

Except to be killed again? Who can thrive
On the poverty of this world, its husks and holes?
His wisdom watches for each sacrifice.

Raymond McDaniel

Assault to Abjury

Rain commenced, and wind did.

A crippled ship slid ashore.

Our swimmer's limbs went heavy.

The sand had been flattened.

The primary dune, the secondary dune, both leveled.

The maritime forest, extracted.

Every yard of the shore was shocked with jellyfish.

The blue pillow of the man o' war empty in the afterlight.

The threads of the jellyfish, spent.

Disaster weirdly neatened the beach.

We cultivated the debris field.

Castaway trash, our treasure.

Jewel box, spoon ring, sack of rock candy.

A bicycle exoskeleton without wheels, grasshopper green.

Our dead ten speed.

We rested in red mangrove and sheltered in sheets.

Our bruises blushed backwards, our blisters did.

is it true is it true

God help us we tried to stay shattered but we just got better.

We grew adept, we caught the fish as they fled.

We skinned the fish, our knife clicked like an edict.

We were harmed, and then we healed.

Sen Jak's Advice to the Tropically Depressed

As for palm-food, pinched face on the fruit
in your hands: that milk is too sweet

to be trusted. For my part I prefer lime
mingled with rum in the eddies

of this tattoo. While waiting this out,
you should eat, burn your fingers then suck them

clean, lament the singe and savor the sediment.
Not to remind you: to anchor.

Mistake a cult, fail a quiz, watch your washing
waste away to a burial. I afflict. I affix.

I wish constantly to impress. I save
sweets for my suitors, my chevaliers.

Between us we had corpse-weight
like a pair of jackasses, tails and fates.

We bray and balk. All this costume,
it comes from theater, bespeaks bellyaches

of joy and starvation, suffers satin
and deadly serious, gasoline a bounty

no less for burning. I tinker soldiers
made of tin, rusted sailormen.

I impress upon you no clemency
but the mercy of my inhabitation.

You are all shipwreck stories. No, it is just
this room, falling into water. Of that,

even the dirt remembers. Taste the bread
we've made, hien? You, too, will have souls.

Sandra McPherson

On Being Transparent:
Cedar Rapids Airport
(October 2001)

If they raise a picture
Of three ingots afloat, or suspended

In discrete shadow-prone directions,
    And do not know
What I am carrying between
The soap's diminished oblong
    And the underslip's commercial lace,
If they do not recognize these sandbars aiming through
The small and doleful stones in soles,
    It is my duty to guide their hands
By voice down into baggage of their doubt,
Carry-on of risk, make common
    The roots
(Inside the hunting ducks) of lead
That held them stable in the streaming lakes
    Or swaying upright in the homely slough.
No battle, just ballast. Then I nod respect
To soldiers at their jobs,
    Two genders in identical camouflage,
And to the searchers far far younger
Than the bachelor scaup and widgeon couple
    I am bearing home. Of personalities —
The winning, the horrific —
There really isn't any mortal scrutiny
    Trained enough to sort
Transcendence from the gross ungodly.
I want such a machine.
    And a machine will suffice: a god
Is too boundless for mere citizens' safety,
Too unwieldy for my preemie-diaphanous-hair's-breadth
    Mysticism — uninspected
But true-to-soul: the one-time visitation
I cling to of a presence glowing … like a
    Golden mayfly.
It came aboard my nerves, lodged
In a reading-light-sized chamber
    Over my left eye,
Where it could radiate unquestionable security,
Peace, and rest. I still carry the gift
    Of its short but sacred flight.

W. S. Merwin

To the Light of September

When you are already here
you appear to be only
a name that tells of you
whether you are present or not

and for now it seems as though
you are still summer
still the high familiar
endless summer
yet with a glint
of bronze in the chill mornings
and the late yellow petals
of the mullein fluttering
on the stalks that lean
over their broken
shadows across the cracked ground

but they all know
that you have come
the seed heads of the sage
the whispering birds
with nowhere to hide you
to keep you for later

you
who fly with them

you who are neither
before nor after
you who arrive
with blue plums
that have fallen through the night

perfect in the dew

September 10, 2001

To the Words

When it happens you are not there

O you beyond numbers
beyond recollection
passed on from breath to breath
given again
from day to day from age
to age
charged with knowledge
knowing nothing

indifferent elders
indispensable and sleepless

keepers of our names
before ever we came
to be called by them

you that were
formed to begin with
you that were cried out
you that were spoken
to begin with
to say what could not be said

ancient precious
and helpless ones

say it

September 17, 2001

To the Grass of Autumn

You could never believe
it would come to this
one still morning
when before you noticed
the birds already
were all but gone

even though year upon year
the rehearsal of it
must have surprised
your speechless parents
and unknown antecedents
long ago gathered to dust
and though even the children
have been taught how to say
the word *withereth*

no you were known to be
cool and countless
the bright vision on all
the green hills
rippling in unmeasured waves
through the days in flower

now you are as the fog
that sifts among you
gray in the chill daybreak
the voles scratch the dry earth
around your roots
hoping to find something
before winter
and when the white air stirs
you whisper to yourselves
without expectation
or the need to know

September 18, 2001

To Ashes

All the green trees bring
their rings to you
the widening
circles of their years to you
late and soon casting
down their crowns into
you at once they are gone
not to appear
as themselves again

O season of your own

from whom now even
the fire has moved on
out of the green voices
and the days of summer
out of the spoken
names and the words between them
the mingled nights the hands
the hope the faces
those circling ages dancing
in flames as we see now
afterward
here before you

O you with no
beginning that we can conceive of
no end that we can foresee
you of whom once we were made
before we knew ourselves

in this season of our own

September 19, 2001

To the Coming Winter

Sometime after eleven the fireworks
of the last fête of this autumn begin
popping down in the valley a few sparks
here and there climbing slowly through thin rain
into the darkness until they are gone
above the carnival din and the caught
faces lit by wheeling rides in that one
moment looking up still and shining what
are they celebrating now that the fine
days are finished and the old leaves falling
and fields empty this year when a season
has ended and we stand again watching
those brief flares in the silence of heaven
without knowing what they are signalling.

September 23, 2001

Philip Metres

From "Hung Lyres"

When the bombs fell, she could barely raise
    her pendulous head, wept shrapnel
        until her mother capped the fire

with her breast. She teetered,
    on the highwire of herself. She
        lay down & the armies retreated, never

showing their backs. She lifted her mouth
    to the nipple, & the planes returned to earth.
        She unlatched from the breast, & planes

took off again. She fought the furies
    in her gut, the armies unloading
        all they swallowed. The wires pulled the dictator

down, the invasion proceeded. She hoisted
    her body against the laws of gravity
        & night. The stubborn stars refused to fall...

When the invasion ended, she could hold her torso up.
    The statue toppled, & she could almost stand.

Asymmetries

After Spencer Tunick

Longing to grasp the familiar, names
    against the anonymous
appendages & naked flesh, a nipple the eye
    could nuzzle, to hide in
dark islands of hair, I near the photo —

    as if the body erotic
could shield against the camera's scalpel.
    In its distance, the bodies
without faces line a river bank, shade
    into some darker shadow,

obeying the desire of gravity. I'm thinking
        of Iraq, how they lay out
each disinterred nest of femurs & ribs
        on separate sackcloths,
trying to punctuate the run-on sentence

        of oppression & unfettered
blood. All's asymmetry. After making love,
        once you said every face,
split in half, fit so precariously, so comically,
        we spent the next half

-hour shading one side of our faces in the mirror,
        then the other. This world
is centaur: half dream, half nightmare.
        Wandering the gallery,
we drift onto an imagined balcony

        & gape at the traffic
of bodies jamming the crossroads, im
        -mobile sculpture of
pure fact, dangling odd-angled & earth
        -bound us.

Testimony

                                   After Spencer Tunick

I sit in a hotel room and draw this Iraqi.
The question is: how to fill the frame
With each etched face, each bound body.
They stripped the father and son, this man says,
████████████████████████████

They made the father strike the son.

Son and father   the stripped they, I write.
I listen as I draw and try to disappear
And make the father strike his son
Hover in words around his unbound head.
While I draw and try to disappear
Scratches turn into words, ██████ .

Hovering in words around his unbound head,
Like a hovering mother or torturer

Scratches turn into words, ███████ :
They could not make son hit the father.
████████████████████████████

I sketch with a stylus on a copper plate

Father ████ hit son   make not   could they
████████████████████████

How *they made the father dig a hole*
The words scratched backwards, as in a mirror.
And *they made the son get into the hole.*

How they made the father dig a hole
I have to write very quickly
How they made the son get into the hole
And made the father bury him up to his neck.
I have to write very quickly
So I do not lose the ██████████
And made the father bury him up to his neck
And later ride him like a donkey.
So I do not lose ████████████ —
Each etched face, each bound body
And later ride him like a donkey —
I sit in a hotel room and draw this Iraqi.

Compline

That we await a blessed hope, & that we will be struck
With great fear, like a baby taken into the night, that every boot,

Every improvised explosive, Talon & Hornet, Molotov
& rubber-coated bullet, every unexploded cluster bomblet,

Every Kevlar & suicide vest & unpiloted drone raining fire
On wedding parties will be burned as fuel in the dark season.

That we will learn the awful hunger of God, the nerve-fraying
Cry of God, the curdy vomit of God, the soiled swaddle of God,

The constant wakefulness of God, alongside the sweet scalp
Of God, the contented murmur of God, the limb-twitched dream-

Reaching of God. We're dizzy in every departure, limb-lost.
We cannot sleep in the wake of God, & God will not sleep

The infant dream for long. We lift the blinds, look out into ink
For light. My God, my God, open the spine binding our sight.

From "Homefront/Removes"

You look at me / looking at you. How close the words
creation and *cremation*. How in Hebrew, Adam is kin to *dust*,
how the stars swam in Abraham's eyes, his profligate future.
Uncountable windows of light, flashing open-eyed. The
towers burned down into themselves — just like a cigarette,
the poet laureate wanted to say, and did, on air, knowing that
distance makes metaphors terrifying and the world less so,
dividing the night from night. How to describe the twisted
angles and planes? Picasso: *a picture is a sum of destructions*, a
way of saying the wind draws dust into us. Thus, my friend
E — who held klieg lights at Ground Zero carries the towers
in lung roots. A kind of seeding, this seeing. We are
windows, half-open, half-reflecting, trying to impersonate
someone who can breathe.

Naomi Shihab Nye

Dictionary in the Dark

A retired general said
"the beautiful thing about it"
discussing war.
We were making "progress"
in our war effort.
"The appropriate time to launch the bombers"
pierced the A section with artillery as
"awe" huddled in a corner
clutching its small chest.
Someone else repeated, "in harm's way,"
strangely popular lately,

and "weapons of mass destruction"
felt gravely confused about their identity.
"Friendly" gasped. Fierce and terminal.
It had never agreed to sit beside fire, never.

Interview, Saudi Arabia

The fathers do not know
what the sons have done.
They are waiting for the sons to call home,
to say it was a mistake,
it was not me.
Somewhere on another street
their boys in short white pants
are walking proudly
in a world they love.
Oranges peeled by hand,
frying onions,
marbles in dust.
Whatever might happen
is shiny, strong.

One of the sons was sad sometimes.
No one knew why.
There is *no way*, says his brother,
he could fly a plane.

The fathers blink back tears.
They have no evidence at all.
Please tell them something better.
Their sons went to school,
were normal, good.
Whatever would happen
might still be changed.

I Never Realized They Had Aspirations Like Ours
(An Israeli, about the Palestinians)

Cranes which land in a Texas river
have flown for thousands of miles.
Dipping long beaks into green water,

they pretend not to notice us.
Graceful necks,
a curved, close world.
Still, a feather fluffs
or a wing stays wide
if we pass.

What else but the long stroke of hope?
Some have said it fifty years.
By now the sorrowing people
make secret refuge in the sky.
If the ground satisfied their dreams,
the sky would miss them.

Geoffrey O'Brien

A History

1.

In the middle of drinking wine
and of studying the curve
of the companion's shoulder,
curve defined by angle and her distance
from the light source, in the middle
of the middle —

2.

Afterwards
there will be the memory
of the exploded room,

a space of perfect freedom.

3.

They had forgotten what city they were in.
So temperate the day

they had forgotten almost their names
for as long as it took the sun,
shifting from faucet
toward the casual heap of cotton and leather,
to catch a zigzag stitch.

4.

Woke to the taste of ashes.

5.

The ancient world
of breached walls and famine tactics —
spies who hid in the gully —
they were living in it
and surrounded by it.
The position of the city in the river.
From those moorings
they traced a history of unladed bolts
of silk, stacks of etched boxes.
Wet stones, an air of arrival.

6.

The ancient world
of stolen glimpses. Outriders
describe the shapes of things.

Bulked masses,
what light hits from a distance.

The ancient world of borders.

7.

"And if I could invent
the air of that room, spin it
out of myself

like the gold thread in the story,

the room
to be made a permanent resort,

its windows guarded, and point of entry
hung with ornament —

what days would be celebrated,
festivals of breath
not written in any history —"

9.

A piece of wall
having had time to lose its markings
is border. Market in another city,
shored up by eroded diggings.

The wall ends
where something ended
to make place for river light
shifting through the accumulated passages.

One city resembles another
as one day resembles another,
as one face resembles itself
in an altered light.

10.

The room.
A view of buildings and water.

Paris, September 11–New York, October 5, 2001

Sharon Olds

September, 2001

A week later, I said to a friend: I don't
think I could ever write about it.

Maybe in a year I could write something.
There is something in me maybe someday
to be written; now it is folded, and folded,
and folded, like a note in school. And in my dream
someone was playing jacks, and in the air there was a
huge, thrown, tilted jack
on fire. And when I woke up, I found myself
counting the days since I had last seen
my ex-husband — only two years, and some weeks
and hours. We had signed the papers and come down to the
ground floor of the Chrysler Building,
the intact beauty of its lobby around us
like a king's tomb, on the ceiling the little
painted plane, in the mural, flying. And it
entered my strictured heart, this morning,
slightly, shyly as if warily,
untamed, a greater sense of the sweetness
and plenty of his ongoing life,
unknown to me, unseen by me,
unheard by me, untouched by me,
but known by others, seen by others,
heard, touched. And it came to me,
for moments at a time, moment after moment,
to be glad for him that he is with the one
he feels was meant for him now. And I thought of my
mother, minutes from her death, eighty-five
years from her birth, the almost warbler
bones of her shoulder under my hand, the
eggshell skull, as she lay in some peace
in the clean sheets, and I could tell her the best
of my poor, partial love, I could sing her
out, with it, I saw the luck
and the luxury of that hour.

Robert Pinsky

Poem of Disconnected Parts

At Robben Island the political prisoners studied.
They coined the motto *Each one Teach one.*

In Argentina the torturers demanded the prisoners
Address them always as *"Profesor."*

Many of my friends are moved by guilt, but I
Am a creature of shame, I am ashamed to say.

Culture the lock, culture the key. Imagination
That calls boiled sheep heads in the market "Smileys."

The first year at Guantánamo, Abdul Rahim Dost
Incised his Pashto poems into styrofoam cups.

*"The Sangomo says in our Zulu culture we do not
Worship our ancestors: we consult them."*

Becky is abandoned in 1902 and Rose dies giving
Birth in 1924 and Sylvia falls in 1951.

Still falling still dying still abandoned in 2006
Still nothing finished among the descendants.

I support the War, says the comic, it's just the Troops
I'm against: can't stand those Young People.

Proud of the fallen, proud of her son the bomber.
Ashamed of the government. Skeptical.

After the Klansman was found Not Guilty one juror
Said she just couldn't vote to convict a pastor.

Who do you write for? I write for dead people:
For Emily Dickinson, for my grandfather.

*"The Ancestors say the problem with your Knees
Began in your Feet. It could move up your Back."*

But later the Americans gave Dost not only paper
And pen but books. Hemingway, Dickens.

Old Aegyptius said, Whoever has called this Assembly,
For whatever reason — it is a good in itself.

O thirsty shades who regard the offering, O stained earth.
There are many fake Sangomos. This one is real.

Coloured prisoners got different meals and could wear
Long pants and underwear, Blacks got only shorts.

No he says he cannot regret the three years in prison:
Otherwise he would not have written those poems.

I have a small-town mind. Like the Greeks and Trojans.
Shame. Pride. Importance of looking bad or good.

Did he see anything like the prisoner on a leash? Yes,
In Afghanistan. In Guantánamo he was isolated.

Our enemies "disassemble" says the President.
Not that anyone at all couldn't mis-speak.

The *profesores* created nicknames for torture devices:
The Airplane. The Frog. Burping the Baby.

Not that those who behead the helpless in the name
Of God or tradition don't also write poetry.

Guilts, metaphors, traditions. Hunger strikes.
Culture the penalty. Culture the escape.

What could your children boast about you? What
Will your father say, down among the shades?

The Sangomo told Marvin, "*You are crushed by some
Weight. Only your own Ancestors can help you.*"

The Forgetting

The forgetting I notice most as I get older is really a form of memory:
The undergrowth of things unknown to you young, that I have forgotten.

Memory of so much crap, jumbled with so much that seems to matter.
Lieutenant Calley. Captain Easy. Mayling Soong. Sibby Sisti.

And all the forgettings that preceded my own: Baghdad, Egypt, Greece,
The Plains, centuries of lootings of antiquities. Obscure atrocities.

Imagine!— a big tent filled with mostly kids, yelling for poetry. In fact
It happened, I was there in New Jersey at the famous poetry show.

I used to wonder, what if the Baseball Hall of Fame overflowed
With too many thousands of greats all in time unremembered?

Hardly anybody can name all eight of their great-grandparents.
Can you? Will your children's grandchildren remember your name?

You'll see, you little young jerks: your favorite music and your political
Furors, too, will need to get sorted in dusty electronic corridors.

In 1972, Chou En-lai was asked the lasting effects of the French
Revolution: "Too soon to tell." Remember?—or was it Mao Tse-tung?

Poetry made of air strains to reach back to Begats and suspiring
Forward into air, grunting to beget the hungry or overfed Future.

Ezra Pound praises the Emperor who appointed a committee of scholars
To pick the best 450 Noh plays and destroy all the rest, the fascist.

The stand-up master Stephen Wright says he thinks he suffers from
Both amnesia and déjà vu: "I feel like I have forgotten this before."

Who remembers the arguments when jurors gave Pound the only prize
For poetry awarded by the United States Government? Until then.

I was in the big tent when the guy read his poem about how the Jews
Were warned to get out of the Twin Towers before the planes hit.

The crowd was applauding and screaming, they were happy—it isn't
That they were anti–Semitic, or anything. They just weren't listening. Or

No, they were listening, but that certain way. In it comes, you hear it, and
That selfsame second you swallow it or expel it: an ecstasy of forgetting.

The Anniversary

We adore images, we like the spectacle
Of speed and size, the working of prodigious
Systems. So on television we watched

The terrible spectacle, repetitiously gazing
Until we were sick not only of the sight
Of our prodigious systems turned against us

But of the very systems of our watching.
The date became a word, an anniversary
We inscribed with meanings — who keep so few,

More likely to name an airport for an actor
Or athlete than "First of May" or "Fourth of July."
In the movies we dream up, our captured heroes

Tell the interrogator their commanding officer's name
Is Colonel Donald Duck — he writes it down, code
Of a lowbrow memory so assured it's nearly

Aristocratic. Some say the doomed firefighters
Before they hurried into the doomed towers wrote
Their Social Security numbers on their forearms.

We can imagine them kidding about it a little.
"*No man is great if he thinks he is*" — Will Rogers:
A kidder, a skeptic. A Cherokee, a survivor

Of expropriation. A roper, a card. Remembered
A while yet. He had turned sixteen the year
That Frederick Douglass died. Douglass was twelve

When Emily Dickinson was born. Is even Donald
Half-forgotten? — Who are the Americans, not
A people by blood or religion? As it turned out,

The donated blood not needed, except as meaning.
At a Sports Bar the night before, the guy
Who shaved off all his body hair and screamed

The name of God with his box cutter in his hand.
O Americans — as Marianne Moore would say,
Whence is our courage? Is what holds us together

A gluttonous dreamy thriving? Whence our being?
In the dark roots of our music, impudent and profound?
We inscribed God's name onto the dollar bill

In 1958, and who remembers why, among
Forgotten glyphs and meanings, the Deistic
Mystical and Masonic totems of the Founders:

The Eye afloat above the uncapped Pyramid,
Hexagram of Stars protecting the Eagle's head
From terror of pox, from plague and radiation.

The Western face of the pyramid is dark.
And if they blow up the Statue of Liberty —
Then the survivors might likely in grief, terror

And excess build a dozen more, or produce
A catchy song about it, its meaning as beyond
Meaning as those old symbols. The *wilds of thought*

Of Katherine Lee Bates: *Till selfish gain*
No longer stain the banner of the free. O
Beautiful for patriot dream that sees

Beyond the years, and Ray Charles singing it,
Alabaster cities, amber waves, purple majesties.
Thine every flaw. Thy liberty in law. O beautiful.

The Raelettes in sequins and high heels for a live
Performance — or in the studio to burn the record
In sneakers and headphones, engineers at soundboards,

Musicians, all concentrating, faces as grave with
What purpose as the harbor Statue herself, *O*
Beautiful for liberating strife: the broken

Shackles visible at her feet, her Elvis lips —
Liberty: not Abundance and not Beatitude —
Her enigmatic scowl, her spikey crown.

Kevin Prufer

National Anthem

And the shopping center said, *Give me, give me.*

And the moon turning on its pole said, *I love you, you who have so much to give.*

And you said, *Darling, if you could just wait in the car for ten minutes and I'll*
be right out—

And the sliding doors opened for you like a coat.

Then the car ticked like the contented in the catatonic snow

and the black boys at the bus stop laughed in their hoods until a bus dragged them through the night and away —

And a woman paced beneath the store.

Sometimes, I can hear the nation speak through the accumulation of the sub-urbs —

Olive Garden and Exxon; Bed, Bath & Beyond, the stars that throw their dimes around us all

until the eyes say, *Love* and the streets say, *Yes!* and the parking lot

fills with angels blowing past the lines of freezing cars.

You had been inside for longer than you said, and when you reemerged

I went to help you with the bags. *I'm sorry, sorry*— into the cold air *—I couldn't help—*

What was the body but a vessel, and what was the store but another,

larger vessel? The keys sang in my numb fingers. The flag applauded in the wind.

And then I saw that you were smiling up at it.

Dead Soldier

Where the living are, no one's missed him yet.
The best of them
                    will sing themselves to sleep.
The others laugh too loud and swallow pills
until their wet cells burst
                              beneath the skin like grapes
or bloom like urchins in a lukewarm sea.

—

High above,
              the green moon glows in a windy sky
like a half-dead cat and its one good eye.

—

And who will coin his eyes,
                              and who would care?
He who failed in school has failed again. And he
who slept last night in a narrow bed
                                        will sleep in tents of sand
with the collapsing dead.

Those Who Could Not Flee

The rain, like Caesar's army —
                                  And the city, aghast —
The old ladies huddled in the doorways,
                                          obliterated
in the downpour, ladies like ghosts of themselves —
And you were saying,
                      Why shouldn't we adopt?
A Chinese? A Romanian? A noble thing to do, these days,
and if the buildings burned
                              we wouldn't see them
through the weather.

—

                        Then the enemy
stealing through the thickets — blue faced and strange.
Our legions far outnumbered, the legions of Paulinus —
so who would save us?
                        The aged and infirm who couldn't
leave the city?
                  They'd string them up on posts,
they'd light the streets
                          with slowly burning bodies.

—

How they hate us for our freedom, someone told me once,
How they loathe our freedom —
An old man tottered in the street;
                                    or the clubfoot
where his retreating family left him, huddled in his bed,

asleep —
      The killers in the thicket —

  —

A child from far away, a Russian
                    or a black one.
You pulled your coat a little tighter
at the throat,
          the thicket trilled with ghosts.
assembled half of rain — and then of flesh.
                   A bus
approached, not ours, and in my dented mind I swore
a black man dragged behind it —

  —

                  They'd burn the city
and the ones who couldn't flee
they'd skin and nail to posts.

  —

             I only mean this
if we can't conceive. Our bus approached,
the crying of the brakes —
           and some in their tattered
useless wings, and others curled in doorways,
their breath that filled the streets with fog —
How they hate our freedoms —
           the doors and the pneumatic hiss —

  —

Caesar's pointless extras and their ragged shields,
the white-faced files.
         Those who had the legs to march
prepared to march away.
         A good thing, you said, *a noble thing* —
a clatter of retreat, the pistons squeaked.
            We had no choice.
We left the weak to perish in the street.

Recent History

All night, angels
                          crashed through the trees,
so the yard was a scatter
                          of bent, failing bodies.
You said: *Another!* to the crackling of branches.
Their scraps are so sweet where they sway with the leaves.

—

From the garden, the asters said: *Love was their weakness.*
The firefly's bright little heart disagreed.

—

Then down fell another, where it cracked on a low branch,
waking the neighbors
                          who leaned from their windows
and peered toward the trees.

—

A crowd had collected
                          in bathrobes and nightgowns,
their faces lit greenly in the angels' dim glow.
I'd like to have known them
                          when they were more vibrant,
you said, looking down,

—

where one gurgled strangely,
                          its wings come undone.
A child had collected a handful of feathers.
Another threw sticks
                          at one caught on a limb.
We'd better get digging, our neighbor said softly.
They'll stink in the sun.

God Bless Our Troops

The sun went up
                    like a burning tent.
The troops we'd planted
                    had sprouted by then,
their sharp leaves glistening in the morning glare.
God bless them, we said
as the bees flared past.
God bless our troops who sway in the breeze.

—

And soon the first troops bloomed on their stems,
hot as marigolds
                    or burst grenades,
The sun caught fire like a tank of gas
and in its flames we grew to love
the flying shrapnel
                    that buzzed the petals,
and sipped the oil
                    the troops provided.

—

God bless our troops, we told ourselves,
while the sun went down like a jet on fire
and lit the fields
                    we'd tended all year.
The troops by then were thick with sap
and heavy with bombs
                    that hung like fruit
from their outstretched fronds.

—

And we ate well
                    all year long
until our troops expired, their leaves gone crisp,
their bones
                    dead stalks in the fertile earth.
Then the snows came down to numb the field.
Like a sinking ship,
                    its deck on fire,
the sun went out with a hiss of flame
and a barely noticed
                    wince of smoke.

Claudia Rankine

From Don't Let Me Be Lonely: An American Lyric

Cornel West makes the point that hope is different from American optimism. After the initial presidential election results come in, I stop watching the news. I want to continue watching, charting, and discussing the counts, the recounts, the hand counts, but I cannot. I lose hope. However Bush came to have won, he would still be winning ten days later and we would still be in the throes of our American optimism. All the non-reporting is a distraction from Bush himself, the same Bush who can't remember if two or three people were con-

victed for dragging a black man to his death in his home state of Texas.

You don't remember because you don't care. Sometimes my mother's voice swells and fills my forehead. Mostly I resist the flooding, but in Bush's case I find myself talking to the television screen: *You don't know because you don't care.*

Then, like all things impassioned, this voice takes on a life of its own: *You don't know because you don't bloody care. Do you?*

I forget things too. It makes me sad. Or it makes me the saddest. The sadness is not really about George W. or our American optimism; the sadness lives in the recognition that a life can not matter. Or, as there are billions of lives, my sadness is alive inside the

recognition that billions of lives never mattered. I write this without breaking my heart, without bursting into anything. Perhaps, this is the real source of my sadness. Or perhaps, Emily Dickinson, my love, hope was never a thing with feathers. I don't know, I just find when the news comes on I switch the channel. This new tendency might be indicative of a deepening personality flaw: IMH, The Inability to Maintain Hope, which translates into no innate trust in the supreme laws that govern us. Cornel West says this is what is wrong with black people today — too nihilistic. Too scarred by hope to hope, too experienced to experience, too close to dead is what I think.

From Don't Let Me Be Lonely: An American Lyric

Timothy McVeigh died at 7:14 A.M. and a news reporter asks relatives of his 168 victims if they have forgiven him. Perhaps because McVeigh is visually the American boy next door, this is yet another attempt by the media to immunize him from his actions. Still it is unclear to me why the reporter asks this now, but I nonetheless continue watching to hear what is said. Many say, No, no I have not forgiven him. A few say, Yes.

What does it mean to forgive and how does forgiveness show itself? "Forgiveness forgives only the unforgivable," Jacques Derrida claims. Timothy McVeigh never asked to be forgiven. He managed to suggest that both condemnation and forgiveness were irrelevant by quoting William Earnest Henley's poem "Invictus":

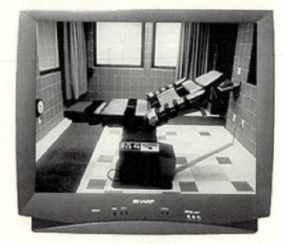

"It matters not how strait the gate, How charged with punishments the scroll, I am the master of my fate: I am the captain of my soul." The need for forgiveness does not seem to enter into McVeigh's final statement to the media. Even as his judicial execution by lethal injection is televised over closed-circuit television for the victims' families, he makes no sign that forgiveness is necessary to him.

So what is forgiveness and how does it show itself? Forgiveness, I finally decide, is not the death of amnesia, nor is it a form of madness, as Derrida claims. For the one who forgives, it is simply a death, a dying down in the heart, the position of the already dead. It is in the end of the living through, the understanding that this has happened, is happening, happens. Period. It is a feeling of nothingness that cannot be communicated to another, an absence, a bottomless vacancy held by the living, beyond all that is hated or loved.

Donald Revell

Given Days

September 11, 2001

The attacks were tall, and then they burned.
I'd been reading, and then it was time
To take our son to school before the mustangs,
As they do every day, fled
The schoolyard for quieter fields up high.

The news was far, then close.
Something had towered above the sky,
And now the sky was alone. At bedtime,
I began to read where I had broken off:
Walt Whitman, a kosmos, of Manhattan the son...

Somewhere between, a little before dinner,
I'd gone out walking.

I passed the fat lady and her lovely daughter,
A three-year-old, on the stoop where they spend every day.
Between them was an orange with a face cut into it,
A tiny jack-o-lantern five weeks early.
                                        A kosmos

Suspended in 1912, the Brooklyn Ferry resumes tomorrow,
And the sky reclaims it own,
And the river reclaims its own,
And we are the despised.

October 16, 2001

Strange new flight paths

                                    chains of the smallest pearls

And glint of the Colorado

                        small so
                        chained so

YOU COULD IMAGINE A CHILD'S DOWNY WRIST
Where never before
Mist showed over water
To the east of our wings

YOU COULD SEE THE CHILD
(Village of Blue Diamond, Nevada)
RUNNING WITH MUSTANGS
Signs of the times, no, these are brighter, these are heavens and damn all
    murderers.

October 22, 2001

I am angry (10/22

                        The house I was raised in
                        Still my mother's alone house
                        1022 Vincent Avenue, Bronx, New York

With my dog for being angry
At Jack Spicer on the radio
Or afraid

LOOK THERE HE IS

Under the table with his diarrhea
And bandanna covered with jack-o-lanterns

> *The house is falling away*
> *My father's death my sister's death the*
>   *Halloween I was ill*
> *And doled out treats in my devil's suit to the*
>   *healthy children*
> *And our turtle died under a Woolworth*
>   *palm tree in a Woolworth pond*

"Believe the birds"
All's well now the dog's asleep now
In tough tender strophes.

October 30, 2001

All around the table
Words before bedtime —
Psalms from King James and some of the Wyatt translations;
A *Greensward*, author I cannot remember;
And tortoises, all those poems
By Lawrence, the best wisdom
Re sorrows and abasements, women and men.

WHERE IS THE REST, THE DEAREST PORTION OF MY FAMILY?
Safe at home

> *In the morning, water*
> *Dowsed a white spider*
> *Out of my razor*
> *When I'd done*

(My son, I hear, has covered the house in fake spiderwebs.)

Over the phone, the word is
Stay at home tomorrow, Halloween.
Anonymous tips from somewhere in Brooklyn,
Anthrax and explosions.

"There are no just wars."
Happy birthday, Ezra Pound.
Happy birthday, Claudia Keelan.

God help John Keats tomorrow.

November 3, 2001

Cake and icing on her lips
After dancing a little
Because of the new trees
(Palo verde and acacia)
And our roses thriving into November,
Claudia kisses me.

Flowers never spoil. (*They are doors to Heaven op. cit. D. H. Lawrence*
   "Bavarian Gentians"
Singers never age. (*They are doors to Heaven c.f. Walt Whitman somewhere*
On the television screen
Cross-legged before a wacky harmonium
Someone from England sings
To weeping firemen.

So, sometimes, flowers never spoil,
Even in the long days after
Lightning strikes the well.

                    (I am far away writing this —
                    Tell me, is there water?
                    How are the trees?

November 30, 2001

A winter night in Salt Lake City

In a bright window   In the dripping bus shelter
Alone in a tender display   A school girl smiles far away
A stylist teases her own hair   Into her paperback *The Hobbit*

SOMEONE ELSEWHERE I'M THINKING

Comes ridiculous news
Disappeared remains
Of a hermaphroditic moose

Comes really sad news
Death of George Harrison
I remember impossibly elusive
The prettiest girl in our class
Loved him so

By first light
The snow falls heavily
And, I'm thinking,
More difficultly.
Someone elsewhere
Bringing my good shoes to the ceremony
Flies to meet me.
Every blessed thing is elusive.
All's muddled.
This must pass.

December 8, 2001

These sentiments grow hair, and wings too.
Just look at the drains, look at the clouds.
John Lennon's death turns 21 today, and one hour
From now, in the theater over there, the curtain
Rises on the blind kids' matinee: *The Nutcracker.*

Comes terrible news: Shahid Ali dead
Who wept at my kitchen table for his mother dead
And balanced then every wild animal slain
In the mts of Kashmir on a silken thread.
He died blind. He was good news.

As I left my hotel this morning,
The television was still talking. It said
These: "like a weapon on its wings" and
"Like a housewife knows her eggbeater."

What do you make of *that*? America   (Arcady)

Is a country of many faults without a flaw.
Why make similes? Why be blind? All we need is love.

In the theater over there.
Beautiful young bodies
Are dancing in total darkness,
And the darkness cannot touch them.

December 19, 2001

Mornings of the war that is no war but,
As the man said, new reasons for spitefulness.
All's paused. And inside of that another,
A pause between shepherds and kings.
Dead winter, and the sap is rising.
At the raffle in Blue Diamond, we got the palm tree,
And we drove it home in a wagon under white stars.

Began where?
A place in Brooklyn and the spine of a book
On a shelf—*Journey to the End of the Night*, a trip
I would believe myself taking, ending
In a child who'd traveled for me the whole time.
Mornings of the war are sex in a toilet.
Real sunrise rests today in darkest night
Under a palm tree scarcely visible.
It drinks myrrh direct from Heaven.
When it's full, look for a good day.

Vietnam Epic Treatment

It doesn't matter
A damn what's playing —
In the dead of winter
You go, days of 1978-
79, and we went
Because the soldiers were beautiful
And doomed as Asian jungles
Kept afire Christ-like
In the hopeless war

I did not go to in the end
Because it ended.

The 20th century?
It was a war
Between peasants on the one side,
Hallucinations on the other.
A peasant is a fire that burns
But is not consumed.
His movie never ends.
It will be beautiful
Every winter of our lives, my love,
As Christ crushes fire into his wounds
And the wounds are a jungle.
Equally, no matter when their movies end,
Hallucinations destroy the destroyers.
That's all.
There has never been a President of the United States.

And the 21st century?
Hallucination vs. hallucination
In cold battle, in dubious battle,
No battle at all because the peasants
Have gone away far
Into the lost traveler's dream,
Into a passage from Homer,
A woodcutter's hillside
Peacetime superstition movie.

On a cold night, Hector.
On a cold night, Achilles.
Around the savage and the maniac
The woodcutter draws a ring of fire.
It burns all winter long.
He never tires of it
And for good reason:
Every face of the flames is doomed and beautiful;
Every spark that shoots out into the freezing air
Is God's truth
Given us all over again
In the bitter weather of men's
Hallucinations. There has never been

A President of the United States.
There has never been a just war.
There has never been any life
Beyond this circle of firelight
Until now if now is no dream but an Asia.

Election Year

A jet of mere phantom
Is a brook, as the land around
Turns rocky and hollow.
Those airplane sounds
Are the drowning of bicyclists.
Leaping, a bridesmaid leaps.
You asked for my autobiography.
Imagine the greeny clicking sound
Of hummingbirds in a dry wood,
And there you'd have it. Other birds
Pour over the walls now.
I'd never suspected: every day,
Although the nation is done for,
I find new flowers.

Frederick Seidel

God Exploding

They all claim responsibility for inventing God,
Including the ruthless suicides who call themselves God Exploding.
All the rival groups, of course, immediately take credit
For terrorist atrocities they did not commit.

One of the terrorist acts they did not commit
Was inventing rock 'n' roll, but, hey,
The birth of Elvis/Jesus is as absolute as the temperature
Of the background radiation, 4°K.

1, 2, 3, 4 — I sing of a maiden that is makeles.

King of alle kings to here sone che ches.
He cam also stille
Ther his moder was,

As dew in Aprille that fallith on the gras.
He cam also stille to his moderes browr
As dew in Aprille that fallith on the flowr.
He cam also stille

Ther his moder lay,
As dew in Aprille that fallith on the spray.
Moder and maiden
Was never non but che;

Wel may switch a lady Godes moder be.
I hate seeing the anus of a beautiful woman.
I should not be looking. It should not be there.
It started in darkness and ended up a star.

Jewish star on the L.A. freeway in Jewish cars
Take the off ramp to the manger
Somewhere in the fields of Harlem,
Bearing gifts of gold and frankincense and myrrh.

Rock 'n' roll in front of the Wailing Wall and weep.
With the stump where your hand was blown off beat your chest.
Hutu rebel soldiers crucify the mountain gorillas.
Hodie Christus natus est.

The Black-Eyed Virgins

A terrorist rides the rails underwater
From one language to another in a packed train of London
Rugby fans on their way to the big match in Paris
And a flock of Japanese schoolgirls ready to be fucked
In their school uniforms in paradise.
This is all just after Madrid in the reign of terror.
This is the girls' first trip outside Japan.
The terrorist swings in the hammock of their small skirts and black socks.
The chunnel train in the tunnel with an announcement
That everyone now alive is already human remains.

The terrorists have seen to it that trains
Swap human body parts around with bombs.
The Japanese schoolgirls say so sorry.
Their new pubic hair is made of light.

Eurostar

Japanese schoolgirls in their school uniforms with their school chaperones
Ride underwater on a train
Every terrorist in the world would dearly love to bomb
For the publicity and to drown everybody.
The Eurostar dashes into the waves.
The other passengers are watching the Japanese girls eat
Little sweeties they bought with their own money
In London. President Bush the younger is making ice cream.
Ice cream for dessert
Is what Iraq is, without the courses that normally come before.
You eat dessert to start and then you have dessert.
One of them is a Balthus in her short school skirt standing on the seat.
She reaches up too high to get something out of her bag.
She turns around smiling because she knows where you are looking.

Song: "The Swollen River Overthrows Its Banks"

The terrorists are out of breath with success.
And cancer is eating American women's breasts.
The terrorists are bombing Madrid
And everywhere serious and nice.
They put the backpacks on
Without a word and leave
The Italian premier talking to an empty room because
They leave the TV on and leave.
One of the many networks Mr. Berlusconi owns
Carries him live denouncing terror. The man
By now has reached Milan
Who has the man in London for Miami.
Both will board the train,
As in the swollen river overthrows its banks.

The Bush Administration

I

The darkness coming from the mouth
Must be the entrance to a cave.
The heart of darkness took another form
And inside is the Congo in the man.
I think the Bush administration is as crazy as Sparta was.
Sparta has swallowed Congo and is famished.
The steel Spartan abs turn to fevered slush
While it digests the good that it is doing
In the desert heat. I felt a drop of rain,
Which is the next Ice Age being born.

II

I stood on Madison. The sun was shining.
I felt large drops of rain as warm as tears.
I held my hand out, palm up, the way one does.
The sun was shining and the rain really started.
Maybe there must have been a rainbow somewhere.
I hailed a cab and as I hopped in
That was the first thing
The radio said:
They had beheaded an American.
There was a thunderclap and it poured.

III

The downpour drumming on my taxi gets the Hutu in me dancing.
Il rombo della Desmosedici makes machete music.
I crawl into a crocodile
And I go native.
The white cannibals in cowboy boots
Return to the bush
And the darkness of the brutes.
I am on all fours eating grass.
So I can throw up because I like the feeling.
I crouch over a carcass and practice my eating.

IV

The United States of America preemptively eats the world.
The doctrine of eat lest you be eaten

Is famished, roars
And tears their heads off before its own is sawed off.
The human being sawing screams *God is Great!*
God is — and pours cicadas
By the tens of millions through the air.
They have risen from underground.
The voices of the risen make a summer sound.
It is pouring cicadas on Madison Avenue, making the street thick.

V

Every human being who has ever lived has died,
Except the living. The sun is shining and
The countless generations rise from underground this afternoon
And fall like rain.
I never thought that I would see your face again.
The savage wore a necklace made of beads,
And then I saw the beads were tiny human faces talking.
He started crying and the tears were raindrops.
The raindrops were more faces.
Everybody dies, but they come back as salt and water.

VI

I am charmed by my taxi's sunny yellow reflection
Keeping abreast of the speeding taxi I'm in,
Playful and happy as a dolphin,
All the way down York Avenue to the hospital,
Right up to the bank of elevators to heaven.
I take an elevator to the floor.
Outside the picture window, rain is falling on the sunshine.
In the squeeze-hush silence, the ventilator keeps breathing.
A special ops comes in to check the hoses and the flow.
A visitor holds out his palm to taste the radiant rain.

VII

The Bush Administration likes its rain sunny-side up.
I feel a mania of happiness at being alive
As I write you this suicide note.
I have never been so cheerily suicidal, so sui–Seidel.
I am too cheery to be well.
I am cheeriest
Crawling around on all fours eating gentle grass

And pretending I am eating broken glass.
Then I throw up the pasture.

VIII

CENTCOM is drawing up war plans.
They will drop snow on Congo.
It will melt without leaving a trace, at great expense.
America will pay any price to whiten darkness.
My fellow citizen cicadas rise to the tops of the vanished Twin Towers
And float back down white as ashes
To introduce a new Ice Age.
The countless generations rise from underground this afternoon
And fall like rain.
I never thought that I would live to see the towers fall again.

Hugh Seidman

Found Poem: Microloans

Fifty dollars is a fortune.
Nations flout women.
Banks scorn mothers.
Usurers steal capital.

Nations flout women.
Poverty lacks collateral.
Usurers steal capital.
Hoping is dependence.

Poverty lacks collateral.
A woman fears risk.
Hoping is dependence.
Microloans lift women.

A woman fears risk.
Mothers feed families.
Microloans lift women.
Women form groups.

Mothers feed families.
How do I contribute?
Women form groups.
A group backs payback.

How do I contribute?
A woman wove cloth.
A group backs payback.
A woman sold bread.

A woman wove cloth.
A woman fired bricks.
A woman sold bread.
No mouth is exempt.

A woman fired bricks.
Children sicken.
No mouth is exempt.
One-fifth of Earth starves.

Children sicken.
Banks scorn mothers.
One-fifth of Earth starves.
Fifty dollars is a fortune.

Thinking of Baghdad

Flesh gorging on oxygen.
Apes of smoke and debris writhing and struggling in air.

Wails of the *infidels* and *assassins*.
Mutilations from the centuries of bronze.

I wanted to exonerate the infants.
The event horizon was white hot.

The infernos were igniting the armor between myself and the infants.
The projectiles were piercing the armor between myself and the infants.

•

There, city, just past imploded brick.
There, city, just past the trope for black holes.

Here, I resented the price of a loaf of bread.
Here, I sat on a park bench in the sun.

Here, I dozed — numb, livid (nine hours from bombs).
Here, I paid tax — to forge the uranium tanks.

Here, I tongued language.
Here, I pled: country! country! country!

•

It is good to be made naïve.
It is good that blood forces in gut, as in brain.

Dreams bloom to the chroma of terror.
Long ago I swore to uphold the *imperial power* of dream.

Shrapnel purifies the eye of the testifier.
Protozoa bore harder into the fly.

The warplane graphic rotates slowly on the vengeful news channel.
Fate reiterates: thirst, starve, curse, scream, burn.

Lisa Sewell

The Anatomy of Melancholy

*Apt to loathe, dislike, disdain, and weary
when the heart-strings do burn and beat
and the heart itself faints like fits of the mother*

he said he wished he were interred
not in the compact car discussing wishes
and requiring analysis

to be inert and uninterpreted, without meaning
for many cannot tell to express themselves in words
or how it holds them.

I do things slowly.
The future seems endless.
I am bothered by things that do not affect me.

Now the chest, now belly and sides
then heart and head aches
now heat, then wind, now this, now that—

When the Sunday bomber blew
at a funeral in Tikrit
and he slept another night behind the office door

hard sleep on the cluttered floor
to keep the indignation clean and glowing
at least fifteen were killed and seventeen wounded.

The researchers repeated the experiment three times
zeroing in on the amygdala, thimble-sized trigger point
for fear and craving and wild euphoric highs
that sits 2½ inches behind the bridge of the nose.

He is weary of all and yet will not, cannot tell
how, where, or what offends him.

The colonel said no coalition soldier was responsible
for the murder of that family, the rape
and murder of that little girl.

I am all appetite.
I have crying spells.
It is hard to concentrate on not reading.

And though very modest themselves,
sober, religious, virtuous and well given,
they cannot make resistance and are violently carried away
with this inward torrent of humors.

Refugees fleeing bombardment talked of chemical
attacks and people melting to death
pieces of bombs exploding in fires
that burn the skin even when water is thrown on the area.

So when he lay face down on the bed
(*hirsute and lean, with broad flat veins*
and thick blood churning) in broad daylight
all the curtains drawn and said
"I wish I was dead," why did she correct his grammar?

It may be the most detailed snapshot ever taken
mapping melancholy on the gray matter of the brain
and exactly what goes wrong in a mind overwhelmed
by the downward spiral of despair.

Everything I do is an effort.
My sleep is restless.
I'm not as good as other people.
I have trouble keeping my mind.

Fastened onto one thing without an ague
better marry than burn saith the apostles
but they are otherwise persuaded.

He was going to get a memorial tattoo
of all the guys who were killed
but there was no more room on his arm
below the elbow.

In the parking lot, we parted, despondent
and prone to weeping, so far gone, so stupefied
and distracted we thought ourselves bewitched.

Susan Stewart

When I'm crying, I'm not speaking

Barred back from the glare
gone gripped along
the rail run down
running from or
toward no matter
no mind never
hell for leather
scraped across
night's increment
torn from the sedge
the salvage
shorn at
the edge forlorn

forewarned
hefting waxed
breached waning
whine needling
half heard
then hearing
help wound in
the wind

When I'm speaking, I'm not crying

The personal is artificially political just as
the political is artificially personal.

War profiteering has many means, including
the sale of poems against war.

Those who destroy the garden and poison
the well think that streets
will be named for them in the future.

When Aeneas, son of the goddess of love, strides out
        alone on the empty
            field, so recklessly
                    to meet the radiant killer Achilles, it's not
                    Love, but the god of earthquakes,
            who takes pity
        and lifts him, just
        in time,
right off the earth.

Meeting with slaughter, the mind breaks into parts.
Salvation hides below us and entire.

Elegy Against the Massacre at the Amish School in West Nickel Mines, Pennsylvania, Autumn 2006

Lena, Mary Liz, and Anna Mae
Marian, Naomi Rose
when time has stopped

where time has slowed
the horses wear the rain

Mary Liz, Anna Mae, Marian
Naomi Rose and Lena
the lanterns lit
at midday dark
pain's processional

Anna Mae, Marian, Naomi Rose
Lena, Mary Liz
innocence has no
argument, justice
returns in a leaf

Naomi Rose, Lena, and Mary Liz
Anna Mae and Marian
a girl is not a kind of girl
she knows her rhyme
she has her name

Lena, Naomi Rose, and Mary Liz
Marian and Anna Mae
zinnias mixed with cosmos,
lupines caught
in hay

Mary Liz, Lena, and Anna Mae
Marian, Naomi Rose
someone had a newborn
calf that died into the light,
and someone knew the night

Anna Mae, Mary Liz, and Marian
Lena and Naomi Rose
someone knew the night
holiness mere meaning
when someone knew the night

Marian, Anna Mae, Naomi
Rose, Mary Liz and Lena
the mad put on death's
mantle, the mad
on fire with shame

Naomi Rose, Marian and Lena
Anna Mae and Mary Liz
The mother of the god you knew
was reading in her chair
and down came interruption

Naomi Rose, Lena and Marian
Mary Liz and Anne Mae
down came endless care
visitation's presence
bookmarked in a book

Anna Mae, Naomi Rose and
Mary Liz, Lena and Marian
your names in stone
your footprints kept
in mud between the stalks

Marian, Anna Mae and Lena
Naomi Rose and Mary Liz
iron bells toss
the clouds at dusk
and elders turn away

Mary Liz, Marian, Naomi
Rose, Anna Mae and Lena
empty-handed, hold their cups
with lead seams
supplicant

Lena, Mary Liz and Anna
Mae, Marian, Naomi Rose
a length of serge
so plain, so plain
the morning grass turned down

Anna Mae, Mary Liz and Marian
Lena, Naomi Rose
when time has stopped
where time has slowed
the horses wear the rain

David Wagoner

In Rubble

Right after the bomb, even before the ceiling
   And walls and floor are rearranging
      You and themselves into a different world,
You must hold still, must wait for them
   To settle down in unpredictable ways,
      To bring their wars, shuddering,
To an end, and only then should you begin
   Numbly to feel what freedom may be left
      To your feet or knees, to your elbows
Or clenched fingers. Where you used to walk
   Or lean or lie down or fix your attention
      At a whim or stomp your foot
Or slump in a chair, you'll find a new
   Architecturally unsound floor-plan
      To contend with, if you can move
At all. Now you may remember others
   Who were somewhere near you before
      This breakdown of circumstances. Caught by surprise
Like you, they may be waiting separately
   At their own levels, inside their own portions
      Of your incoherent flat. They may be thinking
Of you, as you are of them, and wondering
   Whether some common passageway, no matter
      How crooked or narrow, might still exist
Between you, through which you might share the absence
   Of food and water and the cold comfort
      Of daylight. They may be expecting you
To arrive at any moment, to crawl through dust
   And fire to their rescue as they find their bodies
      Growing more stiff, assuming even more
Unusual attitudes at every turn
   Of a second hand, at every sound
      Of a bell or an alarm, at every pounding
Of a door or a heart, so if you can't reach them
   Now and they can't reach you, remember, please
      Remember, whatever you say,

Whatever you hear or keep to yourself, whatever
You scream or whisper, will need to make
Some kind of sense, perhaps for days and days.

C. K. Williams

War
September–October 2001

1.

I keep rereading an article I found recently about how Mayan scribes,
who also were historians, polemicists, and probably poets as well,
when their side lost a war, not a rare occurrence apparently,

there having been a number of belligerent kingdoms
struggling for supremacy, would be disgraced and tortured,
their fingers broken and the nails torn out, and then be sacrificed.

Poor things — the reproduction from a mural shows three:
one sprawls in slack despair, gingerly cradling his left hand with his right,
another gazes at his injuries with furious incomprehension,

while the last lifts his mutilated fingers to the conquering warriors
as though to elicit compassion for what's been done to him: they,
elaborately armored, glowering at one another, don't bother to look.

2.

Like bomber pilots in our day, one might think, with their radar
and their infallible infrared, who soar, unheard, unseen, over generalized,
digital targets that mystically ignite, billowing out from vaporized cores.

Or like the Greek and Trojan gods, when they'd tire of their creatures,
"flesh ripped by the ruthless bronze," and wander off, or like the god
we think of as ours, who found mouths for him to speak, then left.

They fought until nothing remained but rock and dust and shattered bone,
Troy's walls a waste, the stupendous Mesoamerican cities abandoned
to devouring jungle, tumbling on themselves like children's blocks.

And we, alone again under an oblivious sky, were quick to learn
how our best construals of divinity, our *Do unto, Love, Don't kill,*
could easily be garbled to canticles of vengeance and battle-prayers.

3.

Fall's first freshness, strange: the season's ceaseless wheel,
starlings starting south, the annealed leaves ready to release,
yet still those columns of nothingness rise from their own ruins,

their twisted carcasses of steel and ash still fume, and still,
one by one, tacked up by hopeful lovers, husbands, wives,
the absent faces wait, already tattering, fading, going out.

These things that happen in the particle of time we have to be alive,
these violations which almost more than any ark or altar
embody sanctity by enacting so precisely sanctity's desecration.

These broken voices of bereavement asking of us what isn't to be given.
These suddenly smudged images of consonance and peace.
These fearful burdens to be borne, complicity, contrition, grief.

Fear
September 2001–August 2002

1.

At almost the very moment an exterminator's panel truck,
the blow-up of a cockroach air-brushed on its side,
pulls up at a house across the way from our neighborhood park,
a battalion of transient grackles invades the picnic ground,

and the odd thought comes to me how much in their rich sheen,
their sheer abundance, their hunger without end, if I let them
they can seem akin to roaches; even their curt, coarse cry:
mightn't those subversive voices beneath us sound like that?

Roaches, though…Last year, our apartment house was overrun,
insecticides didn't work, there'd be roaches on our toothbrushes and combs.
The widower downstairs — this is awful — who'd gone through deportation
and the camps and was close to dying now and would sometimes faint,

was found one morning lying wedged between his toilet and a wall,
naked, barely breathing, the entire surface of his skin alive
with the insolent, impervious brutes, who were no longer daunted
by the light, or us — the Samaritan neighbor had to scrape them off.

2.

Vermin, poison, atrocious death: what different resonance they have
in our age of suicide as armament, anthrax, resurrected pox.
Every other week brings new warnings, new false alarms;
it's hard to know how much to be afraid, or even how.

Once I knew, too well; I was of the generation of the bomb —
Hiroshima, the broiling bubble at Bikini, ICBMs.
The second world war was barely over, in annihilated cities
children just my age still foraged for scraps of bread,

and we were being taught our war would be nuclear,
that if we weren't incinerated, the flesh would rot from our bones.
By the time Kennedy and Khrushchev faced off over Cuba,
rockets primed and aimed, we were sick with it, insane.

And now these bewildering times, when those whose interest is
to consternate us hardly bother to conceal their purposes.
Yet, we have antagonists, some of their grievances are just,
but is no one blameless, are we all to be combatants, prey?

3.

We have offended very grievously, and been most tyrannous,
wrote Coleridge, invasion imminent from radical France;
*the wretched plead against us...*Then, *Father and God,*
spare us, he begged, as I suppose one day I will as well.

I still want to believe we'll cure the human heart, heal it
of its anxieties, and the mistrust and barbarousness they spawn,
but hasn't that metaphorical heart been slashed, dissected,
cauterized and slashed again, and has the carnage relented, ever?

Night nearly, the exterminator's gone, the park deserted,
the swings and slides my grandsons play on forsaken.
In the windows all around, the flicker of the television news:
more politics of terror; war, threats of war, war without end.

A half-chorus of grackles still ransacks the trash;
in their intricate iridescence they seem eerily otherworldly,
negative celestials, risen from some counter-realm to rescue us,
but now, scattering toward the deepening darkness, they go, too.

The Future

That was the future I came back from
vomiting the taste of the sulfur of my lowest
intestine on my tongue the taste of active
not theoretical not imagined despair.

It wasn't only the deserts impinging
encroaching devouring nor the fevers
charring the last damp from the rivers
the last lick of sap from the withering wheat.

Nor only the ruins of cities spilled out
on highways like coal like kindling the men
groin to groin bound in their rage and despair
like Siamese twins Siamese hordes.

It wasn't the women cowled like turbines
howling like turbines and the children
sentried on cliffs with nothing to nourish
their genius but shrapnels of scrub.

It was grasping rather that their desires
were like mine without limit like mine
checked only by vile chance not rational
supply and demand as I'd been taught.

That their fear was so fierce they wanted
to no longer be endowed with matter
so when houses were built they were razed
when food was grown it was despoiled.

We were locusts we were scorpions
husks hooked on thorns seeds without soil
wombs of a world without portal
flesh and dream we breathed and we slept.

Cassandra, Iraq

1

She's magnificent, as we imagine women must be
who foresee and foretell and are right and disdained.

This is the difference between we who are like her
in having been right and disdained, and us as we are.

Because we, in our foreseeings, our having been right,
are repulsive to ourselves, fat and immobile, like toads.

Not toads in the garden, who after all are what they are,
but toads in the tale of death in the desert of sludge.

2

In this tale of lies, of treachery, of superfluous dead,
were there ever so many who were right and disdained?

With no notion of what to do next? If we were true seers,
as prescient as she, as frenzied, we'd know what to do next.

We'd twitter, as she did, like birds; we'd warble, we'd trill.
But what would it be really, to *twitter*, to *warble*, to *trill*?

Is it *ee-ee-ee*, like having a child? Is it *uh-uh-uh*, like a wound?
Or is it inside, like a blow, silent to everyone but yourself?

3

Yes, inside, I remember, *oh-oh-oh*: it's where grief
is just about to be spoken, but all at once can't be: *oh*.

When you no longer can "think" of what things like lies,
like superfluous dead, so many, might mean: *oh*.

Cassandra will be abducted at the end of her tale, and die.
Even she can't predict how. Stabbed? Shot? Blown to bits?

Her abductor dies, too, though, in a gush of gore, in a net.
That we know; she foresaw that — in a gush of gore, in a net.

Lies

Surely because in childhood we're taught our inner lives,
what we feel and think, those matters most intimate to us,
are open to interpretation, and not rarely contradiction
("You *can't* be hungry now…" "You don't mean *that*…"),

by adults, even other kids, there's a stage of growing up
when children conclude that reality is a negotiable,
not absolute matter, that what is "true" is determined
not by the case, but by agreement between parties,

and therefore if one can state one's own version of events
with sufficient conviction (eyes sincerely widened,
mouth ajar with disbelief at someone else's disbelief),
it will overwhelm the other's less passionately desired

version of what's happened or hasn't, might or might not be,
and sure enough, often enough, the other, even older other,
bored, will let the whole thing drop, confirming our canny
supposition: victory to the liar, all power to the lie.

The politics of relation, call it, or, more depressingly,
just politics: a president with features like a child,
so blankly guileful in his lying that one might half-believe
he half-believes himself, though not, never not, for long.

Eleanor Wilner

Found in the Free Library

> Write as if you lived in an occupied country.
> — Edwin Rolfe

And we were made afraid, and being afraid
we made him bigger than he was, a little man
and ignorant, wrapped like a vase of glass
in bubble wrap all his life, who never felt
a single lurch or bump, carried over

the rough surface of other lives like
the spoiled children of the sultans of old
in sedan chairs, on the backs of slaves,
the gold curtains on the chair
pulled shut against the dust and shit
of the road on which the people walked,
over whose heads he rode, no more aware
than a wave that rattles pebbles on a beach.

And being afraid we forgot to see
who pulled his golden strings — how
their banks overflowed while
the public coffers emptied, how
they stole our pensions, poured their smoke
into our lungs, how they beat our ploughshares
into swords, sold power to the lords of oil,
closed their fists to crush the children
of Iraq, took the future from our failing grasp
into their hoards, ignored our votes,
broke our treaties with the world,
and when our hungry children cried, the doctors
drugged them so they wouldn't fuss,
and prisons swelled enormously to hold
the desperate sons and daughters of the poor.
To us, they just said war, and war, and war.

For when they saw we were afraid,
how knowingly they played on every fear —
so conned, we scarcely saw their scorn,
hardly noticed as they took our funds, our rights,
and tapped our phones, turned back our clocks,
and then, to quell dissent, they sent
(*but here the document is torn*)

In a Time of War

Flies, caught in the sap of the living
tree, someday will be
precious, dressed in amber — just so
the past appears to the present, gem-
like in its perfect preservation,

the hardened gold of yesterday, a relic
through which today's sun shines.

But those who are caught in the sticky
sap of actual time, insects in the odds
against them, who struggle in the ooze,
slowly sink into the mass,
the numberless anonymous dead...
till the atrocious becomes
the mundane, our senses numb
from the sheer litany of repetition.

Let us, then, just watch this one small
desperate fly, stuck first by the feet,
and then, in its struggles, entangled
entirely in the glob of sap, its wings
heavy as a brass angel's, until it is
all at once still, a dark speck
in a bubble of sap
oozing from the felled tree
in a forest marked for the mill.

How many millennia will pass
before a tear-drop lavaliere of amber
carrying its cargo of loss
will adorn the vanity of another
creature, the fly a fossil of a species
no longer present on the Earth,
the Earth itself a speck in a cosmos where
galaxies are carded like cotton on a comb
and pulled out into a distance
where some new fabric is being spun
and shimmers in the firelight
of countless burning suns.

Back Then, We Called It "The War"

And though, since that time, I have read many books,
have followed the smoke trail of countless thoughts
rising from the burning libraries;
though I have inquired in the ruins of many cities,

in the writing on the fallen walls,
in the blank stares of skulls in the killing fields,
in places hidden and open:
nevertheless, I do not understand.

For though, when as a child, I watched the news unreel
at the movies: the smoke and guns, the stirring symphonic music
rousing the blood, the black-and-white legions marching
on film, the flare of anti-aircraft guns, the little planes turning
in a slow spiral as they went down in flames, the heavy-bellied
bombers opening their doors, and the bombs falling,
and where each one fell, a rising pillar of fire; and though
the voice of the announcer was manly and confident, the news
always good, we were winning, we were certainly winning, and
everyone was so proud, and collected cans, and went without
nylons and chewing gum and butter, and clustered around radios
speaking in hushed tones as if in a holy place:
nevertheless I did not understand.

And though, since that time, I have followed Freud's trail, and Adler's,
tracked bad parents, bacteria, the rotting culture in the Petri dish,
followed Nietzsche to the knife in Raskolnikov's hand, with Pip
have seen God's foot on the treadle of the loom, watched goats lick
the pillar of salt that is the whole history of grief: though
I have followed Socrates into the bathhouses of Athens, observed
how he drank the poison that certainty decrees to doubt;
though I have watched 10,000 Iagos ply betrayal's artful
trade; though I have looked in my own heart,
and knowing myself no better than most, and worse than many,
nevertheless, I do not understand.

For, today, when I follow the signs of distress
back to their source, I find only mourners
weeping at the cemetery we have made
of what was once their home.
And playing in the rubble, a little girl
who will never understand, who
nevertheless
is picking up stone after stone,
trying to piece it together again.

The Show Must Go On

> I just want to remember
> the dead piled high behind the curtain.
> — Mahmoud Darwish

The play had been staged as long as we could remember,
a sordid drama in which truth kept changing sides,
the name of the enemy was never the same;

sometimes the players poured over the edge
of the proscenium, spilling into the audience,
who ran terrified from the house

that had become a scene of massacre; sometimes
the drama played at a distance relaxingly remote,
caught and burnished in the bright little

dollhouse screen, so far away it was no more
than fireflies in a bottle, mere hiccups of light —
the carpet bombing, the village, torched.

So that — unless the street were yours,
and the terrible crying of the wounded
your own — it was impossible

to tell what was real, so much was not
what it seemed, was simply *not*:
not at all, not anymore, not this, not that —

yet the music was upbeat, the messenger
smiling, the voiceover a reassuring pour
of syrup in the artificial light. Meanwhile,

though the labels changed, and the set
was rearranged for every act — the plot
remained unvarying, never veering off

from the foretold end. So, when the curtain falls,
we know for certain what is going to be
piled high behind it. Yet we wait, we go on

waiting, as if the bodies might still move,

the actors untwine themselves from the pile,
step through the opening in the folded-back curtain

into the brightly lit house, the resounding applause,
the audience pulling on coats to go home,
the silent streets filling again with laughter and talk;

while deep within the darkened hall, the actors
by their lit mirrors, lift from their sweat-soaked
faces, the eyeless masks.

Rendition, with Flag

The net was spread last night, catching beavers
who have been teething on the trees.

Around the bend, the verge is littered
with gnawed trees, some scraped raw
at the base, some fallen, some about to fall.
The lights of the hunters star the pond.

Thanksgiving? It is a time of anguish,
secrets bagged and hidden under silken flags,
stripes stretched to breaking at the threads,
stars darkening from an unseen source,
red seeping out of all the straining seams.
A US soldier smokes, while Fallujah burns.

The cold is growing now, ice waits in the wings.
The beavers all removed, or fugitive,
dead leaves begin to settle in the silt,
the work of winter will go on, dislodging
what the earnest animals had built.

Thanksgiving 2004

Colony Collapse Disorder (CCD)

...in the demise of honey bee health...the interaction between pesticides, diseases and varroa [mites] and the newly identified Israel acute paralysis virus (IAPV), are likely contributing factors.

Nothing more definite than that we awoke
the next morning (*were we dreaming?*) to
the same droning sound, as the bombers flew on,
named with an A, a B, or an F, plus a number —
                              as if the letters
of the sacred alphabet and the Arabic numerals
(so much more efficient for measuring the stars
and the playful motions of matter
than the clumsy Roman numerals, though those
were fine for incising on the foundations) —
                              as if these signs
were like locusts that, once released from their shells,
spelled only death, the devouring of the grain...

really, we can't say anything more definite
just now (*we must have been dreaming*) — for an hour
we were like children again, our hearts
were *that* high — how we cheered
                              as if to drown out
the keening, the raven caws, the orphaned
sound of the wind blowing over the ruined walls,
the F-16s going on making their runs,
and drones from the sickened hive...

when the beekeepers arrive to see to their bees
in the spring, the colonies have collapsed,
the dead bees tumble out like pieces from
an old game, the dried comb crumbles
at a touch, no milk and honey left to spill...
in the rutted rows of stumps, the olive grove
(*what were we thinking?*) cut down, the hum,
a wind in the ghostly trees,
grown louder now — dead bees
in the phosphorescent flowers
tossed in an open tomb.

C. D. Wright

From Rising, Falling, Hovering

He slept with the dead then   nothing roused him
Did she mention a missing spleen   had she warned him
she shaved down there   the night before

One glimpse of the paper was too much
the number of their dead to remain unknown

So the sleepless one hectored the sleeper:

About the other night   I know you are sorry   I am sorry too   We were
tired   Me and my open-shut-case mouth   You and your clockwork disci-
plines   And I know it is too far to go   But we can't leave it to the forces
to rub out the color of the world

What is said has been said before   This is no time for poetry

From Rising, Falling, Hovering

One bright night: we will see through the oaths of threat and protection

We will get out of our white cars in our white dresses

We will join the black dogs in a circle of the light

We will turn in the circle of the night

Memory murdered

Not so; instead:

They are spared the television except in passing through the lobby. She
struggles with the dailies in Spanish. BÁRBARO ATAQUE: MÁS DE MIL BOMBAS

CAYERON EN LA CAPITAL. The headlines transparent. Except on the eternal bottom of the pyramid, expressions of outrage are everywhere, except on the bottom where hunger numbs even anger.

In Mexico's capital, which is teeming, which is sinking by inches, which is ringed by cardboard colonias, which are teeming, the day after the bombs have begun to drop on Baghdad, the florists are bringing their blooms to the heart, de costumbre, on Fridays, to the hotels and restaurants, the markets and sidewalk vendors.

And this Friday, no different, except the bombs are blooming in Baghdad, and in the heart of the capital of Old Mexico, which is sinking, the florists deliver to the zocalo, forming a quiet convoy, which stops traffic for miles, and the florists unload in early quiet, first light.

They empty their pungent cargo and begin to make a mosaic which can be read by the guests in the Gran Hotel and the Majestic, which spells NO A LA GUERRA Y SI A LA PAZ. And the blooms left over which are given away to passersby.

And in Oaxaca City, on the roof of their hotel, looking over the zocalo: papier-mâché effigies, calla lilies, vigil by candle, graffiti on the walls of the gringo watering hole, and a wasted apparition circling the center, panhandling for smokes.

And in the following days the taxi drivers head for the Alameda, in Mexico City, flying pennants of peace from their aerials, and traffic, which is teeming, is stopped for miles. All quiet in the capital of the old Aztec Empire. Silence in the heart, habitat of 22,000,000 souls, which is sinking by centimeters. Which in inches equals eight a year.

From Rising, Falling, Hovering

I was just thinking

I hadn't worn a dress in so long	the current between my legs
witching as I head for the truck	library shutting ahead of time
clock set to remember something	cars abandoned on the off-ramp

plows forming a convoy on Wampanoag Trail   in advance of the whiteout
juncos blown through frantic branches   snow disappearing

                        the rhododendron

                     Allied military reports

Deadliest day for the forces   Super Stallion crash   not
counting the number of their dead   no such estimates exist
sandstorms on the AccuWeather map   near Ar Rutba
in the western region   town of 22,000   not counting their dead

In his suddenly-grown-small room   the boy freestyling to lifted beats
Telling him through the door   The dog has to go out now
turn down the freaking sound   and No Fumar in the house
The handle turning clockwise   the hood obscuring all
but the slow open mouth   These are not the limits of my world
but the limits of my words tonight   He is writing something down
he does not care to share   folding the paper over with cold hands

---

Robert Wrigley

Exxon

Behold the amazing artificial arm, a machine
eerily similar to the arm it replaced, machined
to exacting *tolerances*, as its engineers say,
to "the limits of allowable error."
Think of the hand in the glove, the piston
in the cylinder, the cartridge in the chamber
of an arm: a weapon, that is, a firearm,
to say it more primitively, more exactingly,

more ceremonially, and with more appropriate awe.
Behold then the arm from which fire comes, the hand
of a god hurling lightning. Behold the digital trigger, tick of
the finger on the hand separated from its body by the bomb

at the police station, the rifle smoking
just beyond it, as though it might yet shoot again,
the digital tick of the bomb's timer also disembodied now.

Study the artificial arm, its array of hex-
head setscrews, its titanium armatures and axes,
its silicone skins from light pink to dark brown.
Here is this, from the company's catalogue: "The upper
and lower forearm tubes are secured
to a four-position, manually locked elbow mechanism,"
and this, from God himself, having slain the man's family
and saying to Job, *Or hast thou an arm like God?*

And, *Wilt thou also disannul my judgment?*
Wilt thou condemn me, that thou mayest be righteous?
The nerve, and the lack. Beyond the limits of allowable error,
beyond the art of it, the story of Job, the trajectory
of narrative, the flight of the bearings and nails,
the improvised explosive device; beyond war itself, that honored
aesthetic ever-present evil alive and vile in the story
that is a lie about the truth and the truth, great engineer

help us, of the lie. Consider the ongoing
problem of tactile sensitivity, the elusiveness
of feeling, those of us otherwise untouched touched
for many dollars a gallon. And see the soldier in parade dress
easing with his other, non-silicone fingers a credit card into
and removing it rapidly from the slot
in the pump, and entering through its portal
the world of disembodied money

and the exacting tolerances of the world banking
system: behold this soldier, and know of his doubts
about the surrendering of arms, which is to say not only
the ambiguous tolerances of the Second Amendment
but the limb abandoned in Baghdad;
the soldier who has entered also into the system
of government surveillance — the porn sites,
the blogs, the maimed-in-the-line-of-duty

collectorates, the whiskeys and women, the rehabilitations.
See the soldier who nods and whose left
intact hand extended to your extended right one

confuses you an instant, but who nods again
to relieve you in your awkwardness. And behold them,
your untouched touched hands, as he nestles his man-made
right one over both of yours on his left, feeling,
between his old self and his new, a responsible citizen.

The Poets: Profiles
and Statements

Rae Armantrout (1947–)

A founding member of the West Coast group of language poets, Armantrout was born and raised in California. She studied at the University of California, Berkeley, and San Francisco State. She has published numerous collections of poems: *Money Shot* (2011), *Versed* (2009) — which won the Pulitzer Prize — *Next Life* (2007), *Up to Speed* (2004), *Veil: New and Selected Poems* (2001), *The Pretext* (2001), *Made to Seem* (1995), *Necromance* (1991), *Precedence* (1985), *The Invention of Hunger* (1979), and *Extremities* (1978). She has also authored a prose memoir, *True* (1998), and her *Collected Prose* was published in 2007. She is a professor of writing at University of California, San Diego, where she also directed the New Writing Series.

STATEMENT

The American public has been serially deceived. We all know that, however we may choose to frame it. Bush lured America and a few of its allies into war under false pretenses. People were lured into unaffordable mortgages by dishonest lenders eager for a quick buck. Those quick bucks were being generated by a stock market that had become indistinguishable from a Ponzi scheme, a market where value is almost entirely divorced from anything material and in which computers buy a share to sell it within seconds without, needless to say, any concept of the companies or products it supposedly represents. When looked at from a distance, this "war on terror" and these "credit default swaps" may sound absurd and even amusing, but, of course, real people are killed in the wars; real people lose their homes and their savings to financial manipulations.

In my poems, I am interested in the way these realities affect us psychologically and linguistically. How do we process this deception and how is it processed for us by our popular culture? In general, my poems often deal with ideology, of one sort or another, and with what Marxist theorists call "false consciousness." As it happens, two of the poems selected for this anthology respond to recent films. For instance, the second section of "Action Poem" replaces Leonardo DiCaprio with "America" as the star of the movie *Inception*. I want to take a little side trip here and mention how interesting it is that, in the last couple of years, DiCaprio has starred in two films (*Inception* and *Shutter Island*) in which the hero is trapped within a deliberately constructed illusion.

In *Shutter Island* the protagonist believes he is investigating a sinister mental hospital/prison for the criminally insane where brainwashing experiments are being conducted. These experiments are (deliberately?) reminiscent of those conducted by Ewan Cameron with CIA backing in the 1950s and recently described by Naomi Klein in her book *The Shock Doctrine.* In the film, however, it turns out that the protagonist, with whom we have identified, *is* a paranoid schizophrenic and that the elaborate deception has been set up by a benevolent doctor in order to help him realize that he is mad. *Really?* In *Inception* DiCaprio's character is in the business of invading other people's dreams in order to steal their secrets. It's sci-fi corporate spying played out in the individual psyche. Such dream espionage involves being able to create believable worlds in which the action can plausibly occur. As the plot unfolds, we realize there are dreams within dreams — and, of course, the film itself is *just* such a dream. The director must create a momentarily plausible world in which his script can unfold. At the end of the movie, we see that the protagonist, who has seemed so capable throughout the film, may himself be caught in one of the constructions.

It seems we can't get enough of such "paranoid" entertainments. Clearly they both mirror and deflect something about our cultural moment. I'm "just saying." But I want to do more than say. I hope that, in my poems, words, lines, stanzas, sentences can sometimes mean more (or perhaps less) or simply other than what they first appear to mean. I want to activate a state of heightened alertness in the reader. So are my poems similar to the films I've described? Yes and no. I think these films are simultaneously exciting and paralyzing A reader *should* ask what he/she is missing. But she/he should not be rendered powerless as the movies' protagonists so often seem to be.

Frank Bidart (1939–)

Frank Bidart was born in California and educated at the University of California, Riverside, and Harvard University, where he studied with Robert Lowell and later helped Lowell revise poems for publication. He has published eight collections of poetry: *Golden State* (1973), *The Book of the Body* (1977), *The Sacrifice* (1983), *In the Western Night: Collected Poems, 1965–90* (1990), *Desire* (1997), *Music Like Dirt* (2002) — the only chapbook to be nominated for a Pulitzer Prize — *Star Dust* (2005), and *Watching the Spring Festival* (2008). Bidart served as a chancellor of the Academy of American Poets from 2003–2009; his awards include the Shelley Memorial Award, the Wallace Stevens Award, and the Bollingen Prize. He teaches poetry at Wellesley College.

Of the poem "Curse," Frank Bidart writes, "The 'you' addressed here brought down the World Trade Center towers; when I wrote the poem I didn't imagine that it could be read in any other way, though it has been. The poem springs from the ancient moral idea (the idea of Dante's *Divine Comedy*) that what is suffered for an act should correspond to the nature of the act. Shelly in his "Defense of Poetry" says that 'the great secret of morals is love'—and by love he means not affection or erotic feelings, but sympathetic identification with others. The 'secret,' hidden ground of how to act morally is entering the skin of another, imagination of what is experienced as the result of your act. Identification is here called down as punishment, the great secret of morals reduced to a curse."

STATEMENT

When I first met Robert Lowell, in graduate school, I had already been taught Marvell's "An Horatian Ode Upon Cromwell's Return From Ireland." (Taught it by a great teacher, Thomas R. Edwards; there is a superb essay on it in Edwards' *Imagination and Power*.) Admiration for Marvell's poem — perhaps the greatest political poem in English — is one of the acts of shared judgment that bound me to Lowell. Marvell's poem so balances praise and blame and insight into the forces at work that people ever since have been arguing about whether the poem is an attack on or defense of Cromwell. (I think, on balance, it is an attack.)

A good political poem doesn't preach to the choir. It penetrates to the usually terrible process that is at the heart of whatever is being looked at, a process that may have heroes and villains but that also contains, at its moral center, a mystery. Yeats is the greatest twentieth-century political poet in English; "Easter 1916" exemplifies this. He could more incisively than anyone generalize about human action in the arena of social realities: "We had fed the heart on fantasies, / The heart's grown brutal from the fare" ("Meditations in Time of Civil War").

The air which my "political" poems breathe is one in which America, founded in ideals that I certainly share, has reached an impasse as it enacts them in the world. Coppola's *Apocalypse Now* exemplifies this impasse probably better than anything else. Soldiers who were once idealists and not evil, executing stupid policies, end up lost nihilists. The great enterprise that was America in the beginning leads us into bewilderment. A terrible story. My "political" poems (even "The Soldier Who Guards the Frontier," in impulse a love poem) are little shards of it.

Robert Bly (1926–)

A poet, editor, translator, storyteller, activist, and father of what he has called "the expressive men's movement," Bly remains one of the most debated American artists of the last fifty years. He was born in Minnesota and educated at St. Olaf College, Harvard University, and the University of Iowa. After traveling to Norway and translating poetry on a Fulbright grant, Bly returned to the United States where he founded a literary magazine (called successively *The Fifties, The Sixties,* and *The Seventies*) for poetry in translation. In 1966, Bly co-founded American Writers Against the Vietnam War. He has published numerous collections of poetry, nonfiction studies, and translations and edited a number of poetry anthologies. Among his most notable is his 1967 collection of poetry *The Light Around the Body*, which won the National Book Award. His 1990 analysis of the Grimms' "Iron John," *Iron John: A Book About Men*, was an international bestseller. His most recent collection of poems is *Talking into the Ear of a Donkey* (2011).

STATEMENT: INTUITIONS AND IDEAS

People are amazed now when they read about the Lincoln-Douglas debates. The two of them would debate for six hours in the afternoon to large crowds, then take a break and come back for two or three hours more at night. Watching these men speak for hours, the listeners could see if the speakers' words fit the speakers' bodies. Is the language coming out of the face we see in front of us? Is that a genuine Lincoln and a genuine Douglas? But in the many plays we see on television each day, the speakers are always pretending to be someone else. So our citizens at a debate watch to see if the politicians are performing well in pretending to be someone else. Most voters have lost the ability to decide if a speaker's words do fit his or her body. That's why Bush — with the help of the Supreme Court — won the election. No one knows what to do about it.

* * *

More and more I've learned to respect the power of the phrase "the greedy soul." We all understand what is hinted at with that phrase. It is the purpose of the United Nations to check the greedy soul in nations. It is the purpose of police to check the greedy soul in people. We know our soul has enormous abilities in worship and intuition coming to us from a very ancient past. But the greedy part of the soul — what the Muslims call "the nafs" — also receives its energy from a very ancient past. The nafs is the covetous, desirous, shameless energy that steals food from neighboring tribes, wants what it wants, and is willing to destroy anyone who receives more good things than itself. In a writer, it wants praise. I wrote three lines about it:

> I live very close to my greedy soul.
> When I see a book published two thousand years ago,
> I check to see if my name is mentioned.

If the covetous soul feels that its national "sphere of influence" is being threatened by another country, it will kill recklessly and brutally, impoverish millions, order thousands of young men in its own country to be killed, only to find out thirty years later that the whole thing was a mistake. In politics, The Fog of War could also be called The Fog of the Greedy Soul.

* * *

England had an educated civil service that administered its empire. But the United States is more and more out of step with other Western nations, both in the intelligence of its leaders and the ability of its civil servants. We are shamefully behind France, Germany, Norway and Sweden, and far behind ourselves at the time of the Second World War.

You'll notice that we don't count civilian Iraqi casualties in this war. We only count the American bodies. That's even more self-obsessed than the counting of bodies we did during the Vietnam War. We don't call up the hospitals; we don't call up the morgues. There's something shameful about that refusal and that silence.

* * *

The invasion of Iraq is the biggest mistake any American Administration has ever made. The most dangerous and greatest confrontation is between twentieth-century capitalist fundamentalism and eleventh-century Muslim fundamentalism. There is much to admire in Muslim culture — immense delicacy and passion — but we're also looking at a society without any division between church and state, made monolithic by the mullahs in the eleventh century.

To increase the antagonism between the two systems is the worst choice possible for a Western country, and that is exactly what George Bush did. Bush Sr. was intelligent enough to pull back and not go towards Baghdad. To tear apart the beehive without any bee hats is a crazy act.

* * *

Many observers have noticed that even though the United States and Canada have many resemblances, we have so many more murders per thousand people than Canada does. Why is that? Perhaps it's because we kept slaves and later fought a vicious civil war to free or keep them. We know from Vietnam that the violence men witness or perform remains trapped in their bodies. That suffering Martín Prechtel has called "unmetabolized grief." To metabolize such grief would mean bringing the body slowly and gradually to absorb the grief into its own system, as it might some sort of poison. But the veterans of the Civil War received no such help. Once the Civil War was over, soldiers on both sides simply took off their uniforms. Some went west and became the Indian fighters. We have the stupidity typical of a country that doesn't realize what the killing of war can do to a human being. When the violent grief is unmetabolized, it demands to be repeated. One could say that we now have a compulsion to repeat the killing. Our Westerns have made that clear for decades.

Bush and Wolfowitz and Cheney are merely the highest placed men involved in the repetition compulsion. The need goes on below the level of rational thought. But it's wrong to give in to such men. We have veered off our own path, which after the Vietnam War has been for a while the path of repentance. In our mad way, we are spending millions to bomb and rebuild Iraq at the expense of our own health system, of education on all levels, and of the support of culture and science. Only the greedy soul could set aside five hundred million for a useless war in the same year that Oregon takes nineteen days off their school calendar.

The careful long-range planning that Eisenhower and others performed during and after the Second World War now seems beyond our power. We are not capable of empire, and we should admit that. The war is a hundred thousand men wandering about in the fog of the greedy soul.

Bruce Bond (1954–)

A poet, professor, and classical and jazz guitarist, Bond has studied both English and music, earning degrees from the University of Denver, Claremont Graduate School, and Pomona College. His published books include *The Visible* (2012), *Peal* (2009), *Blind Rain* (2008), *The Anteroom of Paradise*, revised edition (2007), *Cinder* (2003), *The Throats of Narcissus* (2001), *Radiography* (1997), *National Blood* (1996), *The Possible* (1995), *The Broken Circle* (1995), *The Anteroom of Paradise* (1991), *Independence Days* (1990), and *The Ivory Hours* (1989). His volume *Choir of the Wells* is forthcoming. He teaches at the University of North Texas, where he is also the poetry editor of the *American Literary Review*.

STATEMENT: SUFFICIENCY AND THE ACT OF THE POEM

> The poem of the mind in the act of finding
> What will suffice. It has not always had
> To find: the scene was set; it repeated what
> Was in the script.
> > Then the theatre was changed
> To something else. Its past was a souvenir.
> — Wallace Stevens, "Of Modern Poetry"

Art, like us, is a problem. Or it loves one at least. And what could be better than a problem, the gap in the puzzle that eyes you, draws you, where looking back on a day, a year, a century, you would swear you were looking forward? And you are. We all are. If we read and write the poetry of our time, we give voice to it as a living creature, possessed of heart, mind, and body, all three seeking the community in the one, and the one in the community.

It is true that the period of the eighties, marked by relative peace, the rise of the personal computer, and the flourishing of French theory, had the luxury to indulge an increased sense of unreality, a sense that somehow all our experience was made up of language, by nature unstable, constructed, contextual and thus individualized, making problematic if not impossible the experience of communication. Of course the wonderful paradox of language and literature remains that it is both private and public at the same time, that it is our most illuminating realm where the public and private manifest their animating tension. Perhaps ironically, what Jacque Derrida had to teach us above all was that no system of totality can accommodate the otherness upon which it depends; thus there is always something it leaves out, that impinges on it nonetheless, the way, as Stevens argued during the war years, the sense of the real impinges on the imagination. The critical error of so many intellectuals has been to give voice to the notion that language is the totality of our experience. Nothing could be more dangerous, in both ethics and epistemology, and arrogant in terms of crediting human ingenuity with the construction of a universe. Where language is everything, the body disappears.

How odd, when one looks back, that Jean Baudrillard's popular critique of what was ridiculous about American culture in the eighties, that it was dominated by a worship of signs and imitations versus immediate presences, should morph into a kind of epistemology that would then undermine and hold in suspicion the very category of the authentic (see "Language Poetry and the Lyric Subject" by Marjorie Perloff). And poetry responded with a poetics of irony for its own sake, an effect that is a lot like television: here is one channel, one point of view, then boink, we flip the channel, never lingering, committing, following through. This, I would argue, is the poetry of an adolescent culture, where it is just too embarrassing to aspire to be sincere or wise, to be authentic, and yet still write a poem of great wonder, surprise, intellectual/emotional precision, and lovely difficulty, a poem that contains strong compelling elements of both structure and gesture. Ironic once again that so much of postmodern culture that prides itself on a both/and philosophy is awfully either/or when it comes to stability versus instability, truth versus unreality, control versus abandon, logos versus eros, authenticity versus inauthenticity, the poem as thing versus the poem as process. I understand that the poem of radical irony or opaque nonsense often identifies with being politically aware, invested, and liberal (see Charles Bernstein's *A Poetics*) insofar as it would undermine the sense of an author or more largely of our subjectivity, or that it returns us to some Marxist sense of priorities of the poem as material object. More precisely, subjectivity (which is not specific to the lyric) is less negated by a poem, *any* poem, than it is brought into relationship with otherness. The commerce between self and other, however embedded in a single instant, is what drives the imagination. And in truth Marx was interested in the investment of our consciousness in material process, as opposed to a feeling of being alienated from our work, our making, our world. I doubt he would think much of Bernstein's ideal poem as opaque. How instructively destabilizing to bring into dialogue a sense of the hegemony of logos with George Orwell's "Politics and the English Language," where we see that ambiguity's resistance to logos also suggests the language of the lazy *ad hominem* and of many a totalitarian agenda.

And yes, there has always been resistance to the adolescent poem of unreality with its affinities to an immature and uncommitted poetics of nostalgia. You see such resistance in the poem that, as Stevens would say, registers the "pressure of the real" without relaxing into mere reportage. It is the poetry of an imaginative transfiguration of immediate circumstance, where the events of our time, however large or small, occupy both a deeply inward and outward space, a place where facts struggle and engage an imaginative authentication of human values. It is the poetry of the mind, yes, but the mind as both a public and private space. "The poem of the mind in the act of finding what will suffice," says Stevens, who teaches as well, in the vision of heaven in "Sunday Morning," that sufficiency is death to the act. One might ask if "finding" can truly be an act? Isn't it the end of an act? Such questions lead to yet another paradox of literature, as sufficient with mystery as the ongoing provocation of understanding. As both an aesthetic object and a relational process, a poem is an answer in the shape of a question, a departing arrival, an eye that opens and closes at the same time.

Joel Brouwer (1968–)

A poet, professor, and critic, Brouwer was born in Michigan and educated at Sarah Lawrence College and Syracuse University. His book-length collections include *And So* (2009), *Centuries* (2003), and *Exactly What Happened* (1999). He teaches writing and literature at The University of Alabama.

STATEMENT: THE CLEANUP CREWS: LA VÉRITÉ, L'ÂPRE VÉRITÉ

After the event come two sets of cleanup crews. The first rearranges the event's physical traces, carting away the rubble left behind by earthquake or missile, soaping crude oil from the seabirds, chain-sawing the loblolly pines spun to earth by the tornado. The second crew undertakes the parallel but subtler task of arranging the event's history from a scattered set of facts and notions. What happened? When? To whom? By whose order? Following or breaking which rules? Who deserves praise? Who should be punished? This second crew is comprised of both professionals (journalists, historians, artists, scientists, politicians) and eager amateurs (the neighbor with the rumor of looting, the waitress with the tale of heroism). We grasp at all its diverse expertise as we struggle to condense a bewildering swarm of memories, experiences, hearsay, and reports into a coherent account, to clear the streets of uncertainty.

Both crews are essential, but also deceitful. The first doesn't *erase* the oil and bricks and branches; it just moves them out of our way, out of our sight. But of course everyone knows that's exactly this crew's task, and it doesn't try to hide it. The second crew's perfidy is more complex. Crew two asks you to discard your own experience of the event (which may be incoherent, but still: it's yours!) and accept in its place a representation: edited, crafted, rationalized, and oh so seductively lucid. Just a few days ago, tornadoes tore my town in two, and already I can't remember how I felt and what I thought in the first hours after the storm, as I rode my bicycle around downtown, trying to learn what had happened. That experience was almost immediately supplanted by the quick and efficient efforts of crew two. Thanks to meteorologists, I know why the storm formed; thanks to the Red Cross, I know how to help the victims; thanks to my Mayor, I know a task force will oversee redevelopment planning; thanks to my co-worker, I know an inspirational story about a family saved by a dog; thanks to the excellent work of local journalists, I know precisely where the tornadoes struck, what those places looked like before the storm, and what they look like today. My actual experience of that afternoon — an opaque stew of ignorance, fear, tension, and excitement — was the purchase price of all this understanding. Was that a raw deal? Of course not. Only a narcissist would claim to prefer the experience of his private sensorium to the representations provided by crew two. Joan Didion wrote, "We tell ourselves stories in order to live," and the reverse is also true: If we fail to tell ourselves stories, we are in some sense not alive. At the same time, we do suffer a loss when we accept the historiographical ministrations of crew two. We forfeit at least a portion of the confusion which is our natural state.

"Lines from the Reports of the Investigative Committees," like other "lines" poems I've been writing for the last few years, constitutes a well-intentioned but inevitably flawed attempt to participate in the crucial cleanup work of crew two in the aftermath of an event — in this case not a natural disaster, but a criminal one — while at the same time preserving some measure of the organic disorder and chaos which follows any such event. What did we know in the days after the Deepwater Horizon explosion on April 20, 2010? Almost nothing. The disaster had happened — was happening — 5000 feet below the surface of the sea. The rig was 41 miles off the coast. The workers who survived the disaster were sequestered and prevented from speaking to the media — and their own families — for days. There was virtually no knowledge, yet torrents of information came at us, relentlessly, as BP, Transocean, and government agencies deployed a mercenary crew two charged with the task of authoring a representation of the accident favorable to themselves.

My hope is that "Lines from the Reports" serves to critique self-serving and fraudulent histories of the Deepwater Horizon explosion, provide a disinterested though necessarily partial account of the incident, and, most importantly but probably least credibly, embody the difficulty of discerning reality from representation in the aftermath of any historic event. The poem is dedicated to the eleven men who died on the Deepwater Horizon:

Jason C. Anderson, 35, Midfield, TX.
Aaron Dale Burkeen, 37, Philadelphia, MS.
Donald Clark, 49, Newellton, LA.
Stephen Ray Curtis, 39, Georgetown, LA.
Roy Wyatt Kemp, 27, Jonesville, LA.
Karl D. Kleppinger Jr., 38, Natchez, MS.
Gordon L. Jones, 28, Baton Rouge, LA.
Keith Blair Manuel, 56, Gonzales, LA.
Dewey A. Revette, 48, State Line, MS.
Shane M. Roshto, 22, Liberty, MS.
Adam Weise, 24, Yorktown, TX.

Tuscaloosa, May 2–6, 2011

Timothy Donnelly (1969–)

Born in Rhode Island, Donnelly was educated at Johns Hopkins University, Columbia University, and Princeton University. He has published two collections of poems: *Twenty-Seven Props for a Production of Eine Lebenszeit* (2003) and *The Cloud Corporation* (2010), winner of the Kingsley Tufts Poetry Award. He has been poetry editor of *Boston Review* since 1995. He is an associate professor in the graduate writing program of Columbia University's School of the Arts.

STATEMENT

The first poem I ever wrote was workshopped the week after. So was the next one. And so were the next several dozen after that. I took poetry workshops throughout my undergraduate career and when that was done I enrolled in a poetry masters program. For years, pretty much everything I wrote was read and commented on by others before the ink was dry. And I wrote what I wrote knowing that this would be the case — knowing that my poems had a guaranteed social life. What I didn't know was what, if anything, drove me to write poems in the first place beyond the simple pleasure I took from putting words together in unexpected ways. These workshops were a way of organizing my writing habits, organizing that pleasure, stimulating it, and putting me in the position of answering a strange external demand for poems. But more importantly, workshops provided my poems with a chance to engage with the rest of the world by meeting regularly with a little segment of it — and for college credit, no less.

At the time I wouldn't have thought of writing as pertaining in any way to a psychic need to connect with the world and to come to terms with it, but I did feel that my writing needed the world, that it depended on it somehow, even if it — or I — would never admit it. My poems were formally complex, loud with music, full of pyrotechnics and wordplay and foreign words and phrases. Maybe they were hermetic. Quite possibly they were frivolous. They weren't at all "relatable." There was no mistaking them for recollections of personal experience or urgent *cris de coeur*. Nor were they prayers to an absent god, elegies for a dog, or lonely-hearted letters to the world. They didn't "reach out" in any clear way. And yet they never seemed finished to me — they never seemed *real*— until they met their audience.

That said, I didn't exactly write for applause. While my craftsmanship was often appreciated, for the most part my poems were criticized — often tenderly, sometimes scornfully — by my peers and teachers (with certain important exceptions) for being just as I describe them above. I was encouraged to write less self-consciously artificial poems, poems that reflected more directly or sincerely on what might be called "the real world." My occasional attempts to do so resulted in work that earned respect and even congratulations — but I still cringe thinking back to it. It felt more false to me than all my ostentatiously confected stuff. Because it's not that I was categorically averse to letting reality into my work. I just hadn't figured out how to do so to my satisfaction. It violated my sensibility to write about things that I was neither innately inclined to nor intellectually or technically equipped to handle with confidence and finesse. I was still playing with the medium, still figuring out what I could do with sentences, stanzas, lines, syntax — experimenting with form was more important to me at that stage in my development than subject matter was. Whenever I set out to write a poem about some weighty thought or event, I simply wasn't able to work it into shape. The music of it fell flat to my ears; the tone felt ponderous, simple, bathetic. Instead of giving me pleasure, these poems — forced into being to satisfy the room, or to fit my idea of what the room wanted from me, or what it was challenging me to attempt — left me feeling embarrassed and untrue to myself.

I internalized this sense of challenge and carried it with me to graduate school. Many of the poems in my first book, *Twenty-seven Props for a Production of Eine Lebenszeit*, were the products of this internalization. Increasingly I came to understand my poems' resistance to explicitly personal topics or subject matter of broader social relevance not as a failing of the past work but as a theme to be explored in future work. The tension between the forces of reality and those of the individual imagination and, more specifically, the mind's retreat from the brute mechanical world and into a space of imaginative speculation and liberty — by turns valiant, tragic, godlike, and pathological — became what I wrote about, or wanted to. I found that admitting reality into my work as a springboard or foil allowed for the kind of tonal complexity and amped-up artfulness I couldn't forsake. The poems in my second book, *The Cloud Corporation*, proceeded in the same direction, only much more doggedly, and with the benefit of a decade's worth of practice and maturity — and not merely maturity as a writer, but as a responsible citizen, spouse, and parent. These poems were all written in New York City after 9/11, while the country was (as it remains) at war, and while a growing awareness of the financial, environmental, and social disastrousness of our times changed who I knew myself to be. There was no retreating from the world that didn't seem to me irresponsible — and no response to it that didn't, when I voiced it all the way, verge on frenzy.

The poem "Partial Inventory of Airborne Debris," included here, moves from guilt, despair, and hysteria into the brownout of a nervous breakdown as it dramatizes an individual's sense of complicity in political atrocity. "Dream of Arabian Hillbillies," more impish in its modus operandi, is composed of words taken from successive pages of Osama bin Laden's 1996 "Declaration of War Against Americans Occupying the Land of the Two Holy Places" and the theme song to *The Beverly Hillbillies* — two texts about oil, economics, and destiny. This poem moves in a direction somewhat opposite to that of the other. While "Partial Inventory" begins with a self-possessed account of reality and ends in drugged stupefaction, "Dream" moves from drunken absurdity into an ironically clear-eyed rallying cry. Both poems were finished in 2009. Had I attempted to write either of them before I had the skills to do it right — or more importantly, before I felt an actual need to grapple with these materials as a way to gain a foothold in the world rather than just to satisfy some self-delighting wish to make a topical poem — they wouldn't deserve to take up space in an anthology. They probably wouldn't deserve to be remembered.

Carolyn Forché (1950–)

Born in Detroit, Forché was educated at Justin Morrill College, Michigan State University and Bowling Green State University. She has published four books of poetry including her most recent, *Blue Hour* (2004). Forché, who coined the phrase "poetry of witness" in the title of her anthology *Against Forgetting: Twentieth-Century Poetry of Witness* (1993), is often praised for her ability to negotiate the personal and the political in her poetry. She is also an editor and translator. Forché is the director of the Lannan Center for Poetics and Social Practice at Georgetown University and a professor at Georgetown.

Katie Ford (1975–)

A poet and professor, Ford has studied English, poetry, and theology at Whitman College, the University of Iowa, and Harvard University, respectively. She has authored the collections *Deposition* (2002) and *Colosseum* (2008), and the chapbook *Storm* (2007). Ford was a resident of New Orleans from 2003 to 2006. She now lives in Philadelphia with her husband, novelist Josh Emmons, and their daughter. She is working on a third collection of poetry and teaching at Franklin & Marshall College.

STATEMENT

I write from a country of natural beauty and human horrors, a country of canyons and electric cities, of floods and slums. My country exports medicine, computers, torture and corn. My country, more often than not, disturbs me, and insofar as I am an American poet who often writes from this particular source of disturbance, I am a political poet. Political poetry, despite its fraught and diminished reputation, is simply poetry concerned with citizens living under a government in a particular moment. When references to a government enter a poem, so do issues of power, power that is shaped, for better or worse, by human folly and human good. This power doesn't simply hover over citizens as an abstract, far-off notion. Such power decides — sometimes blatantly, sometimes quietly — if and how citizens survive. Political poetry, then, is nothing less than poetry about life and death.

Living in New Orleans before and just after Hurricane Katrina made the American government and its failure to protect and aid its citizens an overwhelming and inescapable fact pressing on my mind. To be a New Orleans citizen was to wake up eight months after Katrina to news of skeletons found beneath the ruins of wasted shacks in the Lower 9th Ward. It was to hear that suicide rates had quickly tripled and that depression was considered an epidemic in the city. Respiratory and digestive illnesses multiplied as mold grew like grass inside of abandoned houses. Later, snakes infested some neighborhoods. Three doors down, a neighbor walked onto her porch after she had slit her wrists. Writing about life in that city was inherently political, even if the poem was simply about water, wards, tainted fish, or walks through the streets. New Orleans was now joined to the names of other world cities that ring out immediately with political resonance — Sarajevo, Baghdad, Saigon, Waco.

Adonis writes, "Have you gone mad? Please, /Don't write about these things." And yet he then goes on to write about the dead and dying of Beirut in 1982, a city under siege. Had I gone mad to begin writing poems grounded in such dismal images? Certainly we were all a bit mad in those days down in New Orleans. When I was writing *Colosseum*, the book from which the poems in this anthology come, I admit that Robert Lowell's "Skunk Hour" line, "My mind's not right," went through my head many times. Yet the measuring, ordering impulse to write the poem remained, even if each poem broke open new confusions and forms of dismay at what had been withheld from the essentially abandoned, and largely African

American, New Orleans population. Often content such as this is so ungodly, is so harsh, that to think of it makes the mind feel severed or broken. Imagining what is occurring in the ghostly American programs of rendition and practices of torture do the same to me now.

And so there is a kind of double-madness that is felt as one composes these types of poems: first, the madness that comes at the thought of widespread, preventable death; second, the madness that comes when your poems, too, are full of these deaths, knowing such writing has been warned against as its own kind of madness. It is a deeply destabilizing position to be in poetically, which is just as it should be. I suspect that if a poet does not feel as if she runs a horrible risk — the risk of sensationalizing violence, the risk of sentimentalizing human loss — she is likely writing with too much comfort and too much ease. The poet should feel the same enormous pressure someone would feel writing a eulogy for a funeral attended by the beloved companions of the one who died. Then the poet, in her imagination, should add to that audience the rest of the world.

The admonishing of Adonis should press upon each word the poet writes; such admonishing can bring about the apt word, the hard-won song, the lament deserved by the dead. "In thy book record their groans," John Milton begs God in "On the Late Massacre in Piedmont." Far beyond being political, the poet, too, ought to take up this task: Preserve the groans of the dead, despite the warnings against it.

Forrest Gander (1956–)

Born in the Mojave Desert, Gander has lived in many regions of the United States and Mexico. He attended the College of William & Mary and studied geology, then went on to earn an MA in literature from San Francisco State University. His writing reflects his diverse background: though primarily a poet, he is also an essayist, novelist, translator, and editor. His writing is often attentive to ecological and geological concerns. Gander is the author of over a dozen books; his most recent collection of poetry, *Core Samples from the World*, was published in 2011. He is the Adele Kellenberg Seaver Professor of Literary Arts and Comparative Literature at Brown University.

STATEMENT

I have to admit that looking back on poetics statements I've made in the last twenty years, and reading those of others, I'm not much given to making a new one. Mine start to look like bad tattoos. The lines and colors fade, the context is lost. It seems to me now that definitional statements are better proposed by those with more vibrant egos and less sense of history.

I associate the poem "Background Check" with Mary Ruefle and Kent Johnson, whose respective works I was admiring at the time that I wrote it. When I first read the poem, at an AWP conference, there was no need to mention the context. Everyone had seen the recent newspaper photograph of the U.S. ambassador announcing plans for war, our first war against Iraq, to the United Nations' Security Council. The ambassador was standing in front of a curtain that had been pulled across the reproduction of Picasso's painting of Guernica, which normally hangs in the Security Council foyer. According to *New York Newsday*, "Diplomats at the United Nations, speaking on condition they not be named, have been quoted in recent days telling journalists that they believe the United States leaned on UN officials to cover the tapestry 'because the Bush administration did not consider it appropriate for the ambassador to speak of war with the image of women and children and animals suffering in the background, behind him.'"

Peter Gizzi (1959–)

After growing up in Massachusetts, Gizzi earned degrees at New York University, Brown University, and the State University of New York at Buffalo. The author of several collections of poetry — most recently *Threshold Songs (2011)* and *The Outernationale* (2007) — Gizzi cites Ezra Pound, the Beats, and John Ashbery as influences. Critics have noted that his poetry negotiates the boundary between narrative and lyrical poetry and places meaning just at the edge of understanding in subtle and astonishing ways. His honors include the Lavan Younger Poet Award from the Academy of American Poets, and fellowships in poetry from The Howard Foundation, The Foundation for Contemporary Arts, and the John Simon Guggenheim Memorial Foundation. In 2011 he was the Judith E. Wilson Visiting Fellow in Poetry at Cambridge University. He currently teaches at the University of Massachusetts, Amherst.

STATEMENT

"Protest Song" was the first and only poem I have written on spec. Sequitur, a musical ensemble collective in New York City, commissioned the composer Michael Fiday to write a song for their program on the theme of protest. He asked me to write the libretto, and we discussed various ways to approach it. I tried a few failed attempts and then the fall of 2001 came and went along with the willful hijacking of the situation by the Bush administration and the corrupt policies that emerged.

There were many "political" poems appearing in journals and flying about on line. I could understand the social aspect of poets banding together to show their numbers and be counted as dissenters from the Bush Doctrine. But I felt what I could add was a simple quiet reversal of many of the claims being made for poetry at that time. I was hoping to return the form and occasion of the poem to poetry itself, that is, the beauty of expression and form, plaintiveness, clarity, and song as its primary estate of resistance.

I have always been wary that "political" poetry could ever be meaningful in any way regarding the condition of the state. Though I have always been fascinated by the relationship between poetry and national ideology. The political is always implicit to real writing. It runs through the entire fabric of its meaning and sound. For instance, we know what it is to be a citizen in 1st-century Rome by reading Ovid. We understand Rome's social mores, its sense of power, and its call to duty even though we might be reading the story of a person becoming an animal or a lover disenchanting a suitor.

William Carlos Williams might have stated it best when he wrote in his introduction to *The Wedge* in 1944, "The war is the first and only thing in the world today. The arts generally are not, nor is this writing a diversion from that for relief, a turning away. It *is* the war or part of it, merely a different sector of the field." He reminds us that working in the American lang*wedge* (or any national language) is already working within a vast political architecture and ideology.

W.H. Auden's famous statement that "Poetry makes nothing happen," always seemed an apt perspective from which to consider poetry's inability to shape policy. But perhaps this is too narrow a reading of this famous line. Perhaps poetry is much more effective as it does in fact precisely make "nothing" happen. I find it productive to set his phrase in relation to Emily Dickinson's earlier and more haunted perspective in order to tease out the finer aspect of Auden's thinking. Here is Dickinson: "The human heart is told / Of nothing—/ 'Nothing' is the force / That renovates the World."

Louise Glück (1943–)

Louise Glück was born in New York City and educated at Sarah Lawrence College and Columbia University. She has authored twelve collections of poetry including *The Wild Iris* (1992), which won the Pulitzer Prize. Her most recent, *A Village Life*, was published in 2009. Her poetry is often noted for its use of the first-person personae and technical and linguistic precision. She served as a chancellor of the Academy of American Poets from 1999 to 2005. In 2003, Glück succeeded Billy Collins as the Library of Congress's Poet Laureate Consultant in Poetry. She is currently a Writer-in-Residence at Yale University.

Albert Goldbarth (1948–)

Albert Goldbarth, born in Chicago, was educated at the University of Illinois, Chicago Circle; the University of Iowa; and the University of Utah. He has published a novel, four essay collections, and more than 25 collections of poetry. His poetry is often known for its density, complexity, energy, and diverse subject matter. He resides in Kansas and teaches at Wichita State University.

Kenneth Goldsmith (1961–)

A poet, conceptual artist, radio host, editor, and professor, Goldsmith was born in New York and earned a BFA in sculpture from the Rhode Island School of Design. He has published ten books of poetry and is known for his innovative approach to collage. His newest book, *Uncreative Writing: Managing Language in the Digital Age*, is a collection of critical essays. Goldsmith is the founding editor of the online archive UbuWeb and a senior editor of the online poetry archive PennSound. He teaches writing at the University of Pennsylvania.

STATEMENT: POLITICS

I have written elsewhere that "in their self-reflexive use of appropriated language, conceptual writers embrace the inherent and inherited politics of the borrowed words: far be it from conceptual writers to morally or politically dictate words that aren't theirs. The choice or machine that makes the poem sets the political agenda in motion, which is often times morally or politically reprehensible to the author (in retyping every word of a day's copy of the *New York Times*, am I to exclude an unsavory editorial?). While John Cage claimed that any sound could be music, his moral filter was on too high to accept certain sounds of pop music, agitation, politics, or violence. To Cage, not all sounds were music. Andy Warhol, on the other hand, was a model of permeability, transparency, and silver reflectivity; everything was fodder for Warhol's art, regardless of its often unsavory content. Our world turned out to be Andy's world. Conceptual writing celebrates this circumstance.

I feel that language, by its nature, is political. Every letter is embedded with semantic, semiotic, historical, cultural, political and associative meanings. Think of the letter *a*, and it's anything but neutral. Associations for me include *The Scarlet Letter*, a top grade, the title of Louis Zukofsky's life poem, Andy Warhol's novel, and so forth. When non-objectivist painters tried to rid painting of illusion and metaphor, you can see why they chose geometric forms, not letters, to do so.

As writers, we bend over backwards to try to create meaning without realizing how meaningful and loaded the raw materials of our profession are. My two books, *Day* and *The Day* (excerpted here) set out to explore these implications. *Day* is a transcription of a day's newspaper. I purposely chose a slow news day to transcribe: Friday, September 1, 2000. It's a rather neutral book, filled with fascinating tales I didn't write. For *The Day*, I chose the most loaded-almost cliché-newspaper to transcribe: September 11, 2001. The newspaper was not September 12th — the day of the reportage of the planes going into the World Trade Center — but the day of the attacks, the newspaper people carried to work with them on the morning of the 11th. Far from neutral, it's an emotional and sometimes wrenching document. With these two books, I wanted to show how the identical technique of NOT writing, could produce two entirely different effects.

So, in conceptual writing, it's the choices we make beforehand — the machine we construct — which determines the outcome of the writing we produce.

Jorie Graham (1950–)

Born in New York City, Jorie Graham grew up in Italy. She studied philosophy at the Sorbonne in Paris, filmmaking at New York University, and poetry at the

University of Iowa. Her numerous books of poetry include *The Dream of the Unified Field: Selected Poems 1974–1994*, which won the 1996 Pulitzer Prize for Poetry; *Overlord* (2005); *Sea Change* (2008); and *Place* (2012). Her poetry is known for commenting on current philosophical and political concerns. Graham served as a chancellor of the Academy of American poets from 1997 to 2003. She teaches at Harvard University.

Linda Gregerson (1950–)

Raised in Illinois, Gregerson earned degrees from Oberlin College, Northwestern University, the University of Iowa, and Stanford University. She is the author of two books of literary criticism and four collections of poetry — most recently, *Magnetic North* (2007). She teaches Renaissance literature and creative writing at the University of Michigan.

STATEMENT

"Not Angles, angels," writes Muriel Rukeyser in the very first poem of her very first book: "Not Sappho, Sacco." And contained in these six words is one of the most powerful poetic manifestos I know. Rukeyser had no patience for the artificial sequestrations of poetry and politics, private imagination and collective history. "Prinzep's year bore us," she writes; "see us turning at breast / quietly while the air throbs over Sarajevo." We are creatures of history; we take it in as we take in air and milk; its tenors and textures make us what we are. And, although there is ignorance aplenty, some of it deadly, there is no such thing as perfect innocence, if to be innocent means to be untouched. And there is no such thing as a separate realm of the aesthetic.

"Not Angles, angels": a musical logic, and one that appears on the surface to be choosing the life of the spirit. But the phrase derives from a famous story told by the Venerable Bede. When Pope Gregory, writes Bede, observed a consignment of fair-skinned, fair-haired slaves in the market in Rome one day, he asked his companion who they were. "Angles," said his companion. "*Non Angli, sed angeli*," replied the Pope. Not Angles, angels. A story the English construed for centuries as a sign that they were a chosen people. The lovely, bell-like echoes of a pun are taken to reflect the stamp of heavenly favor, beneath which lies — just barely beneath — a double-sided story of enslavement and racial privilege.

"Not Sappho, Sacco." The notorious trials and execution of Sacco and Vanzetti played out for seven years of Rukeyser's early life, calling into question the very foundations of justice and political tolerance in America, throwing a harsh light on class and ethnic divisions. So when the poet, fresh out of her privileged education at Vassar, claims a muse, she refuses to stay within the proper, decorous boundaries.

The "not" in both of Rukeyser's alliterative formulations has to be taken with a grain of salt: the wit and the music rely upon the yoking of terms, after all, not upon the occlusion of one by the other. "Not only" is how I hear it. Not only, but also.

Which is always easier said than done. Writing a decent poem of any sort is hard. Writing a poem that wishes to make some of its own historical or political underpinnings explicit is harder yet, simply because there are so many ghastly ways of going wrong. I'm always worried — I think it's essential to be worried — about the possibilities of trespass. We've all seen work that hitches an easy ride on the sufferings of others, that borrows intensity from large-scale trauma only to reduce it to the scale of self, that sinks to didacticism. We're all — or those of us who try to make a place in our poems for the world of other people — we're all in constant danger of lapsing into such awfulness ourselves.

Eamon Grennan (1941–)

The Irish poet Eamon Grennan has lived in the United States for over thirty years. He studied at University College in Dublin and Harvard University. He has authored a collection of critical essays on Irish poetry, over ten collections of poetry — most recently, *Matter of Fact* (2008) and *Out of Sight: New & Selected Poems* (2010) — and two translations including *Leopardi: Selected Poems* (1997) which won the PEN award for poetry in translation. He taught at Vassar College until his 2004 retirement. Grennan still lives in Poughkeepsie, and when he can (every summer, for the most part) he migrates to the west of Ireland.

STATEMENT

The question asked, I guess, concerns poetry's relationship to the political. There are so many strands to this, and probably as many answers as there are poets. I remember two such answers in particular. One was that given by the South African oral poet David Manisi years ago in a talk he gave at Vassar College. He said, when asked about the poet's political responsibility, that the poem "should agitate." I like that, like the sense that a poem is not necessarily a comfort, but an agitation — of the nerves, of the intellect, of the feelings. That it should not leave us, as it were, unchanged. And there are so many ways this can be the case, short of express and direct "political action." Another answer I have never forgotten was given by Joseph Brodsky. After a reading he gave — again at Vassar College — I asked him in the Q&A period the same question: What is the poet's political responsibility? Without a second's hesitation, Brodsky shot back his simple three-word answer: "To the language." This seems entirely right. Making the language work so that it adjusts, deepens, maybe expands, our sense of the real — surely this act or at least this ambition has some political implication, whether the subject matter of the poem concerns "public events" or not. Michael Longley's poems about flowers or birds on the western seaboard of Ireland — poems written by a poet from Belfast — have their own political point and weight, no question.

In my own case, where actual "public events" — events that have their meaning in the realm of the political — figure as subject matter, I've found it necessary for the most part to "tell it slant." Hence in "Y2K" — the acronym that became a buzz phrase around the turn of the millennium, that imagination-scratching change —

I just wanted to run a quickened eye over some of the violent occasions that were willy-nilly marking that shift from one century to another — whether those occasions were the despoliation of the environment, or episodes in the war in the Balkans. My "point" was just to point, I guess (the "father carrying his daughter on one shoulder/ over rocky embankments" being something in a news photograph of that time). And to ask "what changes?"

Mostly I don't engage in any direct way with political events. But a poem called "Sea Dog" about a dead (and obviously deliberately killed) dog on the seashore was an oblique touching of the neighbor-killing-neighbor state of things that marked the Troubles in Northern Ireland. And when 9/11 happened, a prose poem I wrote then concerned a class I was teaching on Macbeth, on a particular scene in the play, and on the inability to find language to deal with horror. More recent poems have dwelt on Middle East violence through the prism of my own peaceful part of the west of Ireland. In the end, I guess, I shy away from — as I think many poets do — explicit and direct handlings of the political, of public events, probably wary of the kind of hollow rhetorical gestures that such direct confrontations can generate. Shying away, I suppose, from being too easily judgmental. And in the final analysis I suppose I want, in my own case, to counter the public with the private world, to insist on the value of the ordinary, the everyday, the domestic. As a recent statement of this position I can offer, for what it's worth, the following poem, which has as an epigraph a couple of lines from a poem by Wallace Stevens:

Prayer

Peace means these,
And all things, as before.
                    Wallace Stevens, "Phases"

Though I know the settled sound these cows are making
as they trawl among rushes, buttercups and sweet grass
cannot be heard under the rubble of cities, still I can hope
the voices out of my neighbour's radio as they vanish
among fuchsia flowers and the bees humming from
cup to honey-cup might find the hidden way to peace,
bring ceasefire and silence into the shaken world, let
the smoke settle and the people go indoors again, pick up
their dinner things, fill the glass jugs with water, the flowered
plates with food, taste the olives again, the oranges
and dates, the roast lamb on its bed of yellow rice,
and call down out of nowhere the usual blessings on the food
and the feasters — with no more than the racket of traffic
or the jubilant ramshackle neighbourhood chatter
or the rusty tinkle of goatbells out in the world to disturb them.

Marilyn Hacker (1942–)

Marilyn Hacker is the author of twelve books of poems, including *Names* (Norton, 2009), *Essays on Departure* (Carcanet Press, 2006) and *Desesperanto* (Norton, 2003), and an essay collection *Unauthorized Voices* (University of Michigan Press, 2010). Her eleven volumes of translations from the French include Marie Etienne's *King of a Hundred Horsemen* (Farrar, 2008), which received the 2009 American PEN Award for Poetry in Translation, Hédi Kaddour's *Treason* (Yale University Press, 2010), and Vénus Khoury-Ghata's *Nettles* (Graywolf, 2008). For her own work, she is a past recipient of the Lenore Marshall Award for *Winter Numbers*, the National Book Award for *Presentation Piece*, an Award in Literature from the American Academy of Arts and Letters in 2004, the American PEN Voelcker Award for Poetry in 2010, and the Argana Prize from Morocco's Bayt as-Sh'ir for 2011. She is a chancellor of the Academy of American Poets. She lives in Paris.

Forrest Hamer (1956–)

A poet, psychologist, and psychoanalyst, Hamer was born in North Carolina and educated at Yale University before receiving his master's and doctoral degrees in psychology from the University of California, Berkeley. He has published three volumes of poetry including his most recent, *Rift* (2007). He has a private practice and is part of the faculty of the San Francisco Center for Psychoanalysis.

STATEMENT

I began working on these and other poems some months after a difficult trip to South Africa in 2001. I'd attended the Non-Governmental Organizations' pre-conference of the UN World Conference Against Racism hoping to participate in a global discussion of racism, and related intolerance, from the particular perspective of psychoanalysis. I'd been impressed with the psychotic states of mind intolerance represents, and I hoped to help illuminate unconscious fantasies shaping such states, not only in people whose attitudes and behavior might be characterized as racially intolerant but potentially in everyone given certain circumstances. I'd also hoped to address a skepticism widely held about the value of psychoanalysis for such discussions. The year prior, I'd helped facilitate a discussion about prejudice at a United Nations conference on the millennium, and was shocked by the open hostility from some quarters at the idea that psychoanalysts believed they had anything to contribute to political, economic and social analyses of global concerns.

I attended the Durban conference with another, more private hope — that I would make appreciable progress on a series of poems which had as their theme fractures in connection between peoples and between parts of the self and nature. I set myself the nightly task of writing the first draft of a new poem stirred by the day's conference proceedings. It would be a personal log as well as another means of personal reflection.

The reader may remember some of what happened in Durban that summer — the remarkable contention between Israelis and Palestinians concerning an effort to include language in a final conference document equating Zionism with racism, heated arguments about the notion of political and economic reparations for the transatlantic slave trade, efforts by Dalits ("the untouchables") to draw attention to their domestic situation of discrimination in the face of governmental denial of such problems, and the lingering pall of ethnic conflict and massacre in Rwanda. There were many other issues brought to the forum, each one of them presented with an urgency that belied fantasies about what should happen at such a conference relative to the alleviation of suffering. I became impressed with how little people listened to each other, and how the forum became less a place for discussion and more one for confrontation and attack. Importantly, this NGO conference was (to my mind at least) not well organized — on any given day many workshops were simply not held, and workshops which did happen were not run in a manner which provided for the tolerant consideration of different and opposing viewpoints. It was extremely discouraging, particularly for those of us not representing an organization with certain interests to advocate in the preparation of a conference document to be presented to the governmental meetings occurring just after. The problematic organization of the conference seemed in retrospect to reflect a failure of containment (to use Wilfred Bion's notion of that intrapsychic-interpersonal function which allows us to bear otherwise intolerable anxiety and to effect meaningful thinking); I experienced the failure of containment as an unloosing of chaos.

After only two days, I stopped writing poems. And in reflecting on this, I would come to realize that the attacks I witnessed between groups of people had become attacks on my writing: I was reacting to the violence between people with a violence of my own. And the casualty of this was not only my ability to make creative meaning but my ability to feel hope. I knew somewhere in me that this was likely only a temporary state of affairs, and that all kinds of internal activity would probably occasion some sense of generativity and connection. I returned to the United States on September 10, and the events of the day following became incorporated into a frame of mind still reeling from the events in Durban.

It would be the re-creation of a containing function within me that would allow me to remember and reflect, the very function Donald Winnicott notes as developing initially because the caretaker serves as a container of the infant's aggressive projections. I sought to re-create my own by talking with intimates and colleagues, and I soon realized that psychoanalysis was one of those containing objects, if you will, that I used to help me gain new perspective on the troublesome hatred I had witnessed and introjected. Specifically, I relied on a sense that the situation could be understood, and that I had probably experienced some collapse with regard to feeling safe and generative that had both personal and situational components.

I tell this because it helps me frame much of my own thinking about psychoanalysis in contemporary life. I tell this also because it is another way of describing why I turn to poems — as a reader and, most fortunately, as a writer.

Robert Hass (1941–)

A San Francisco native, Robert Hass was educated at St. Mary's College of California and Stanford University. In addition to authoring seven collections of poetry, Hass is also widely known for his critical work and translations. He served as Poet Laureate Consultant in Poetry to the Library of Congress from 1995 to 1997. He was elected as a chancellor of the Academy of American Poets in 2001 and served until 2007. He lives in California with his wife, fellow poet Brenda Hillman, and teaches at the University of California, Berkeley.

Bob Hicok (1960–)

The author of five collections of poetry — most recently, *Words for Empty and Words for Full* (2010) — Bob Hicok previously worked in the automotive die industry and owned his own business, Progressive Technology. He's often praised for his ability to tell stories with his poetry. He teaches creative writing at Virginia Tech.

Brenda Hillman (1951–)

Born in Arizona, Brenda Hillman was educated at Pomona College and the University of Iowa. She has authored eight poetry collections including her most recent, *Practical Water* (2009). Critics often note the influence of Hillman's religious upbringing when discussing her poetry. She holds the Olivia C. Filippi Chair in Poetry at St. Mary's College of California and serves on the permanent faculty of the Napa Valley Writers' Conference and the Squaw Valley Community of Writers. She has been actively involved with CodePink and the Occupy Movement.

STATEMENT: SEED MATERIALS

(A) Materials for the poem come from the unconscious, a collective storage place, so by definition, they are unavailable to us except through mysterious glimmers of myth, metaphor and dream. This source is the inexhaustible potential and the residue of our experience, a generational wisdom. In this selection of my poetry, mysticism and practical knowledge are sisters. I have always admired occult forms of knowledge wherein the stuff of dream and reverie are tools that can be taken into the corridors of power.

My poetic practice includes spiritual contradiction & paradox in relation to the non-human world. I use trance techniques to visit the blue cave and the yellow tablets. The dream-source is in daily life, the bizarre quotidian where parking meters look like flamingoes. The imagination is where the outer and inner can meet.

(B) I took some young poets outdoors. We saw an endangered creature, a newt, *taricha tarosa*, sequestered under a piece of serpentine, a mineralized green rock that crumbles to produce a useless but pretty soil. Soil is the best library.

Nearby, the seeds of the most immense tree on earth hid under shy spikes: *Sequoia sempervirens* (after Sequoyah, a Cherokee chief who invented a writing system for his native language, plus *sempervirens*, eternally living) or the crisp Anglo-Saxon "redwood."

A syllable seed bank is practical. Denise Lawson and I found a wondrous wild lily in a thicket in West Marin; it was a soap plant — the *Chlorogalum pomeridianum:* part purple and white perkiness. It is described as *a native, perennial forb* with *a basal tuft of wavy, 1-inch wide, linear leaves.... The liliaceous, star-like flowers of soap plant have 3 sepals and 3 petals and are borne on a leafless, paniculate inflorescence composed of racemose axes.* We ordered some seeds from a seed bank in Santa Cruz to do a writing project with our soap plant.

My mother saved her mother's wedding bouquet from the early 20s. Six decades later, she sprouted some seeds from that bouquet in her own garden. Feminism and sources ... Rachel Blau du Plessis writes in *ecopoetics 6–7:* "Argue with Archives." Perhaps she means never let anything stay put; make a restless, process-inflected art. Water molecules and DNA. Strawberry Creek calls to the letters in Berkeley names as it flows under the corners of the buildings of the City Council, with the trace of non-human, gathering force through sense experience.

(C) I spent childhood afternoons looking at dust motes in the suburban library at the edge of a desert in Tucson, Arizona — a room of shallow glowing space close to the dry desert earth. Children sat with the tiny bent dust motes floating up into the stacks of books, dancing on the gray bound books of dead and living writers. For years, I cried in libraries, enchanted by the musty smell, by the words of someone I would never meet, the dancing motes animating all existence; I wrote a series of poems about this mystical dust in *Pieces of Air in the Epic.* Now, having taught Walter Benjamin's *Arcades Project* a number of times as a modernist poem, I think of the dust motes as tiny "flâneurs," ambling through the centuries.

The poet writes in relation to the roots of words, in relation to what has been written; that is her joy, to keep linguistic imagination alive in a society that is increasingly dead to language. The history of our language is not only found in libraries, but they are important, and we can never forget to consult the writings of predecessors from all poetic traditions — from Romantic to post-modernist. As American poetry veers into a minor art of the anti-heroic, other voices call us from the previous times: Blake and Yeats remind us of visionary journeys.

(D) I was recently asked in an interview "What is the role of the writer in the current culture?" To be a radical, to be at the roots of words — to point to what is wrong and to what is savagely beautiful. To be an engaged citizen, taking time to protest injustice, refusing to be complicit with the destruction of the planet and its creatures. To write well.

* * *

The source material for several of these poems is the public record. To expand that record, I fetched the words of the officials from the air, interviewed weapons and munitions sales personnel in hopes of transforming their language. My husband and I traveled to Nevada to protest the use of drones, and we will do this again. The poet can call attention to the misuse of language, such as the use of the word "drone" or the word "spill" about the BP Gulf oil disaster. The place where protest and poetry come together is not a place of results, it is the place where the dreamer meets official language with the force of matter meeting anti-matter. When the poet goes to official places of power it is often in a state of depression & loss of agency, feeling she is powerless. Yet, entering the public sphere she should bring notebooks and recording devices, for many officials and public servants care about how they are depicted; they are scared of poets, since poets are in contact with the eternal realm and they may look bad forever. However fragmented or modernist, your writings can engage with the private and public sphere, to embody spontaneity, subtlety, slantness and doubt. These values serve both activism and poetry.

I am finishing these notes right after Osama bin Laden was killed; I'm shaken by images of the horrific gloating response of people of this nation celebrating the violent lawless execution of a violent lawless man. In the wake of a tragic and absurd decade, in which endless wars are being fought as revenge, to support the greed of the munitions and petroleum industries and the nation's rampant imperialism, the appropriate response to the untold suffering — at the site of violence where poetry fails us — is mourning.

* * *

Yet deeply and boldly the beautiful world comes back, the non-human world of plants and animals and soil, a place of origins in the human heart, the material word, the joy of syllables and the wild lyric, the courage of human logic in the social-political realm. These are some of our sources and these things have a temporary meeting place in poetry.

Galway Kinnell (1927–)

Galway Kinnell earned degrees from Princeton University and the University of Rochester. He has authored ten collections of poetry, including *Selected Poems* (1982), which won the 1983 Pulitzer Prize for Poetry, and his most recent work, *Strong Is Your Hold* (2006). He has also published a novel, a selection of interviews, a children's book, and a number of translations. He has served as the State Poet of Vermont and as a chancellor of the Academy of American Poets. He has taught abroad and in the United States, including at New York University. He was also previously a journalist in Iran, a director of adult education at the University of Chicago's Downtown Center, and a field worker for the Congress of Racial Equality in Louisana. He divides his time between New York City and Vermont.

Yusef Komunyakaa (1947–)

Yusef Komunyakaa was born in Louisiana and served in the U.S. Army from 1969 to 1970 during the Vietnam War. He was a war correspondent and managing editor of the *Southern Cross*, for which service he earned a Bronze Star. After returning, he received degrees from the University of Colorado Springs, Colorado State University, and the University of California, Irvine. Komunyakaa has published prose and poetry, including *Neon Vernacular: New & Selected Poems* (1993), which won him the Pulitzer Prize, and his most recent collection, *The Chameleon Couch* (2011). He has also worked as an editor and translator. In 1999, he was elected a chancellor of the Academy of American Poets. He is currently on the faculty at New York University.

Maxine Kumin (1925–)

Born in Philadelphia, Kumin earned her BA and MA from Radcliffe College. Her seventeenth volume of poetry, *Where I Live: New & Selected Poems 1990–2010* (2011), won the Los Angeles Times Book Prize in 2011. Her 1972 collection, *Up Country: Poems of New England*, earned the Pulitzer Prize in Poetry. She has also published a memoir and four collections of essays. From 1981 to 1982, Kumin served as the Poet Laureate Consultant in Poetry to the Library of Congress and, from 1989 to 1994, as poet laureate of New Hampshire. She was elected as a chancellor of the Academy of American Poets, but, along with fellow chancellor Carolyn Kizer, resigned in 1998, an act that was instrumental in opening the Academy to more female and minority poets. Kumin was a professor for many years, teaching at institutions including Princeton, Columbia, and MIT. She lives on a farm in New Hampshire with her husband of 65 years.

STATEMENT

I never set out to write what are being called my "torture poems." They were wrung from me, arising out of my fury and sense of helplessness as the actual facts emerged (not that all of them have yet emerged, or indeed ever will). Most of the poems are in form: one is a villanelle, another a pantoum. The rigors of writing within a pattern somehow seem to free me to speak out. I'm sure there are other poets who feel the same.

Ann Lauterbach (1942–)

Raised in New York City, Ann Lauterbach graduated from the University of Wisconsin, Madison, and received a Woodrow Wilson Fellowship to Columbia University. She lived in London for seven years, working in publishing and in the visual arts. She has published eight books of poems and an essay collection, *The Night Sky: Writings on the Poetics of Experience* (2005), as well as a number of collaborations with visual artists. Her most recent chapbook is *The Given & The Chosen* (2011). She has been, since 1990, co-chair of writing in the Milton Avery Graduate School of the Arts at Bard College, where she is also Schwab Professor of Languages and Literature, and has been a visiting critic at the Yale School of Art. Her awards include fellowships from the Guggenheim and MacArthur foundations; her last poetry collection, *Or to Begin Again* (2009), was nominated for a National Book Award.

STATEMENT: WRITING IN THE NEAR/FAR

Most of my poems are not about a single event. I like to think of them as arising out of a constellation of materials including, obviously, language itself. For me, the poem's subject is myriad, not singular. Most, if not all, of the poems in my last two books, *Hum* (2005) and *Or To Begin Again* (2009) have the virtually continuous wars in Iraq and Afghanistan as what I might call their *conditions*. The poems arise in part from an awareness that, far from where I live and from the conditions of my life, persons are being trained to go to war, are going to war, and are killing and being killed in the name of certain beliefs about how humans should conduct their lives. Some of these beliefs I share, but not without question, not unconditionally.

To state the obvious: images and reports of events do not bring us closer to events; they serve only to make us conscious of them.

At some point I began to think about the fact that the Internet has further collapsed our sense of spatial relations, making the local, the near, almost indistinguishable from the far, the distant. It has also made us more acutely aware that the temporal present, the *now*, is multifarious and dimensional; there is simply no way to capture it, despite our addiction to the nominal and to the event. The present cannot be reduced to an *it*. These thoughts have led also to a sense that our affective registers, our abilities to respond with our full heartmind, are now so mediated that we are increasingly deprived of what we might call experience, if experience means undergoing something that leaves a trace, that alters our sense of ourselves in the consequential reality of our lives. The root of our faith in empiricism is a trust in our capacity to perceive, witness, observe, discern, and thus, to know; to be present to a present.

The poem "Hum" was, in fact, written as a response to the catastrophic events of September 11, 2001. In this case, I was in fact physically *near*, awakened by the huge roar of a low-flying jet that crashed into the World Trade Center a few blocks south of where I then lived. This singular experience left traces, I might even call them scars. The refrain "the days are beautiful" is both a fact, the weather *was* beautiful, and an assertion of bare life against the massive tragedy and sorrow and spectacle of the events, events which *changed* the local weather that morning: the air turned into raining ashes; tiny bodies fell from the burning towers. Here I was trying to find a way to think through multiple aspects of the transformative scale of near-far in relation to the inadequacy of any single witness and response. Grief, the most private emotion (similar and connected to love), blasted into the public arena as uncontained rage, and from there/then into repercussions without end. I wished for a refrain — "the days are beautiful" — that might push back against the discourse of vituperative violence, as well as the real violence, that was unleashed. I wanted to give solace amid chaos.

"Victory" is partly a meditation on the limits of empiricism set against the evisceration of material or physical presence. My near is not your near, and so you cannot know, for example, the noise of snowmobiles circuiting my house in upstate New York, nor that this sound brings me viscerally back to the 9/11 jet overhead, just as I cannot know the sights and sounds of a soldier in the field. You probably don't know that the "copulating/dolls hung from threads" refers to a Louise Bourgeois sculpture. This embedded or indirect citation leads in the poem to the notion of "solace," which the boys on their machines, or the soldiers in the field, will perhaps never know. Art can give solace. You can know, and the poem says so, that the great writer W.G. Sebald was killed in a car crash, and you may know to whom the philosopher with a poker refers (Wittgenstein), and that there may be a connection between Sebald and Wittgenstein. Knowing these references is not essential to an understanding of the poem, since the group, or constellation, is an example of the vibrating terrain between fact, experience, and knowledge. But the poem also stages an ongoing indictment of the primacy of vision: the eye's sight transcribed into descriptive imagery, linguistic or photographic is, for me, inadequate. *Why I am not a painter* (O'Hara).

"Echo Revision" was written partly in response to the capture, trial for war crimes (at the Hague) and death (in his cell in 2006) of the Serbian (previously Yugoslavian) President Slobodan Milosevic, and to the complex of inconsistent responses to his life and death in his homeland and in the West. These events are mingled with others, including the ongoing war in Iraq, a photograph taken at my nephew Richard's wedding, and another photograph of my uncle Bill, also recently dead, that I had taken. This poem again tries to negotiate the near-far field. It was made by enjambing early and late drafts of the same poem, placing single lines from each in couplets, so that the reader or listener might feel a rip or tear in the narrative continuum: "the war was a separate entity, with its own turning dates." The poem emphasizes the discontinuous. Here, again, I am interested in the impossibility of capturing any present "single" event, either in a poem or on a film or in a photograph, while at the same time conveying the overwhelming pressure of events (I call this "world") on our individual consciousness.

Time as layered space: cadence, sequel, and scale are relative, contingent. The arcs of cause and effect intersect, erupting in simultaneity. Narratives stutter. The etymologies of the words "event" and "happen" exfoliate from their origins in chance, fortune and fate. The complex negotiation between objective data *as information* and subjective interpretation or comprehension *as knowledge* continues to be the site of my poetic concerns. The challenge of an adequate response to the influx of information and the disembodied screen, what I perceive to be the collapse of the logic of single temporal-spatial perspective, is at the crux of my sense of contemporary form.

Ben Lerner (1979–)

Lerner was born in Topeka, Kansas. His books of poetry are *The Lichtenberg Figures* (2004), *Angle of Yaw* (2006), and *Mean Free Path* (2010), all published by Copper Canyon Press. His first novel, *Leaving the Atocha Station*, appeared from Coffee House Press in the fall of 2011. He has been a Fulbright Scholar in Spain, a

Howard Foundation Fellow, and a National Book Award Finalist. In 2011 he became the first American to win the Preis der Stadt Münster für internationale Poesie. He edits poetry for *Critical Quarterly* and teaches in the writing program at Brooklyn College.

STATEMENT

Because "Didactic Elegy" *is* didactic — because it's somewhere between a poem and an essay, and because it comments at length on its own investments and procedures, I'm reluctant to add much of a prose supplement. This poem could be considered, among other things, a kind of protest submission for the WTC memorial — an attempt to imagine a response to September 11th that doesn't utilize the tragedy for a project of violence, an attempt to imagine a negative response that resists spectacularization.

Timothy Liu (1965–)

Timothy Liu is the author of eight books of poems, including *Of Thee I Sing* (2004), a *Publishers Weekly* 2004 Book of the Year, and *Vox Angelica* (1992), awarded the Poetry Society of America's Norma Farber First Book Award. His poems have been translated into ten languages, and his journals and papers are archived in the Berg Collection at the New York Public Library. Liu is a professor of English at William Paterson University and a member of the core faculty at Bennington College's Writing Seminars; he lives in Manhattan.

STATEMENT

With the murder of Bin Laden by Navy Seals almost ten years after the Twin Towers fell, I am thoughtful about the impromptu tailgate parties that sprang up in televised cities right after Obama took full credit as Commander-in-Chief late the other night. As if the U.S. team had just won the World Cup. As if our national collective shame had been momentarily redeemed. No talk anywhere about the price tag on wars waged without end. Now Bin Laden's body is "buried at sea." Today we learn that photos of Bin Laden's bullet-fractured skull will not be released. Yesterday in a Creative Writing workshop, a student of mine turned in a poem that questioned how easy it is to project the shadow of evil onto a figure like Bin Laden and to forget the complicity of our own elected officials in sanctioning mayhem; he was worried that his poem would not be well received by his peers, that his writing would betray him as a traitor. No one in my class, as it turned out, seemed to care one way or another, only thought that the poem was "cool" and might've had something to do with the shooting of Bin Laden if indeed the poem had just been written the night before. What I am getting at here is that dizzying sense of things happening in time from moment to moment, commemorated and just as quickly forgotten via facebook and twitter, far from that Wordsworthian sublime of "emotion reflected in tranquility." Ten years ago, people thought the great poems about 9–11 would have to be written years (if not decades) after the fact, certainly not in the wake of trauma. I'd begged to differ. I thought of Wilfred Owen on the front lines. Of Whitman. And Robert Desnos. And Mandelstam on his death march. Of what they had seen. Twenty years ago, the academic halls I sauntered through were all abuzz with notions of "poetic witness," Milosz's *The Witness of Poetry* and Carolyn Forché's *Against Forgetting* anthology in the foreground, on the frontlines of our poetic imaginations. Where are we now, and by we, I mean both American poets and American citizens? What holds our attention? American Idol? Beheadings on YouTube? Gossip Girl? Torture manuals and bomb-making guides just a Google-search away? RuPaul's Drag Races? Where do we get the news? From poetry? From wiki leaks? I remember sitting at breakfast a few weeks back and not being able to simultaneously eat my instant oatmeal and devote my attention to the Afghanistan Kill-Team photo spread in Rolling Stone that my partner asked if I'd had the chance to see. The literal disgust I felt. All I know is this: I don't want to read or write "sanitized" poems. I don't want poems to participate in a kind of "mind-numbing" mystique. I don't mind if poems fail in their ambitions to enlarge the soul or to bear witness to tragedy however ancient or contemporaneous. I'm not prescribing or proscribing. What I'm looking for is work that snaps me out of my own moral stupors and torpors, art as a wake-up calling to live a more authentic life, whatever that may be, or as Rilke said, whomever we may finally be.

John Matthias (1941–)

Born in Ohio, John Matthias studied at Ohio State University and Stanford University. He has published fourteen volumes of poetry, including his most recent, *Trigons* (2009) and *Collected Shorter Poems* (2011). He is also an editor, a translator, and a literary scholar with a focus on British and American modernism. Though retired from teaching, he continues to serve as the poetry editor of *Notre Dame Review*. His current work includes a book of memoirs and essays, *Who Was Cousin Alice? and Other Questions* (2011). He has also recently begun to dramatize some of his longer poems.

STATEMENT: NOTES ON "COLUMN I, TABLET XIII"

I don't remember where I was when news began to come in about the bombing of the United Nations Baghdad office at the Kanal Hotel on August 19, 2003, but it was clear by the next day that Sergio Vieira de Mello, the top UN envoy in Iraq and perhaps heir apparent for the position of UN Secretary General, had died after spending three hours trying to direct rescue efforts from his cell phone. Eventually, reports began to arrive on the news media about "a man called Gil" who had evidently been the only person rescued from de Mello's part of the building, and who might just possibly survive. By the time my wife got home from work, she knew that "Gil" was Gilburt Loescher, our long-time University of Notre Dame colleague and next-door neighbor, who had recently taken early retirement to live in Oxford and work for the Institute for Strategic Studies. When my wife walked in the door, looking shattered, she said, "Gil Loescher was badly injured in Baghdad. Both of his legs had to be amputated in order to free him from the rubble."

If there was a trouble spot in the world, we were never surprised to hear that Gil had been there or was on his way. At Notre Dame he worked at the Kroc Institute for International Peace and was a fellow of the Kellogg Institute for International Studies. His academic interest and, more importantly, his human calling had to do with refugees. He had probably done humanitarian work in half the refugee camps in the world. When he was at his desk, he wrote books like his official history of the U.N. High Commission on Refugees, but he was more likely to be on a plane than at his desk. He had flown to Baghdad "to assess the human cost of the war and occupation," and he was planning to report his findings to the U.N. He himself became part of the human cost of the war and occupation within 24 hours of arriving.

One does not immediately sit down and write a poem on hearing that a friend has been blown up in a war and may not survive. All of Gil's friends — and they come from all over the world — did what friends try to do in situations like this: give whatever comfort they can from whatever distance by whatever means. Gil's wife and daughters were flown to Germany where Gil was taken for emergency surgery and a long period of recovery. When he was able to write about it himself, this is what he said.

> On our arrival, we went straightaway to the third floor office of Sergio Vieria de Mello, the U.N. envoy to Iraq. At exactly the same time, a cement truck driven by a suicide bomber and loaded with explosives was circling the compound, looking for a way in. As I exchanged greetings with Sergio and with several members of his staff, the suicide attacker was able to turn into the space directly under Sergio's office and detonate his bomb. The deafening explosion collapsed the ceiling of the third floor upon us and crushed to death several of the people in the room. Others were killed or severely injured when the bomb shattered the windows of the building, sending fragments flying everywhere. The bomb killed Arthur Helton and 21 others and left 150 people wounded. I lost both my legs above the knees, severely damaged my right hand and suffered numerous shrapnel wounds. I lay trapped, hanging by my ruined legs that were caught between the floor and the collapsed ceiling of Sergio's office. Later I was to learn that I didn't bleed to death because I was hanging upside down.

Eventually I felt compelled to write something. As part of a generation responsible for glib and self-important political poems during the period of the Viet Nam war, I hesitate to write any longer what is generally considered to be "political poetry." Nonetheless, I couldn't get two things out of my mind: That Gil somehow rhymed with Gilgamesh, hero of the great Mesopotamian epic, and that his life had been saved because he hung upside down in the air. When the Loeschers were still living next door, Gil's wife Ann and I had tried for some time to hang a bird feeder from a wire strung between our two houses. In the end, we found it worked better hanging upside down. Gil found this funny, laughing at us as he looked up from the book he was reading in his garden.

There are only XII tablets in *Gilgamesh*, most in fragments. My fragment is therefore from apocryphal tablet XIII. *Gilgamesh* is about a great friendship, about the search for immortality, about many other things. Enkidu is the friend. Humbaba is a monster. A late version of the poem was first written down by Sin-Lequi-Unninni. It is the one usually followed in translations. My poem is, of course, achingly inadequate. The important thing is that Gil survived and continues to do his work, both for the living and in memory of those who did not survive.

J. D. McClatchy (1945–)

An editor, critic, librettist, teacher, and poet, McClatchy was born in Pennsylvania. He was educated at Georgetown University and Yale University. He has published three books of prose, worked extensively as an editor, and written six books of poetry, including his most recent collection, *Mercury Dressing* (2009). He served as a chancellor of the Academy of American Poets from 1996 to 2003. He lectures at Yale University and edits *The Yale Review*.

STATEMENT

I can't now remember the exact sequence. Since it's impossible that I would simply have sent an unsolicited poem to *The New York Times*, it must be that they asked me — as they have done from time to time — to send them a poem for use on their Op-Ed page. (They usually ask for poems about a season or an election, never about an issue.) In any case, "Jihad" ended up on their desk ... they called excitedly to say they wanted to run it at once ... a proof was faxed to me ... it was set to appear the next day. Then, late that night, I received a call from the Op-Ed editor saying that the *Times'* editorial board had met and overruled him. The poem would not run. When I asked why, he said they thought it would ruffle too many Middle Eastern feathers.

Imagine anyone over there taking time off from the councils of war to read a poem! It says a good deal about the newspaper's bland timorousness. Yes, the poem's italicized sections closely paraphrase the Koran's injunctions, but whom would the Prophet's words offend? And though I try to provide the context for extremism, and a tiny dramatic portrait of a suicide bomber, I think of the poem as descriptive, not polemical. And its middle part explains that "jihad" is, above all, less a murderous theory than a rationale for the cleansing and control of the self. No matter. I knew what I was doing. I had wanted to use cool tongs to hold a hot topic. Maybe that's an impossible poetic task.

I have always thought poetry has two primary subjects, love and power. The poem's argument is to trace how each undermines or fulfills, colludes with or corrodes, the other. Politics can be a convenient arena in which to watch this struggle, though as a rule its *love* is conceited and its *power* is hollow. Still, I have returned to it again and again, mostly to areas of conflict (Palestine and Ireland in particular) where a history of brutality over borders has revealed the fatuity of high-minded purpose and the cost of God-driven conflict.

Bad poems take sides, and the rawest political poems deal with the trials of the heart, the first Eden, the first no-man's land. And that is where poetry's lyric impulses are best served. When the poet takes the world on its own terms, the results are likely to be flat or strident. Of course, there are magnificent exceptions. Yeats comes immediately to mind, then so do Homer and Virgil. But then look at the disaster that Ezra Pound was, and beware. Brecht is someone who topples on the edge, and keeps his balance. Best of all is the Chinese poet who sits on the river bank and watches the bodies of those killed by war in the north float by. His very description is both elegy and warning, but not cast in either mode. What the poet knows is sometimes best kept from his poem.

Raymond McDaniel (1969–)

Raymond McDaniel was born in Florida and educated at the University of Michigan. He has published two collections of poems: *Murder (a Violet)* (2004) — which won the National Poetry Series competition — and *Saltwater Empire* (2008). He is also known for his lively poetry reviews on *The Constant Critic* website. McDaniel teaches at the University of Michigan.

STATEMENT

Politics is a grotesque, ignoble enterprise. To identify something as *political*, then, is to taint it by association. Often, when we deploy the term, we would be better off using the word *civic*, in the sense that it is of citizens. The rhetorical armaments of politics refer to citizens, claim to speak for citizens, but they are not *of them* in any meaningful way.

I don't think of the poems included here as political, because they do not engage directly with the god-awful machinery of politics. But I do think of them as civic, because they concern not just the idea or the abstraction of citizenry, but actual citizens. Much of what happens to people depends on the operation of politics, of course, but because the political is increasingly divorced from the civic, to write "politically" is to place oneself on the wrong side of the fight.

When we focus on the political, the fact of the civic retreats. For me, that fact is that the citizenry includes *everyone*. Politics aggregates people on the basis of the utility of those groupings, but the citizenry itself is messy, contradictory, as various as its membership, as rich and brilliant and mysterious as an orchestra falling into and out of tune. No politics can have an ethics if it does not defer to this cacophony (this euphony), and political industry is at its most dangerous when it depends on the denial of the number and diversity of the people it allegedly serves.

E pluribus unum, the seal reads. This is a lie. *Per plurima, plura*: this is the truth. Tell me what it sounds like.

Sandra McPherson (1943–)

Raised in California, McPherson studied at San Jose State University and the University of Washington. She has published several poetry collections, including her most recent, *Expectation Days* (2007). Her honors and awards include three National Endowment for the Arts fellowships, a Guggenheim fellowship, two Ingram Merrill grants, an Award in Literature from the American Academy and Institute of Arts and Letters, and a nomination for the National Book Award. She taught English at the University of California, Davis from 1995 to 2008.

STATEMENT: WRITING SECURITY

"On Being Transparent: Cedar Rapids Airport" has a sky-level and a floor-level. Airports are among my least favorite places. In the early 1970s I wrote "Holding Pattern" about being stuck in the suspense of a sick airplane: "We have developed / A slight technical difficulty / and may not be able to land / Without a mechanic." Airport nightmares live like disaster film-makers in my unconscious.

And yet, also in the brain is a locus of something sublime, something that ascends. "On Being Transparent" consists of the words that catch between the hellish and the heavenly. Its date indicates its proximity to the 9/11 terror. Airports were secured by the military. Dread compounded dread.

I wrote another piece early on that addressed a skyjacker, Raffaele Minichiello: "they do not paint carbines / the color of fresh fruits or Italy. / I suppose it is practical, suppose / I need one too, have one." Minichiello, a decorated Vietnam veteran, did not want to stand trial in America for a small crime he considered justified, so he hijacked a plane from North America's West Coast and forced it to fly to Rome. The 6,900-mile, 14-hour flight was the longest in hijacking history.

Even earlier than that I needed security clearance to work on defense projects for Honeywell in Seattle. I wrote a couple of poems about that responsibility. How safe was I? And how safe were other people from me?

In my home I had a ceramic Day of the Dead airplane being pulled out of the sky by a skeleton. Over the years I wrote "Centerfold Reflected in a Jet Window," "How to Read an Aerial Map: War Department Field Manual, August 1944," and probably others I haven't found, out of the tension of air travel's environment.

Since in 2001 my husband and I were in the antiques business, I had a lot of unusual items in my suitcases: duck and fish decoys balanced with lead weights. I was suspect and nervous.

I would love to be hijacked by the Golden Mayfly again. It's nothing I can intentionally maneuver. It has occupied me twice in my life and been a great comfort.

W. S. Merwin (1927–)

Born in New York City, W. S. Merwin was raised in New Jersey and Pennsylvania and studied poetry and Romance languages at Princeton University. He has published more than twenty collections of poetry, including *The Carrier of Ladders* (1970) and *The Shadow of Sirius* (2008), both of which won Pulitzer Prizes. His poetry spans decades and many themes, often engaging with current social and political issues such as the Vietnam War and the environmental movement. He has also written prose memoirs, plays, and many volumes of translations. Merwin served as a chancellor of the Academy of the American Poets from 1988 to 2000. In 2010, he was elected as the seventeenth Poet Laureate Consultant in Poetry to the Library of Congress. His most recent volume is *The Shadow of Sirius* (2009). Merwin currently lives and works in Hawaii.

Philip Metres (1970–)

Philip Metres' most recent volumes are the chapbook *abu ghraib arias* (2011) and *To See the Earth* (2008). His edited books include *Come Together: Imagine Peace* (2008), *Catalogue of Comedic Novelties: Selected Poems of Lev Rubinstein* (translation, 2004), and *A Kindred Orphanhood: Selected Poems of Sergey Gandlevsky* (translation, 2003). He is also author of the critical book *Behind the Lines: War Resistance Poetry on the American Homefront since 1941* (2007). His work has appeared in *Best American Poetry* and *Inclined to Speak: Contemporary Arab American Poetry* and has garnered an NEA Fellowship, a Watson Fellowship, two Ohio Arts Council grants, and the Cleveland Arts Prize in 2010. He teaches literature and creative writing at John Carroll University in Cleveland, Ohio. Were it not for Ellis Island, he notes, his last name would be Abourjaili.

STATEMENT

When I was five, at the end of the Vietnam War, my parents decided to "sponsor" a refugee Vietnamese family, to help them into a new life in the United States. My father, who served in Vietnam as a U.S. naval advisor on a South Vietnamese patrol gunboat, and my mother, a lifelong pacifist, navigated the maze of tents stretching into the distance at Camp Pendleton. The fourteen members of the Nguyen family huddled in a dusty tent, among hundreds. We greeted each other without words. I would share my room with Lam and Dùng — boys a few years older than me — while my parents battled racist landlords reluctant to rent to foreigners. Thirty years later, when my wife and I visit the Nguyen's beautiful home, Ba, the patriarch, told the story of how we became one family, and did not hold back his tears — tears of gratitude, tears of sorrow — as memories of that war and its aftermath flooded back.

War always comes home. In Great-uncle Charlie, who spent his entire adult life in an asylum when he returned from the Great War. In the anger and grief of my veteran father. In the men who wept behind dark sunglasses as my father pinned medals onto their worn fatigues during the 1986 Vietnam Veteran parade in Chicago. In the scars in the skull of my Palestinian brother-in-law. In the paranoid gaze that a woman gave me, on an international flight after 9/11, as I, a somewhat swarthy Arab American, slowly removed my shoes.

Writing, for me, has been a practice pitched against the forces of war — the dislocation, trauma, and pain that trail in their wake. As Herodotus said in his History, I write to "prevent these deeds from drifting into oblivion," striving not only to chronicle what has happened, but also articulate the contours and fleeting images of a more just, peaceful, sustainable world. Naomi Shihab Nye articulates this vision of belatedness and hope well in her poem "Jerusalem": "it's late but everything comes next."

In the past ten years, in the post–9/11 world, I have been inexorably drawn into witnessing the depradations of wars in the Middle East. The poems included in this anthology are parts of *Sand Opera*, a book-length meditation on living in a time of war. The poem from the "Homefront/Removes" series particularly addresses the interstice, the hyphen, of Arab-American subjectivity, in which one feels both object and subject, and doubly complicit in the death-grip between the terrorists of 9/11 and the U.S. actions in the Middle East. The poem from "Hung Lyres" tracks the uncanny experience of nurturing a baby while wars bleed across the screen, that simultaneity of domestic joy and international madness. "Asymmetries" emerged from a series of poetic engagements with ekphrasis, juxtaposing the stunningly objectifying photographic nude-landscapes of Spencer Tunick with news of the war in Iraq. "Testimony" is part of a longer meditation on the torture scandal at Abu Ghraib, and relies upon the work of artist and witness Daniel Heyman. Finally, "Compline," named after the last of seven canonical hours of the divine office prayed at night, comprises the end of a sequence of prayer poems written in the Advent season. Witness without love is like death without life. The problem becomes: how to work our way back toward what the Sufi poet Rumi called "the field" — that place of the imagination beyond the realm of good and evil?

Naomi Shihab Nye (1952–)

Born in Missouri, Nye grew up mostly in the United States, with a year in Jerusalem as a teen. She studied English and World Religions at Trinity University in San Antonio, Texas, where she still lives. She has written or edited 32 books, in various genres, the most recent being *Transfer*, a collection of poems published in 2011, and *There Is No Long Distance Now: Very Short Stories*, also in 2011. She has worked as a visiting writer all over the world. In 2010, Nye was elected as a chancellor of the Academy of American Poets.

STATEMENT

Who could have imagined that the opening years of the 21st century would be fraught with so much conflict, turbulence, and war? The geographical map currently (2011) feels dotted with chaos in all directions. As if to keep up, natural disasters of various extravagant styles are occurring with speedy consistence. One catastrophe eclipses another in the news, and in our brains. It's a weird time to be a human. Do cats feel it? Turtles, birds? I think birds do.

As an Arab American child growing up in the United States, I would never have imagined conflicts between the two parts of the world connected to my parents — although Mom and Dad did argue quite a bit. I would also never have imagined so much writing — by myself, or anyone else — relating to ethnic background. But in times of ongoing loss, diaspora, despair, writing which affirms the integrity of memory and the preciousness of culture seems painfully necessary. War erases details — poetry nurtures and protects them. We are always trying to navigate among disparities.

I would much prefer to live in a world where one were not called upon to comment on these subjects but so far I have not found it. Everything is intrinsically woven together. Staring at the grasses by the roadside becomes a political act. Some have no more grasses. Or roads, either. Some would be afraid to go outside and stare at anything. Americans have that luxury, as a Palestinian university student reminded me years ago, and if we don't express and expand beyond our most comfortable perimeters, what are we doing? Of course, one also feels guilty — how dare we speak, when we are living with thermostats and street lamps and no one cuts down our trees unless we pay them to? How dare we?

I have not answered this sufficiently, even to myself. But it's the only thing I ever knew how to do — speak. There is always more sorrowing silence around the words than the words might suggest.

Geoffrey O'Brien (1948–)

Geoffrey O'Brien was born in New York City. His poetry volumes include *A Book of Maps* (2007), *The Hudson Mystery* (1994), *Floating City* (1996), *A View of Buildings and Water* (2002), and *Early Autumn* (2010). He is also the author of a number of prose works including *Dream Time: Chapters from the Sixties* (2002), *The Phantom Empire* (1995), *The Browser's Ecstasy* (2003), and *Sonata for Jukebox* (2005). His latest book, *The Fall of the House of Walworth*, appeared in 2010. O'Brien serves as editor-in-chief of The Library of America.

STATEMENT

In my experience a poem generates its own field of energy into which relevant particles are drawn. These can be of any nature and certainly may include surrounding events, social conditions, premonitions, irrational rages, and found objects bearing traces of the same. They find their way into poems just as they do into dreams or into the corner of the eye (if they do not hit you on the back of the head). The process is not always fully conscious. A poem based on a 1950s jungle movie might turn out to be an oblique response to yesterday's invasion. By the same token an ostensibly political poem might serve as a mask for a more private drama, or for an unconscious recapitulation of a 50s jungle movie. The precipitating event might of course be sufficiently overwhelming to force its way in without asking permission. In the case of "A History" my recollection is that I simply fitted together fragments I had written, with no particular argument or direction in mind, in the immediate aftermath of the September 11 attacks. They were written at a distance because although I lived at the time in the immediate vicinity of the World Trade Center, on the day before the attacks I had just arrived in Paris for a vacation; hence the line about one city resembling another. The tone is probably informed by the fact of looking at one set of surroundings while obsessing about another. It wasn't my intention to write anything further about 9/11, but I note that it did manage to inscribe itself in any number of subsequent poems, occasionally in half-successful disguise.

Sharon Olds (1942–)

Sharon Olds was born in San Francisco. She received a BA at Stanford University and a PhD at Columbia University. Her first collection of poems, *Satan Says* (1980), earned the inaugural San Francisco Poetry Center Award. Olds's follow-up collection, *The Dead & the Living* (1983), received the Lamont Poetry Selection in 1983 and the National Book Critics Circle Award. Olds was one of the founders of NYU's ongoing outreach workshop at Sigismund Goldwater Memorial Hospital 26 years ago, and, more recently, of the NYU writing workshop for veterans of Iraq and Afghanistan.

STATEMENT: SEPTEMBER, 2001

The number of first drafts I've written which have to do with immediate family has been roughly equal to those having to do with world family, with experience not my own. But relatively few of the world family poems have seemed to me worth typing up and working on. I didn't have the art for it, or maybe the soul for it, or enough of a sense of boundaries.

And in September 2001, in New York City — this was clearly a subject I was not up to. More than that — it went without saying, that first week or two, that I would not write poems any more. The possible usefulness of any poem of mine was so small. The families, and the city, and the country, and the wars ongoing and to come — all was so huge, all was in shock, it was all beyond me. And my poems had that particular danger — being personal when it was not appropriate (fools rush in).

But when I woke from the dream of the jack/plane in the air, it felt the way it had felt when a poem had "come to me." I put it off for days, but then, knowing no one else would see it, no one would be hurt by or insulted by it, or scorn it, I sat down to write it — having no idea where it would go.

Later, I found myself willing to read it to others, in among all the poems from all the countries we were all reading to each other in those days. I guess I was willing because it wasn't a brag, it had something to do with gratefulness to fate, and with a sense of others' sufferings being beyond my imagining.

Robert Pinsky (1940–)

Robert Pinsky's *Selected Poems* was published by Farrar, Straus & Giroux in April 2011. Of his numerous individual volumes of poetry, the most recent is *Gulf*

Music (2008). His translation of *The Inferno of Dante* (1994) received the Los Angeles Times Book Prize and the Harold Morton Landon Translation Award. As United States poet laureate from 1997 to 2000, Pinsky founded the historic Favorite Poem Project, including the video segments that can be seen at <www.favoritepoem.org> and an annual one-week institute for K–12 teachers. Among his other awards and honors are the William Carlos Williams Prize, the Harold Washington Award from the City of Chicago, the Italian *Premio Capri*, the PEN-Volcker Award and the Korean Manhae Prize.

STATEMENT: POLITICS / POETICS

For me, a true poem is both itself a reality and includes reality: a new planet made from the sounds of language, it is also based on observation of this planet where we live.

In both these aspects of the poem — not just the second one — political questions arise: to whom, implicitly, does this new thing belong? Whose property is poetry itself? Whose is the language? More explicitly, in the matter of observation, all the material of the editorial page is possible, and more: no subject is excluded or forbidden.

Poetry concerns reality, and politics is a major part of reality. But a poem is not a versified editorial. (Yiddish poetry, said the early 20th-century modernist Zishe Landau, must be more than the rhyme department of the Jewish Labor Movement.) Preaching, like everything else, is possible in art, but it's not for me — especially so, preaching to the choir.

"Poem of Disconnected Parts" was written during the George W. Bush administration. President Bush, his Secretary of Defense Donald Rumsfeld, his Secretary of State Colin Powell, his foreign policy adviser Condoleezza Rice and his powerful adviser Vice President Richard Cheney told the world in general, and us American citizens in particular, that the United States needed to invade Iraq, inflicting "shock and awe," notably in the form of bombing, on that country's population, because the dictator Saddam Hussein had weapons of mass destruction. This falsehood is now presented by the politicians who disseminated it as an honest mistake. To me, the evidence indicates it was an expedient lie. The lying, the bombardment of towns and cities, the torture of helpless captives: all were purposeful, part of a design.

In that same period, the Bush Attorney General, Alberto Gonzales, declared that the ancient, basic principle of *habeas corpus*— the right to liberty, to freedom from false imprisonment — would no longer apply for people whom the government decided, by its own administrative processes, not by any court of justice, to put in categories such as "enemy combatant."

As a citizen, I felt two incapacities: I could not ignore the violence, the falsehood and betrayal of principle by my country's government; and, I could not argue or preach in any deeply informed way about these disgraces — not even in prose, let alone in poetry. I felt outrage, but also confusion, and neither feeling diminished the other: a potential impasse or emotional withdrawal — a temptation to think about something else. It also felt imperative to resist that temptation, to school myself in the facts of those official betrayals.

But in poetry there is a different urgency, different from the civic urgency, propulsive in an almost opposite direction. I was attracted to the *poetic* challenge of making a poem that might include my own distraction and confusion and irritation at the daily news—along with the daily news. Poetically, I had no interest in naming the politicians I have listed here—names on which the pollen of forgetting has already begun to settle. But the drama of outrage and fatigue, looking and looking away, remembering and forgetting: to evoke all that in a poem was interesting.

The separate, mostly end-stopped couplets of "Poem of Disconnected Parts" try to express inward and outward conflict, to honor both realities, to express the actual emotions I felt about public events in 2003–4. The poem begins with Robben Island, where Nelson Mandela was imprisoned by the South African regime in the time of apartheid. I had visited South Africa recently: a country where patriotism, with Mandela alive, had a vivid, living, as well as historical, presence.

The Robben Island prisoners' slogan for making the penal island a scene for education—"each one teach one"—struck an eerie, peculiar chord with something I had read in Jacobo Timmerman's writing about his imprisonment in the days of the monstrous dictatorship in Argentina: that the torturers demanded to be addressed by their victims as "*Profesor.*" The power inhering not just in ideas but in *the idea of learning* seemed related to the struggle in my own mind, as I forced it to concentrate on political realities and their history: a struggle not to turn away. The poem, with its disconnected (but I hope not unconnected) parts is my pledge of allegiance to attention, you might say, or to memory: allegiance to the ancestors.

On my visit to South Africa, a Zulu man took me to see a traditional seer who in a trance communicates with ancestral spirits, a *sangomo*. He prepared me by explaining, in words I quote in the poem, "In our Zulu culture we do not worship our ancestors: we consult them." The *sangomo* I saw did make the statement that concludes the poem: "Only your own ancestors can help you."

That admonition presented me with a profound truth. It inspired me to acknowledge in poems like these the political and cultural reality that I am a particular person, with my own history and descent. My poem and I are in history, not above it or outside of it. So, including my mother Sylvia and her mother Becky, along with other various cultural references and progenitors, including the ancestors I have chosen as well as those I was given by birth, seemed imperative. The different kinds of memory, personal, cultural, historical, political, in some important way felt like one—maybe needed to be felt as one, to get beyond being an unaware preacher or part of an unwitting choir.

The other two poems selected by the editors, "Anniversary" and "The Forgetting," also concern the drama of memory and forgetting. Supporters of the atrocious Bush policies exploited memory of the September 11 terrorist attacks, as justification. "Anniversary" undertakes to recognize that manipulation of memory, while also honoring the legitimate, ineluctable need for communal—even ceremonial—memory. "The Forgetting," approaching similar material in a different way, includes at the end a particular moment when I found myself resisting a choir.

Kevin Prufer (1969–)

Kevin Prufer is the author of several volumes of poetry, the most recent of which is *In a Beautiful Country* (2011) and *National Anthem* (2008), named one of the five best poetry books of the year by *Publishers Weekly*. He is also editor of *New European Poets* (2008), *Dunstan Thompson: On the Life & Work of a Lost American Master* (2010), and *New Young American Poets* (2000), among other volumes. The recipient of three Pushcart prizes, grants from the Lannan Foundation and the NEA, and numerous awards from the Poetry Society of America, he is a professor in the creative writing program at the University of Houston.

STATEMENT

For fifteen years, I lived in Warrensburg, a small town in west-central Missouri. It was a fine, scraggly sort of place surrounded by miles of farms. It had a coffee shop, a college, a string of fast food restaurants along 13 Highway. Through the middle of town ran a train track; no matter where you were, you could hear the horns and the station bells. By the highway exit was a Walmart, where you were guaranteed to run into friends. Up that highway a piece, the B-2 bombers rose from Whiteman Air Force Base and flew low over my house on their way who-knows-where.

In Warrensburg, I felt a connection to the run-ups to our wars in Afghanistan and Iraq that my city friends avoided. The people I ran into in the hardware store or the Blockbuster were sometimes headed to the war, sometimes just back, often worried about being called up. My students balanced military service with studies. And how, listening to the bomber flying low over town, could I not imagine a long dotted line across the map, the plane rumbling along it, over the water and into the futility and horror of our actions abroad?

I thought about military actions that seemed simultaneously far away and all around me, what it meant to live in the rural middle of the country at a time when these things seemed so beyond our control. It felt important to write about this — to think of poetry as a public sort of speech, an act of communication about our responsibilities as citizens, our simultaneous culpability and helplessness.

The ancient Roman historians often composed accounts of the far-off past as veiled ways to criticize the behavior of possibly vengeful rulers of the present. For different reasons, this approach seemed good to me, as it allowed for a kind of distance that removed the terrors of war and the vagaries of citizenship from my own personality and concerns, allowing me to imagine them from other, far-away, broader perspectives. They subverted the pitfalls of didacticism to the complexity (and imagined disinterestedness) of sweeping historical narrative. My first political poems were, at least superficially, about the ancient Roman Empire. "Those Who Would Not Flee," for instance, imagines the revenge of Queen Boudicca on the Roman city of London, overlaying that narrative with an overheard, chauvinistic conversation about the virtues of adopting children from abroad. But it is really about our sense of ourselves, while people "other" than us threaten us from our borders.

Later, I developed different ways of forcing distance on my narratives, setting them in worlds that seemed science fictional, fantastic, futuristic, apocalyptic, or surreal. All of this I now understand to be a kind of swimming away from the immediacy of the events around me — the news reports, the students headed off to military service, the bomber, the idle talk of war in line at Wal-Mart — into more timeless, neutral, imagined territory. That freedom, I hope, allows for a more complex, less didactic, meditation on American might, on our sense of ourselves as citizens and the porosity of our cultural, virtual, and literal borders. That is, anyway, what I hope for my poems.

Claudia Rankine (1963–)

Claudia Rankine is the author of four collections of poetry, including *Don't Let Me Be Lonely* (2004), and the plays *Provenance of Beauty: A South Bronx Travelogue*, commissioned by the Foundry Theatre, and *Existing Conditions* (co-authored with Casey Llewellyn). Rankine is co-editor of the *American Women Poets in the Twenty-First Century* series with Wesleyan University Press. She has also produced the Situation videos in collaboration with John Lucas and organized the Open Letter Project. A recipient of fellowships from the Academy of American Poetry and the National Endowment for the Arts, she teaches at Pomona College.

STATEMENT

Mark Bradford, the Los Angeles artist, while discussing a video installation composed of two videos on opposing walls — a Martin Luther King Day parade in Los Angeles and a marketplace in Egypt — stated that "Black bodies in public space is political, always a political condition ... the Muslim body has become so politically charged so the space is charged." This is perhaps the short answer to why political and public issues have informed my poems. The long answer is always in the arrival at the moment of writing. When I first read the account of James Byrd, Jr.'s death in June of 1998 I was sickened. I am not being hyperbolic — whatever was in my stomach was regurgitated. It was as if my body could not accept his life as he was being dragged behind the pickup until his head and arms were severed. I didn't think to write about him at first because though the death was political the death mostly felt familial and personal to my race and that felt known. The sorrow was deep, it was recognized, and the arbitrariness of the murder made me fearful of the pervasiveness of racism, but that might be a definition of being black in America. It wasn't until October of 2000 when former President Bush misremembered the details around the defendant's punishments — two had the death sentence and one had life imprisonment (he thought all three had the death penalty) — that I began to think of the death as an American experience to enter and critique. Because Bush was the Governor of Texas when Byrd was killed and I had been waiting for him to address this moment nationally for a long time, I became incensed that the first discussion I heard about this heinous crime by him was littered with misinformation and rerouted into a discussion about the death penalty. The writing of the piece became for me a way to redirect the discussion back to Byrd's body, which as Mark Bradford reminds me, was always a political condition. Once I had written the piece, because the violence was tied to nothing more than the visual appearance of the black body, it became necessary to include a visual portrait of James Byrd, Jr., and the sites where his body parts were found. This June 2011 when a number of white male teenagers decided to "F with an N," James Craig Anderson, a 49-year-old auto plant worker in Mississippi, was beaten and run over with a pickup truck. (In the words of Deryl Dedmon, "I just ran that nigger over.") Reading the account of this event I was reminded of James Byrd, Jr., but when I sat down to try to write about James Craig Anderson I could only hear the wheels turning. This suggests to me it is not the body but the public discourse around the black body that starts me writing.

The Timothy McVeigh piece in an unconscious way was also about the inherent political condition of the black body. In April of 1995 when the Alfred P. Murrah Federal Building in downtown Oklahoma City was bombed and 168 people were killed it was immediately identified as a terrorist attack and the assailant was assumed to be Muslim. He was described as an animal and worse but when it became clear that the white American McVeigh was responsible the language in the media changed. Now he was a brother and a son gone wrong. Hence McVeigh's body, by virtue of its whiteness, was redeemable. I wondered if questions of forgiveness would have come up around a Muslim body. I thought this is what concerned me but when I finally sat down to write about McVeigh in June of 2001 I became fascinated with the discussion around forgiveness itself detached from the white body. McVeigh's victims were being asked to forgive him or if they forgave him, and I had been thinking about forgiveness as a national act since South Africa's Truth and Reconciliation Commission, and the genocide in Rwanda had been in the news not long before. I wanted to understand how forgiveness worked and wondered if I believed it was knowable or really possible.

Donald Revell (1954–)

Donald Revell is a graduate of SUNY–Binghamton and SUNY–Buffalo. His first collection of poems, *From the Abandoned Cities*, was published by Harper & Row in 1983. Since then, he has published several collections, including: *The Bitter Withy* (2009), *A Thief of Strings* (2007), *Pennyweight Windows: New And Selected Poems* (2005), *My Mojave* (2003), and *Beautiful Shirt* (1994). Revell's critical writings are *The Art of Attention: A Poet's Eye* (2007) and *Invisible Green: Selected Prose* (2005). His honors include two Pushcart prizes, two Shestack prizes, the Lenore Marshall Prize, the Gertrude Stein Award, two PEN Center USA awards for poetry and one for translation, as well as fellowships from the National Endowment for the Arts and from the Ingram Merrill and John Simon Guggenheim Memorial foundations. Revell has been a poetry editor of *Colorado Review* since 1996. He has taught at the Universities of Tennessee, Missouri, Iowa, Alabama, Utah and Denver. Since 2008, he has been a professor of English at the University of Nevada, Las Vegas. Revell lives in Nevada, with his wife, poet Claudia Keelan, and their children, Benjamin and Lucie.

STATEMENT

Each of the three poems [in this anthology] is, in its way, a minor version of Homer's great woodcutter scene in *The Iliad* ... i.e., each is a reference to how ordinary life goes on, in its essential, quiet, tragic ordinariness, in dogged, humane defiance of the infamies of warfare and of disgraceful strife. The truth plods on through the morass of infamy. Just as poetry does. My dog suffers and dies. Blind children go to the ballet. One goes to any movie that's playing. To notice and record such things is resistance.

Frederick Seidel (1936–)

Frederick Seidel was born in St. Louis, Missouri, and earned an undergraduate degree at Harvard University in 1957. He is the author of numerous collections of poetry, including *Poems: 1959–2009* (2010), *Evening Man* (2008), and *Ooga-Booga* (2007). His awards include a Lamont Poetry Prize and a PEN/Voelcker Award. In 2003, Seidel published *The Cosmos Trilogy*, consisting of three earlier volumes: *The Cosmos Poems, Life on Earth*, and *Area Code 212*. The trilogy of books is loosely modeled on Dante's *Divine Comedy*, though it moves in the opposite direction, beginning in the heavens and ending on the streets of Manhattan, in a post-9/11 landscape. The first section, *The Cosmos Poems*, took shape after the American Museum of Natural History commissioned Seidel to write poems to inaugurate the opening of the new Hayden Planetarium. Many poems from the concluding section, *Area Code 212*, first appeared in the *Wall Street Journal*, where they were serialized monthly for close to two years.

Hugh Seidman (1940–)

Hugh Seidman was born in Brooklyn, New York. His poetry has won several awards, including the 2004 Green Rose Prize from New Issues Press, two New York Foundation for the Arts grants in 1990 and 2003, a New York State Creative Artists Public Service grant in 1971, and three National Endowment for the Arts fellowships in 1970, 1972, and 1985. His first book, *Collecting Evidence*, won the Yale Series of Younger Poets Prize in 1970. Seidman has taught writing at the University of Wisconsin, Yale University, Columbia University, the College of William and Mary, the New School University, and several other institutions.

STATEMENT: CONTAGION

1. Alain Resnais

Somewhere between reportage and exploitation lies the path of art. Alain Resnais, who early on dealt monumentally with the grand themes of love and war, has always been a master in this regard.

A. *Particular → General*

Elle: Hi-ro-shi-ma.

Elle: Hi-ro-shi-ma. C'est ton nom.

Lui: C'est mon nom. Oui.

Lui: Ton nom à toi est Nevers. Ne-vers-en-Fran-ce.

    —*Hiroshima Mon Amour* (Marguerite Duras)

The chronic anxiety of impending atomic catastrophe brings a nameless French actress to Hiroshima to play a Red Cross nurse in a peace film (*eternal nurse of eternal war*). But on the last day before her return to France, she and the nameless Japanese architect consummate a brief and adulterous affair — her second great love — though as she says she is no stranger to adultery. And it is to this man, this stranger, that she tells her story — told until now to no one: head shaved; 20 years old; her shot German lover dead in her arms in Nevers (where she says she went mad with hate) one day before liberation. Thus, in the daylight, post-dawn, of her last morning, obliterated as persons, all of Hiroshima has fallen in love with all of Nevers and vice-versa, forever.

B. *Action → Quietude*

Sun up; work

sundown; to rest

dig well and drink of the water

dig field; eat of the grain

Imperial power is? and to us what is it?

The fourth; the dimension of stillness.

And the power over wild beasts.

    —"Canto 49" (Ezra Pound)

Alphonse in *Muriel* (full title: *Muriel ou le Temps d'un retour*), made after *Hiroshima*, speaks the impossibility of knowing another: "Every person is a private world." But in a different resonance of that remark, we might say that the eponymous, anonymous girl that Bernard and his friend Robert torture (to death) in Algeria has crossed the private/public barrier. Thus, Bernard kills Robert after the war, while the infection of World War II is seen to have distorted the collective memory and physical space (Boulogne) of the older characters like Alphonse and his former lover Hélène (Bernard's stepmother). Yet against this, in the last gesture of the film, the previously static camera at last unmoors to follow Simone, the wife Alphonse has abandoned, from empty room to empty room in Hélène's depopulated apartment — the entropic universe of its space now drained of disturbance.

2. "Thinking of Baghdad"

A. "*The projectiles*" / "*the uranium tanks*"
Background

Because of its high density (1.7 times that of lead), "depleted uranium" (DU) has been used for projectiles (e.g., ammunition and "kinetic energy penetrators") and for warheads (e.g., in so-called "bunker buster" bombs). Also, since 1987, versions of the M1 Abrams tank — deployed in the Gulf War, the Iraq War, and the War in Afghanistan — have incorporated DU in their armor.

DU is a by-product of the process by which uranium (a "heavy" metal) is enriched with U-235 — the fissle isotope of uranium that sustains the chain reaction necessary for the explosion of nuclear bombs and the operation of nuclear reactors.

For example, 141 pounds (64 kg) of naturally occurring uranium contains about 1 pound of U-235, whereas the 141 pounds of enriched uranium in the Hiroshima bomb ("Little Boy") contained about 113 pounds of U-235. By comparison, 141 pounds of DU typically contains somewhat more than a quarter of a pound of U-235.

The military has portrayed DU as an essentially benign substance, but its use remains controversial. Natural uranium is more radioactive, but DU is still radioactive and potentially highly toxic, since DU munitions tend to ignite on impact to form a dust of very small particles (various oxides, 0.2–15 microns in diameter) that can enter wounds, contaminate food and water, and/or be inhaled (probably the most significant type of exposure).[1] However, it has been hard to make definitive statements with regard to health and the environment, since actual DU data is often classified and/or not known.

Example: The Siege of Fallujah (Iraq)

A 2010 study[2] verified an abnormal spike in birth defects, infant deaths, and cancer after the second siege of Fallujah in the fall of 2004 — the first siege occurred in April 2004 — but identified no causal agent(s). The US Central Command (CENTCOM), however, has denied using DU munitions during the second siege but also claims that no records concerning DU use in Fallujah were kept prior to July 2004.[3]

A second Fallujah study,[4] conducted in 2011, did attempt to pinpoint causal agents. The results were unexpected: evidence of *enriched uranium* (my italics) contamination was found but no evidence of DU contamination was found. Was some unknown nuclear device therefore the cause of the spike in birth defects, infant deaths, and cancer observed in Fallujah after 2004? The authors of the 2011 study appear to think so and conclude: "The findings suggest [that] the enriched Uranium exposure is either a primary cause or related to the cause of the congenital anomaly and cancer increases. Questions are thus raised about the characteristics and composition of weapons now being deployed in modern battlefields." As of this writing (November 2011), however, the origin of any actual or hypothetical enriched uranium contamination at Fallujah remains a mystery.

B. "imperial power"

See excerpt from "Canto 49" (above).

C. "Dreams bloom"

i tylko sny nasze nie zostały upokorzone
      —"Raport z oblężonego miasta" (Zbigniew Herbert)

Notes

    1. Briner, Wayne. "The Toxicity of Depleted Uranium." *International Journal of Environmental Research and Public Health*, January (2010), 303–313.
    2. Busby, Chris; Hamdan, Malak; and Ariabi, Entesar. "Cancer, Infant Mortality and Birth Sex-Ratio in Fallujah, Iraq 2005–2009." *Int. J. Environ. Res. Public Health*, July (2010), 2828–2837.
    3. <http://www.bandepleteduranium.org/en/a/406.html> (Website of the International Coalition to Ban Uranium Weapons)
    4. Samira Alaani, Muhammed Tafash, Christopher Busby, Malak Hamdan, Eleonore Blaurock-Busch. "Uranium and other contaminants in hair from the parents of children with congenital anomalies in Fallujah, Iraq." *Conflict and Health,* 2 September (2011), 5:15.

Lisa Sewell (1960–)

    Lisa Sewell is the author of *The Way Out* (2002), *Name Withheld* (2006), and *Long Corridor* (2009), which won the 2008 Keystone Chapbook Award. She is also co-editor with Claudia Rankine, of *American Poets in the 21st Century: The New Poetics* (2007) and *Eleven More American Women Poets in the 21st Century: Poetics Across North America* (2012). Recent work has appeared in *Colorado Review, Tampa Review, American Letters and Commentary, Denver Quarterly, New Letters* and *The Journal*. She lives in Philadelphia and teaches at Villanova University.

Statement

    "In these explanations it is presumed that an experiencing subject is one occasion of a sensitive reaction to an actual world." Alfred North Whitehead

    Recently, in my work, I have begun to question the boundaries between the self and the world, trying to develop a more socially engaged poetics without resorting to polemic. By investigating and meditating on the act of reading, I gesture toward these boundaries: sitting quietly, engaged in a private act that nevertheless involves her in the worlds and words of others, the reader come into existence as she reads and is read. During the years of the Bush administration it became impossible for me to separate my private concerns from the events occurring around me — events I did not condone but could not help but feel implicated in, from the invasion and occupation of Iraq and the on-going degradation of civil rights through the Homeland Security act, to the growing evidence of global warming and environmental destruction. As the weeks and months passed, it became clear that my private feelings of shame, anxiety and depression were as connected to the state of the culture as they were to my personal problems and disappointments. I could no longer bear to listen to the news. Every new day brought new reasons to despair, as soldiers on both sides of the conflict died, as images of Abu Ghraib circulated on the Internet, as new names became familiar — Haditha, Ramidi — and new terms entered my vocabulary: IED, extraordinary rendition, enhanced interrogation. At the same time, I was re-reading Robert Burton's *The Anatomy of Melancholy* and marveling at how apt many of his descriptions were for the contemporary malaise my friends and I were experiencing. My poem of the same title is written at the intersection of ordinary private misery and public shared despair, drawing on Burton's language, my own experiences, newspaper reports about the war in Iraq, and contemporary assessments for determining depression.

Susan Stewart (1952–)

Susan Stewart's most recent books of poetry are *Red Rover* (2008), *Columbarium* (2003), which won the 2003 National Book Critics Circle Award, and *The Forest* (1995). Her translation, *Love Lessons: Selected Poems of Alda Merini*, appeared in 2009 and in 2012 she will publish two co-translations: with Sara Teardo, Laudomia Bonanni's novel *The Reprisal*; and, with Patrizio Ceccagnoli, the most recent two books of poetry by Milo De Angelis, *Theme of Farewell and After-Poems*. She also has translated Euripides' *Andromache* with Wesley Smith and the poetry and selected prose of the Scuola Romana painter Scipione with Brunella Antomarini. Her song cycle, "Songs for Adam," was commissioned by the Chicago Symphony and had its world premiere in October 2009. Her books of criticism include *The Poet's Freedom: A Notebook on Making* (2011); *Poetry and the Fate of the Senses* (2002), which won the Christian Gauss Award in 2003 and the Truman Capote Award in 2004; *The Open Studio: Essays on Art and Aesthetics* (2005); and *On Longing* (1993), *Crimes of Writing* (1994), and *Nonsense* (1989). A former MacArthur Fellow, Stewart recently served as a chancellor of the Academy of American Poets. She was elected to the American Academy of Arts and Sciences in 2005, and in the spring of 2009 she received an Academy Award in Literature from the American Academy of Arts and Letters.

David Wagoner (1926–)

David Wagoner has published 18 books of poems, most recently *A Map of the Night* (2008) and *After the Point of No Return* (2012). He has also published ten novels, one of which, *The Escape Artist* (1982), was made into a movie by Francis Ford Coppola. He won the Lilly Prize in 1991, six yearly prizes from *Poetry,* and the Arthur Rense Prize for Poetry from the American Academy of Arts and Letters in 2011. He was a chancellor of the Academy of American Poets for 23 years. Co-founder and editor of *Poetry Northwest* from 1966 to 2002, he is professor emeritus of English at the University of Washington. He teaches at the low-residency MFA program of the Whidbey Island Writers Workshop.

STATEMENT: MY PUBLIC POEMS

I grew up in a politically corrupt territory where the chief contenders for control were large corporations and the Mafia: Lake County, Indiana. I think I may be the only American poet ever to have had a city council resolution passed against him. While I was in my thirties, I published a poem in *The New Yorker* called "A Valedictory to Standard Oil of Indiana" which complained bitterly about their treatment of my high school classmates. The majority of them were the children of immigrants born in Poland, Hungary, Czechoslovakia, and Yugoslavia, and they felt less at home in the English language than I did. I assumed the role of their spokesperson, though I was teaching college in a Seattle by then. The poem was reprinted in the Chicago *Sun-Times* with photos of polluted air and shabby company houses under the title "A Valedictory to Whiting, Indiana." The city council didn't appreciate the publicity.

I had been a newspaper reporter on the very tame, polite Hammond (Indiana) *Times* briefly before going west to teach and had had a good look at the ways local politicians obeyed and prospered, but hadn't had the skill, the audacity, or the editor's permission to say or do much about it. Those feelings have continued to find their outlets in my fiction and poems, though most of the focus shifted to the lumber industry.

"In Rubble" is one of a large number of poems I've written about people in serious trouble through no fault of their own, suffering from the violence of war, the indifference of authority, official incompetence, and the general hazards involved in nearly all human activity. I'm not sure why I've felt the need to talk about it so often. Maybe I'm still trying to speak up for the ones who keep quiet out of shyness or embarrassment or because they don't have time to put their feelings into words.

C. K. Williams (1936–)

C. K. Williams was born in Newark, New Jersey. He is the author of numerous books of poetry, including *Wait: Poems* (2011), *The Singing* (2004), which won the National Book Award; *Repair* (2000), winner of the Pulitzer Prize; and others. Williams has also published five works of translation: *Selected Poems of Francis Ponge* (1994); *Canvas*, by Adam Zagajewski (with Renata Gorczynski and Benjamin Ivry, 1991); *The Bacchae of Euripides* (1990); *The Lark. The Thrush. The Starling: Poems from Issa* (1983); and *Women of Trachis*, by Sophocles (with Gregory Dickerson, 1978). His honors include an American Academy of Arts and Letters Award, a Guggenheim Fellowship, the Lila Wallace-Reader's Digest Award, the PEN/Voelcker Award for Poetry, and a Pushcart Prize. He has served as a chancellor of the Academy of American Poets. Williams teaches in the creative writing program at Princeton University.

STATEMENT

There are times I've asked myself in all seriousness how it came to be that a certain proportion of my poems were dealing with public matters, mostly dark matters: war, injustice, poverty, suffering and misery of all sorts, and, lately, most insistently, environmental immolation.

There's no question that on our splendidly multi-languaged planet there've been a greater number of poems written that have to do with more overtly personal events and emotions, light or dark, happy or sad, tragic or ecstatic, but private. The evocation and enactment of a "self" in the world, a particular self chanting or singing or whispering or crying aloud in measured language, is in truth the very ground of the poetic act.

So poetry doesn't have to concern itself with public sadnesses, and there are readers who would prefer poems that don't. And yet at some point early on I realized that there was a portion of myself, of my deepest self, that consisted of my responses to and my reflections on such larger matters, and it became essential to my belief in myself and my work that I take such moral struggles into account in what was clearly the most vital activity in which I was engaged, the writing of poems.

I've wondered if the real ground of my decision might actually have had its roots in the part of psyche which remains eternally a child's, and that perhaps what I really want is just to be "a good boy." But then maybe everyone does, maybe our most sophisticated concepts, our ten commandments, our "categorical imperatives," ultimately arise from that source. For myself, though, whatever the origin of this choice, once I made it, or perhaps even before that, perhaps once I even entertained its possibility, I found I was committed to it.

And certainly there's no question that many of the most powerful emotions I've felt and still feel have had to do with my despair or my rage at beholding and helplessly, haplessly participating in the stupidities, absurdities, and cruelties of our common life.

Injustice is the most common manifestation of our human limitations, and war their most dramatic enactment. I'm almost stunned to have to realize how many times in the relatively short segment of history I've lived through I've had to behold war presented as a solution to a problem, and how often actual wars, large and small — though is there ever a war which is "small" for those who are afflicted by? — have been committed.

Committed, most rendingly and enragingly, all too often by my own nation, a nation whose population I know consists of people who are for the most part "good," good boys, good girls, good men, good women; people who are not fools, although many are apparently ignorant of how their political system works and how they participate without realizing it in the evils their government perpetrates. The heart breaks to behold the whole of our sad human history: it's thrice torn by the portion that is one's own.

Sometimes lately I feel that there must be another element of my child's mind being resurrected in me, the part that wants just to hide its eyes when the bad thing, the monster, looms large, in a dream, or a movie, or, these days, the world. "Leave me alone, go away, don't *be* there" — how often does that reflexive whimper take me?

It might be that trying to live as consciously as one can entails a dialectical struggle between those two parts of the soul, the self as possible agent of change, and the self as the partial obliviousness one lives in every day. It is a conflict that may by definition be tragic, because neither impulse can ever entirely triumph: I suppose all we can do is hang on and try to convey the attempt.

Eleanor Wilner (1937–)

Eleanor Wilner has published seven collections of poetry, including: *Tourist in Hell* (2010), *The Girl with Bees in Her Hair* (2004), and *Reversing the Spell: New and Selected Poems* (1997). She has also written a verse translation of Euripides's *Medea* and a book on visionary imagination, *Gathering the Winds* (1975). Her work has appeared in more than forty anthologies, including *Best American Poetry 1990* and *The Norton Anthology of Poetry* (fourth edition). Wilner has received numerous awards, including fellowships from the MacArthur Foundation and the National Endowment for the Arts, the Juniper Prize, and three Pushcart Prizes. She holds an interdepartmental PhD from Johns Hopkins University; has taught, most recently, at the University of Chicago, Northwestern, and Smith College; and is currently on the faculty of the MFA Program for Writers at Warren Wilson College. She lives in Philadelphia.

STATEMENT

Susan Howe, in her *Europe of Trusts*, wrote: "For me there was no silence before armies." We were born in the same year: 1937. Fascism was rising in Europe: the Spanish Civil War was on; it was the year of Guernica, the first aerial bombing of a city and a civilian population, which was to become commonplace in the wars to follow. I was four years old when America entered World War II, and the War entered us; everyone had someone "over there," everything shaped itself around "the war effort," we had blackout curtains and air raid wardens, and people lived from one radio broadcast to the next. When I was eight, bombing missions (now called "air strikes" to make them sound less catastrophic to those on the ground) reached their crescendo in the atom bombs the U.S. dropped on Hiroshima and Nagasaki. And the Nazi concentration camps were opened. Of course, none of this was suffered directly, but I absorbed the brutal images, in *Life* magazine, in movie newsreels, on early television. Their effect — because it was a less cynical time, and because I was a child and not inured to such atrocities — was internal and indelible. We were the fortunate ones — we lived, our house still stood, but all that I had been taught to believe in was in ruins. No one had clean hands, and there was no sanctuary.

A new, truer set of meanings had to be constructed out of that history. We needed to see the slaughter of our own kind for what it was, in the blinding light of new technologies of mass death, stripped of the old justifications. And, as with the revisionist historians, the past in our poetry began to change when viewed, not through the winners who write the self-approving, sanctified versions we learn, but through those on whose bodies and lost chances history has always been made. And with this change, the violence of the present also appeared.

I speak of this public history in relation to my little life because it explains why one of these poems, "Back Then, We Called It 'The War,'" goes against my usual practice, and speaks in a first person voice that is autobiographical. And because it answers a question I've often been asked: why don't you write about the personal? That question shrinks the notion of what is personal. For me, partly out of these events that ended my childhood early, the savagery of history burned its brand in my brain; what happens out there has always since felt painfully personal.

It is hard to imagine many American children of today being similarly affected. Today's wars are distant, canned, unreal, virtual TV spectaculars, in which the distracted public, spoon-fed on media spin, soon lose interest. With the draft gone, too many of our citizens can easily choose not to be involved. Besides, aren't we given grand abstractions, like "freedom" and "democracy," to replace reality? The D.C. PR mill covers mortal wounds with the gauze of euphemism: "disinformation" for lying; "detainees" for prisoners without rights; "contractors" for mercenary soldiers answerable to no authority; nothing is called what it is. So poetry's concern with calling things by the right name becomes ever more urgent. Nor is it surprising that the larger world bleeds more and more into our poetry; it has always been so in the more afflicted and troubled regions of the world, and I believe that we, who have lived too well off their trouble, are in the midst of joining them.

It was always good to know that Plato wanted poets banned from his top-down Republic. It meant that the kind of knowing that poems provide — from what he called the "furor poeticus," as if we were all out of our minds — was somehow a threat to rulers. A comforting thought for those of us whose dreams are troubled by the actions of our rulers who, in the words of George W. Bush, "sleep well." I hear again Hamlet: "I could be bounded in a nutshell and be king of infinite space, were it not that I have bad dreams." So perhaps the bad dreams are instructive, as they reprove that vaunted ambition which madly links oneself, kingship and infinite space.

Since I have invoked our intellectual ancestors, I think of Plato's saner counterpart, Aristotle, who, in his often quoted definition of tragedy, said that tragedy is not simply about what happened, but about what happens. In their introduction, the editors of this anthology set Robert Lowell's imperative, "say what happened," as the necessarily problematic call to an engaged poetry. The tragic part of this — and what also makes "saying what happened" poetry and not just reportage — is that what actually happened, the events of today's history are, in some terrible way, also "what happens," what goes on happening, what repeats until it seems impossible to tell prophecy from memory — the local forms shift, but the pattern recurs. Since what was, in the 1940s called "the War," with that now ironic definite article, we have as a nation waged The Korean War, The Vietnam War, and now the wars in Afghanistan and Iraq. That deadly repetition is the burden of many of these poems, the context in which today's wars and atrocities are set, a pattern the poems record and whose blindness and waste they mourn. The imagination reminds us of the value of what is lost in the pursuit of a deadly and forever elusive "victory," and says, along with what happened, and what happens: enough.

C. D. Wright (1949–)

C. D. Wright was born in Mountain Home, Arkansas, and lives in Rhode Island. She has published numerous volumes of poetry, including *One with Others* (2011), a finalist for the National Book Award, winner of the National Book Critics

Circle Award and of the Lenore Marshall Prize; *Rising, Falling, Hovering* (2009), which won the Griffin Poetry Prize; and *Cooling Time: An American Poetry Vigil* (2005). Other books include *Just Whistle* (1993), *Deepstep Come Shining* (2000), *Tremble* (1997), and *String Light* (1991), which won the Poetry Center Book Award. Much of Wright's early work is narrative; her later poetry is characterized by formal experimentation while retaining a notably rooted sense of idiom and terrain. Among her numerous honors are fellowships from the National Endowment for the Arts, the Guggenheim Foundation, MacArthur Foundation, the Bunting Institute, as well as awards from the Lannan Foundation, a Whiting Award and the Robert Creeley Prize. Wright is on the faculty of Brown University in Providence. She is married to the poet and translator Forrest Gander. They have a son, Brecht.

Robert Wrigley (1951–)

Robert Wrigley received his BA with honors in English Language and Literature at Southern Illinois University in 1974, and his MFA in Poetry from the University of Montana in 1976. His collections of poetry include *Beautiful Country* (2010), *Lives of the Animals* (2003), *Reign of Snakes* (1999), winner of the Kingsley Tufts Award, *In the Bank of Beautiful Sins* (1995), winner of the San Francisco Poetry Center Book Award and Lenore Marshall Award finalist, and others. His work has also been published in various anthologies and literary journals. Wrigley's awards and honors include fellowships from the National Endowment for the Arts, the Idaho State Commission on the Arts, and the Guggenheim Foundation, as well as the J. Howard and Barbara M.J. Wood Prize, the Frederick Bock Prize from *Poetry* magazine, the Wagner Award from the Poetry Society of America, the Theodore Roethke Award from *Poetry Northwest,* and two Pushcart prizes. From 1987 until 1988 he served as the state of Idaho's writer-in-residence. Wrigley lives with his wife, the writer Kim Barnes, and their children, in Moscow Mountain, North Idaho. He has taught at Lewis and Clark College, at the University of Oregon, and at the University of Montana. He now teaches at the University of Idaho.

STATEMENT: THE POEM AS A DIFFICULT MACHINE

Having something to say is not the optimal situation for a poet sitting down to write. Having a point to make can be a recipe for disaster; worse still, having an ax to grind. I'm interested in how I've already resorted to two ready-made phrases — clichés, really — simply trying to talk about a poetics that can accommodate "public or political issues." Frankly, I'm never especially happy trying to articulate how it is I work. I began "Exxon" as a kind of meditation on the word "tolerance," in its context as a term in mechanical engineering. That sort of tolerance is a measurable distance or space between parts of a system, or as one definition I found described it, "the limits of allowable error." Complicated machinery, from an automobile engine to a Cruise missile or, as it turned out as I discovered in my research, an artificial arm, must all be designed and manufactured according to tight or restrictive tolerances. Any machine not so made will likely fail. It might be said that the Constitution of the United States, and the nation it governs as well, is just such a machine. So, of course, is a poem.

Therefore I have to say that, in following my usual strategy in composing a poem, I was simply finding my way through what had been, in Richard Hugo's term, the poem's "triggering subject," in order to arrive at what it might actually be about. Or come to be about. In Hugo's terms, that's its "true subject." I did not set out to write a poem about the responsibility of all citizens for their nation's behavior, but that's part of what the poem became. That sort of exploratory, even accidental, voyaging toward the possibilities of meaning is why the poem succeeds, assuming that it does. I like to think it does, but time alone will tell.

In all honesty, I've never shied away from poems that engage public or political issues, though I like to think I've gone to great lengths to avoid turning a poem into a mechanism that merely propagandizes. And as far as I can tell, the only way to avoid mere propaganda — no matter how righteous and well-intentioned — is to craft the poem according to the most demanding tolerances one can ask of oneself. But what, exactly, does that mean? I'm not sure I know. I'm not sure anyone knows, really. Auden claimed to despise his "September 1, 1939." When the poem was reprinted with four others in an anthology called *Poetry of the Thirties* (Penguin, 1964), he said in a note to accompany the poems, "Mr. W.H. Auden considers these five poems to be trash which he is ashamed to have written." He was wrong about that, the "trash" part, but it's also admirable that he imposed such stringent demands on his work. He was particularly "ashamed" of the now-famous line near the end of the poem, "We must love one another or die." He later changed it to "We must love one another *and* die," but that particular revision bleeds the imperative necessity right out of the passage. The anger and disgust, as well as the slim possibility of hope, that drove the original, is vital to the poem, which — sorry, Mr. Auden — is great.

Which brings me to rage. It's not a positive emotion. It should be avoided whenever and wherever possible; this seems utterly clear. And yet, anyone who is not appalled by political chicanery and mendacity would seem to be in denial. In other words, though rage is in some way toxic to the individual and to the culture, it may often be in response to something of far greater toxicity. Such rage, in order to be usefully marshaled, must be managed. Therefore, most of my poems that might be said to address public or political grievances have necessarily begun in something like rage and then had to be managed into problems of poetic engineering. For me, that means discovering ways to build a unified creation, a poem in which all the parts connect seamlessly with all the others, a poem the whole of which cannot have been said in any other way.

I've never believed that the poet bears any more responsibility toward his culture's public and political situation than any other citizen. That's one of the points "Exxon" means to make, I suppose. I believe the poet's only responsibility is to the machine he's making. He needs to make it with precision and clarity and richness, and by "clarity" I don't mean ease of understanding. By "richness" I mean the possibility of several ways to see and know, including the possibility of multiple, even contradictory, ways of fathoming what it says. By "precision" I mean the way its parts — line, rhythm, diction, figure, symbol, and more — fit together to make a whole. And if that whole is assembled to the most demanding tolerances the poet can muster, then it stands a chance of transcending mere opinion and becoming a work of poetic art. Any purpose served beyond the crafting of the poem itself is not incidental, then, but earned.

That's the aim, anyway. It's not easy. I'm glad it's not easy. What's kept me writing for nearly forty years is the difficulty, as well as the possibility, however remote, of success. The same might be said of citizenship too.

Index

"A1" from The Day 54
A contrail's white scimitar unsheathes 137
A giant poplar shades the summer square. 80
A History 151
A jet of mere phantom 174
A retired general said 149
A terrorist rides the rails underwater 175
A week later, I said to a friend: I don't 153
Absolutely, I agree. It's what we all 98
Action Poem 19
After a nightlong white-hot hellfire 115
Aftermath 83
All night, angels 163
All the green trees bring 144
"All the News 54
The Altars of September 28
Always more. No, we aren't too ashamed to prod celestial beings 116
AMERICA 18
The Anatomy of Melancholy 181
And the shopping center said, Give me, give me. 159
And though, since that time, I have read many books, 195
And we were made afraid, and being afraid 193
The Anniversary 157
Apt to loathe, dislike, disdain, and weary 181
Armantrout, Rae 17
As for palm-food, pinched face on the fruit 139
As they loaded the dead onto the gurneys 32
Assault to Abjury 139
Asymmetries 146

At almost the very moment an exterminator's panel truck, 189
At Robben Island the political prisoners studied. 154

Back Then We Called It "The War" 195
Background Check 46
Barred back from the glare 183
Beauty 135
Beauty is sexual, and sexuality 88
Behold the amazing artificial arm, a machine 202
Beneath three thousand feet, the sea is wholly dark. 32
Bidart, Frank 20
The Black-eyed Virgins 175
Bly, Robert 23
Bond, Bruce 28
Brouwer, Joel 32
Bubble Wrap 18
The Bush Administration 177

Call and Answer 23
Cassandra, Iraq 192
Clouds 117
Colony Collapse Disorder (CCD) 199
Column I, Tablet XIII 136
Compline 148
Conference 84
Cornel West makes the point that hope is different from American optimism. 165
Cranes which land in a Texas river 150
Curse 20

Dead Soldier 160
Dear Hayden, I have owed you a letter for 78

259

Dictionary in the Dark 149
Didactic Elegy 129
Donnelly, Timothy 34
Don't Let Me Be Lonely: An American Lyric 165–167
Dream of Arabian Hillbillies 38

Each shot three times at least, thrice 96
Earth 44
Echo Revision 125
Election Year 174
Elegy Against the Massacre at the Amish School in West Nickel Mines, Pennsylvania, Autumn 2006 184
Elegy for Oum Kolsoum Written Across the Sky 135
Employment 66
Entering Houses at Night 120
Eurostar 176
Extraordinary Rendition 118
Exxon 202
Ezra Pound's Proposition 88

Father Mercy, Mother Tongue 70
Fear 189
Fifty dollars is a fortune 179
Fish Market 44
Flag 29
Flee 43
Flesh gorging on oxygen. 180
Flies, caught in the sap of the living 194
Forche, Carolyn 41
Ford, Katie 43
The Forgetting 156
Found in the Free Library 193
Found Poem: Microloans 179
From hills, from storm drains 105
From my position as a woman 102
From our high windows we saw them 107
Full Flight 94
The Future 191

Gander, Forrest 46
Ghazal: min al-hobbi m'a qatal for Deema Shehabi 82
The Ghost of Heaven 41
Given Days 167
Gizzi, Peter 47
Gluck, Louise 47
God Bless Our Troops 164
God Exploding 174
Goldbarth, Albert 53
Goldsmith, Kenneth 54
Graham, Jorie 61

Gregerson, Linda 68
Grenade 113
Grennan, Eamon 78
Guantanamo 64

Hacker, Marilyn 78
Hamer, Forrest 83
Happy Anniversary 93
Hass, Robert 85
He has bribed the thorns 115
He slept with the dead then nothing roused him 200
Heavy Metal Soliloquy 115
Here, the old masters of Shock & Awe 112
Here the Sleepers Sleep 27
Here the sleepers sleep, here the Rams and the Bears play. 27
Hicok, Bob 93
Hillman, Brenda 99
His ears his mouth his 72
Homefront/Removes 149
Hum 123
Hundreds of bodies identified. Others 135
Hung Lyres 146

I Am Your Waiter Tonight and My Name Is Dmitri 85
I dreamt I saw a caravan of the dead 22
I heard from people after the shootings. People 97
I keep rereading an article I found recently about how Mayan scribes, 188
I made a winged 99
I Never Realized They Had Aspirations Like Ours 150
I read this curious Victorian novel 119
I sit in a hotel room and draw this Iraqi. 147
I was just thinking 201
If the English language was good enough for Jesus 70
If they raise a picture 140
If yellow 17
If you respect the dead 44
I'm in a plane that will not be flown into a building. 94
In a Senate Armed Services Hearing 102
In a Time of War 194
In High Desert Under the Drones 107
In Rubble 187
In the Loop 97
In the middle of drinking wine 151
Inauguration Day 23

Intention draws a bold, black line across an otherwise white field. 129
Interview, Saudi Arabia 150
Is it winter again, is it cold again, 47
Is, more or less, the title of a poem by John Ashbery and has 85
It doesn't matter 172
It is agreed that life as we know it must come to the end of its tether 121

Japanese schoolgirls in their school uniforms with their school chaperones 176
Jihad 137
Just Deserts 121

Kinnell, Galway 107
Komunyakaa, Yusef 112
Kumin, Maxine 118

Lauterbach, Ann 122
Lena, Mary Liz, and Anna Mae 184
Lerner, Ben 129
Lest, forgetting, the branch-maiden lopped off. 125
Let Sympathy Pass 24
Letter to Hayden Carruth 78
Lies 193
Linda, said my mother when the buildings fell, 68
Lines from the Reports of the Investigative Committees 32
Listen the voice is American it would reach you it has writing in its swan's neck 66
Little Exercise 61
Liu, Timothy 134
Longing to grasp the familiar, names 146
Love in the Time of War 112

Matthias, John 136
May breath for a dead moment cease as jerking your 20
McClatchy, J.D. 137
McDaniel, Raymond 139
McPherson, Sandra 140
Merwin, W.S. 142
Metres, Philip 146
Missing-persons photo plastered onto a van. 134
Mostly broken, but assumed to be 136
Mutant-engineered bloodsucker djinns, invisibility rays, 53
Mutation of bells. Chapels vanishing in fog. 78

Names 80
National Anthem 159
New 17
Nine Untitled Epyllions 99
None of us spoke their language and 120
Northern lights illumine the storm-troll's house. 25
Nothing more definite than that we awoke 199
Now the suicidal drift 44
Nye, Naomi Shihab 149

O'Brien, Geoffrey 151
October 47
Olds, Sharon 153
On Being Transparent: Cedar Rapids Airport 140
On Reading The Age of Innocence in a Troubled Time 119
On screen 19
On South African TV, the nightly news is broadcast four times — 84
On the surface of the earth 21
On Visiting the DMZ at Panmunjom: A Haibun 89
One bright night: we will see through the oaths of threat and protection 200
Only the oak and the beech hang onto their leaves 118

Partial Inventory of Airborne Debris 34
People vote for what will harm them: everywhere 24
Pinsky, Robert 154
Poem of Disconnected Parts 154
Praying (Attempt of June 14 '03) 62
Previews 18
Protest Song 47
Prufer, Kevin 159

Rain commenced, and wind did. 139
Rankine, Claudia 165
Ready-Mades 134
Recent History 163
Rendition, with Flag 198
Reportorial poetics can be used to record detail with immediacy while 102
Reportorial Poetry, Trance & Activism An Essay 102
Request to the Berkeley City Council Concerning Strawberry Creek 105
Revell, Donald 167
Reverence for that dust. 122

Right after the bomb, even before the ceiling 187
Ringtone 32
Rising, Falling, Hovering 200–202

Salutations from the all-encompassing 38
Seidel, Frederick 174
Seidman, Hugh 179
The Selvage 76
Sen Jak's Advice to the Tropically Depressed 139
September, 2001 153
Sewell, Lisa 181
She's magnificent, as we imagine women must be 192
The Show Must Go On 197
Sleep to sleep through thirty years of night 41
Small wonder I recoil 34
So door to door among the shotgun 76
The Soldier Who Guards the Frontier 21
Some Common Terms in Latin That Are Longer Than Our Lives 53
Some of David's Story 89
Sometime after eleven the fireworks 145
Somewhere there are omens. 83
Song: "The Swollen River Overthrows Its Banks" 176
The Stew of Discontents 25
Stewart, Susan 183
Still Life 72
Still We Take Joy 120
Stop-loss 98
Surely because in childhood we're taught our inner lives, 193
Surge 116
Sweet 68

Tell me why it is we don't lift our voices these days 23
Testimony 147
"That first time I met her, at the party, she said, 89
That night she closed her eyes and saw 28
That was the future I came back from 191
That we await a blessed hope, & that we will be struck 148
The attacks were tall, and then they burned. 167
The body begs for a system that will not break— 45
The century's greatest Arabic voice 135
The cry of those being eaten by America, 26
The darkness coming from the mouth 177

The days are beautiful 123
The fathers do not know 150
The forgetting I notice most as I get older is really a form of memory: 156
The human imagination does not do very well with large numbers. 89
The neck and head of a horse, but with the seam of the jaw 46
The net was spread last night, catching beavers 198
The personal is artificially political just as 184
The plane bobs like a cork 117
The play had been staged as long as we could remember, 197
The rain, like Caesar's army— 161
The screen is full of voices, all of them holding their tongues. 61
The sun went up 164
The terrorists are out of breath with success. 176
There is a war. 93
There's no rehearsal to turn flesh into dust so quickly. A hair-trigger, a 113
These nights in all their smoke 29
They all claim responsibility for inventing God, 174
Thinking of Baghdad 180
This is not a declaration of love or song of war 47
This morning before dawn no stars I try again. 62
Those Being Eaten 26
Those Who Could Not Flee 161
Timothy McVeigh died at 7:14 A.M. and a news reporter asks relatives of his 166
To Ashes 144
To eke out spirits on a bomb-damaged site. 135
To say about it one thing. No, two. It was a horror. It could not be spoken. 84
To the Coming Winter 145
To the Grass of Autumn 143
To the Light of September 142
To the Republic 22
To the Words 143
Today, despite what is dead 23
The Towers 113
Troubled Times 96

The Vessel Bends The Water 45
Victory 122
Vietnam Epic Treatment 172
Vita Breva 135

Wagoner, David 187
Waning moon. Rising now. Creak, it goes.
  Deep 64
"Want to turn on CNN, 18
War 188
The Warlord's Garden 115
We adore images, we like the spectacle 157
We are western creatures; we stand for
  hours in the sun. We read 107
What Happened 84
When I'm crying, I'm not speaking 183
When I'm speaking, I'm not crying 184
When it happens you are not there 143
When the bombs fell, she could barely raise
  146
When the Towers Fell 107
When the transistor said *killing wind* 43

When you are already here 142
Where the living are, no one's missed him
  yet. 160
While in Baghdad sewage infiltrates 120
Williams, C.K. 188
Wilner, Eleanor 193
Wright, C.D. 200
Wrigley, Robert 202

Y2K 78
Yes, dear son 113
You could never believe 143
You look at me / looking at you. How close
  the words 149
You, old friend, leave, but who releases me
  from the love that 82